Java Outside In

This book treats learning a programming language much like learning a spoken language: Programming is best learned by immersion. Through building interesting programs and addressing real design issues much earlier than other texts, this one is able to move beyond the placement of semicolons and other syntactic details in order to discuss the architecture of serious programs: how delegation and inheritance allow objects to cooperate to do useful work.

Throughout the text, the authors deal with programs that implement applications close enough to real to be convincing. These programs are more like those students encounter in the real world than ones they are likely to find in traditional programming texts. The authors constantly revise the programs as they grow in sophistication so students learn another important aspect of programming – that, in the real world, programs are constantly updated and improved. Finally, in the exercises, the authors encourage students to write programs that interact with and extend programs discussed in the text and then ask them to write about those programs. After completing this one-semester course, students emerge as programmers.

Ethan D. Bolker is a professor in the departments of Mathematics and Computer Science at the University of Massachusetts, Boston. Dr. Bolker's research interests include combinatorics and geometry (in mathematics) and the performance modeling of operating systems (in computer science). He has consulted at BMC Software (which acquired BGS Systems) for twenty years, writing queueing theory algorithms, designing software, building tools, managing projects, and enjoying his work with many former students. He is the author of three texts, on number theory, calculus, and applied mathematics at an elementary level.

Bill Campbell is an associate professor in the department of Computer Science at the University of Massachusetts, Boston. His professional areas of expertise are software engineering, object-oriented analysis, design and programming, and programming language implementation. He has been teaching for more than fifteen years. He has worked for AT&T and Intermetrics Inc. and has been a consultant to Apple Computer and EntitleNet, Inc. He wrote UMB Scheme, a portable public-domain implementation of the Scheme programming language. UMB Scheme is distributed with Linux.

To Joan – *Ethan*

To Nora, Fiona, and Amy – *Bill*

Java Outside In

ETHAN D. BOLKER

BILL CAMPBELL

University of Massachusetts, Boston

CAMBRIDGE
UNIVERSITY PRESS

PUBLISHED BY THE PRESS SYNDICATE OF THE UNIVERSITY OF CAMBRIDGE
The Pitt Building, Trumpington Street, Cambridge, United Kingdom

CAMBRIDGE UNIVERSITY PRESS
The Edinburgh Building, Cambridge CB2 2RU, UK
40 West 20th Street, New York, NY 10011-4211, USA
477 Williamstown Road, Port Melbourne, VIC 3207, Australia
Ruiz de Alarcón 13, 28014 Madrid, Spain
Dock House, The Waterfront, Cape Town 8001, South Africa

http://www.cambridge.org

First published 2003

Printed in the United States of America

Typefaces ITC Century Book 10/12 pt., Gill Sans, Courier   *System* LaTeX 2_ε [TB]

A catalog record for this book is available from the British Library.

Library of Congress Cataloging in Publication Data

Bolker, Ethan D.
Java outside in / Ethan Bolker, Bill Campbell.
    p.   cm.
Includes bibliographical references and index.
ISBN 0-521-81198-8 – ISBN 0-521-01087-X (pb.)
1. Java (Computer program language)   I. Campbell, Bill, 1950–   II. Title.
QA76.73.J38 B65   2003
005.13′3–dc21   2002073692

ISBN 0 521 81198 8 hardback
ISBN 0 521 01087 X paperback

Contents

Preface

Programming a computer can be

* fun
* hard work
* an intellectual adventure that requires both understanding new ideas and careful attention to detail
* a career

Several years ago Java was invented. Java is

* elegant and powerful
* easy to learn
* easy to use
* fun to write
* fashionable
* practical
* object oriented

So it's just right for beginners (as well as professionals). We decided to use it in our first programming course and looked around for a textbook we thought our students would enjoy. We hoped for one that immersed them early in programs they would want to understand, ones that introduced programming as a craft and a culture. When we couldn't find one, we wrote lecture notes for our students as we designed the course. Five years later, this book is the result. It can help you learn what computer programming in general and object-oriented programming in particular are really all about.

The title, *Java Outside In*, reflects our teaching philosophy. We immerse you in Java, presenting complete and interesting programs in Chapter 1 in order to show you how such programs behave and how programmers design them. We count on you to master the details in time.

We love programming: reading programs, writing programs, reading about programs, writing about programs, and teaching students to program. We hope this book will help you come to love programming as much as we do.

For the Instructor (and the Student)

We work with objects from the start. When Pascal replaced BASIC as the language of instruction in CS1, procedures (particularly procedures with parameters) were often introduced only after students had learned to program without them. In time, educators began to understand that structure wasn't what you learned after you learned to program but that students needed to be writing structured programs right from the start. We need to make a similar transition now. Object-oriented programming is the standard programming paradigm, not a new, difficult, advanced technique to learn after you've learned to program. When students find objects in their first programs, they don't think of them as particularly strange or puzzling. They are just what you build programs out of.

We think students learn programming best by immersion. We begin not with "Hello, world" but with a simulated banking system built from bank, bank account, and automatic teller machine objects. We find that students can read and understand this 200-line application, and can modify it, well before they can understand all the language features that make it work. We believe students can learn the details of Java by starting from a view that studies how object-oriented programs are built.

We think it's important to read programs. Code reading is common in industry, and in advanced courses in software engineering. We think it has an important place in beginning courses, too. When students read code, they learn what good code looks like. They can absorb the idioms that make correct programs easy to read as well as to modify.

We think it's important to write about programs. We ask students to write about the programs they write, documenting design choices and problems met and solved (or not solved) and telling us how they tested their programs and what help they received from fellow students and other sources. They complain at first but quite often come to agree in the end that doing so helped them learn. And the narratives help us – after reading them, it's easier to read the students' code.

How we teach from the book. In lectures we read code with the class, stressing the ideas the code expresses. We answer some questions with "You don't need to understand that now – we'll let you know when you do." That's occasionally necessary because the code we are reading often must use features we haven't yet covered.

The structure of the book. In Chapter 1 we introduce two applications as examples that illustrate object-oriented programming: a banking system and a simulated traffic light. We use the successive iterations of these and other application programs to introduce the important features of Java and object-oriented design: declarations and arithmetic in Chapter 2, objects and message passing in Chapter 3, collections in Chapter 4, inheritance and polymorphism in Chapter 5, an extended discussion of

Juno (a command-line interface to a simulated hierarchical file system) in Chapter 6, error handling and exceptions in Chapter 7, strings in Chapter 8, files and persistence in Chapter 9, and finally, interfaces and graphical user interface programming in Chapter 10. We can cover almost all of this material in one intense semester.

The exposition is carefully organized so that new language features can be illustrated as the sample programs grow. For example, in Chapter 4 we give our banks a collection of bank accounts. In Chapter 7 we enable error handling, so that users may not withdraw more money than an account contains. The first time you teach from this book you should probably resist the temptation to improve the applications prematurely.

Often the answer to an exercise in one chapter is used in the text in succeeding ones. We have marked those exercises with an asterisk. If you assign them to your class you should be aware of the fact that students who read ahead may find solutions. If you do not assign them you may need to discuss them in later lectures.

What you won't see. We tend to let the compiler rather than the text teach syntax lessons, although we do provide small demonstration programs for each significant language construct.

There is essentially no graphical user interface programming, save for an example in Chapter 1 and a small applet and a large application in Chapter 10. That choice was dictated at first by hardware limitations at UMass-Boston. But we now think the command-line focus is wise for its own sake. Students can more easily grasp a larger fraction of programs that work from a command-line interface. Less of what the computer does for them looks like magic.

CD-ROM and Online Resources

All of the source code that is referred to in this text can be found on the accompanying CD-ROM. We supply the code in several forms, including ASCII text for compilation and line-numbered PDF for printing.

All the source code can be found also at `http://www.cs.umb.edu/joi`, in several forms: ASCII text for downloading and compilation, PDF for printing, and in a browsable version. That Web site also contains information about development environments for students and classes. You can usually see how we teach from this text by visiting `http://www.cs.umb.edu/cs110`. That Web site starts afresh each semester and grows as the course progresses. We have home pages at `http://www.cs.umb.edu/~eb/` and `http://www.cs.umb.edu/~bill/`.

License to use: All code is copyright 2003 by Ethan Bolker and William Campbell. All rights reserved. A non-exclusive license is hereby granted to use, distribute, and modify the programs herein free of charge for educational purposes only. All commercial use and rights to republication of the programs are reserved.

Acknowledgments

Java Outside In grew out of our experience teaching CS1 at the University of Massachusetts, Boston. Our first debt is to our students, who cheered us on, corrected our errors, and forced us toward clarity (which we hope we have achieved). One, Mike Ozorowski, suggested *Java Inside Out* for the title. We had help from colleagues (faculty and graduate students) who taught from early drafts of the text – Colin Godfrey, Joan Linskey, Jack Lutts, Bob Morris, Eric Rich, Denis Rinfret, Gabriel Rodriguez, Dennis Wortman, and Lei Xia. Our agent, David Miller, sent a draft to Alan Harvey at Cambridge University Press. His endorsement of our vision made it possible for us to rewrite (and rewrite and rewrite) in order to turn course lecture notes into this text. John Zukowski provided a thoughtful, detailed reading of a near-final draft. We accepted most of his fine suggestions. Eric Newman's careful copyediting focused our attention in a last revision.

Chapter 1

Computing with Objects

Computers are at work in surprisingly many everyday (and not-so-everyday) places. They control watches, home appliances, cars, airplanes, multinational banking systems, underwater probes, and orbital telescopes. We can use our home computers for everything from word processing, surfing the Internet for business or pleasure, budgeting, and electronic mail to virtual stargazing, language learning, and intergalactic war games. What is remarkable is that all these computers are essentially alike. A computer is a general-purpose machine that can be ***programmed*** to behave as if it were a machine built for a special purpose – a machine for controlling the mixture of gasoline and oxygen in an automobile engine or one for controlling a set of traffic lights. Moreover, the program can be changed without rebuilding the computer, which is why we can use our home computers for so many different tasks. Each ***application*** is a separate program that runs on our computer.

A computer program is a set of instructions (the ***software***) that tells a general-purpose computer (the ***hardware***) how to behave like some special-purpose machine. A computer program is written in a ***programming language***. There are many programming languages; this text uses ***Java***, a general-purpose language based on the modern, object-oriented style of program design that allows one to write programs that focus more on the problem the program must solve than on the computer on which the program will run.

You will learn the craft of programming the way a prospective writer learns the craft of writing. Writers learn by reading. You'll read lots of programs. Writers learn by writing. You'll write many programs.

In this first chapter, we introduce object-oriented programming by studying two applications. The first makes the computer act as if it were an automatic teller machine connected to a bank. The second makes the computer act as if it were a traffic light at an intersection. These programs are longer than those you customarily see in the first chapter of an introductory text. Read them in order to capture a sense of what a Java program looks like. Don't try to understand all the details.

Simulating a Simple Banking System

How does our automatic teller machine (ATM) work? This question is really two different important questions:

- How does the ATM behave? More precisely: How do you interact with the computer when it pretends to be an ATM and you pretend to be a customer? What is the ATM's ***user interface***?

- How does the program we have written cause the computer to behave like an ATM? What is the ATM's *implementation*?

The Banking System's Behavior

In order to understand the program, we think first about the user interface of the real ATM[1] we are simulating. We insert our bank card into a slot. The ATM reads the card to determine which bank account we want to access. Then it asks for our personal identification number (PIN). When we've entered it correctly, the ATM knows we're entitled to access that account. Then it waits for us to tell it what transactions we want to perform. When we tell it we're done, it returns our card and waits for the next customer.

To keep our simulation simple, our bank will have just two bank accounts. The ATM won't read cards, ask for PINs, or dispense real money. And it will manage its fake money only in whole dollar amounts. We communicate with our ATM by typing messages at the computer keyboard and reading what the computer displays on the screen.

When we start the program, we are telling our computer to behave as if it were an ATM. The computer responds by displaying a welcome message and a prompt asking us to enter an account number. Typing the account number identifies the account we wish to work with – on a real ATM, inserting a bank card does that.

```
Welcome to Engulf and Devour
Account number (1 or 2), 0 to shut down: 1
```

In this example and throughout this book, we use **bold monospaced font** to identify what the computer types and `monospaced font` for what we enter at the keyboard. Remember to press the Return (or Enter) key on your keyboard at the end of each line; until you do, the program will not know that you have typed anything.

Once we choose an account to work with (in this case, account 1), the program offers a list of available transactions and then repeatedly prompts for transactions to process. The program carries out each transaction request, prompting for additional information when necessary. For example, while pretending to be the first customer we might interact with the ATM as follows:

```
Transactions: exit, help, deposit, withdraw, balance
transaction: balance [followed by Return or Enter!]
200
transaction: deposit
amount: 40
transaction: balance
240
```

---

[1] "Cashpoint" in Canada and the United Kingdom.

```
transaction: withdraw
amount: 25
transaction: balance
215
transaction: help
Transactions: exit, help, deposit, withdraw, balance
transaction: exit
```

When we're finished with an account, we type `exit` as a final transaction. The program ends the transaction cycle for the current account, welcomes the next customer, and prompts for an account number. This in turn begins another transaction cycle for the next account selected:

```
Account number (1 or 2), 0 to shut down: 2
transaction: balance
200
transaction: exit
```

If the first customer now revisits account 1, she will find that her balance is 215.

To shut down the program,[2] we type 0 for an account number:

```
Account number (1 or 2), 0 to shut down: 0
Goodbye from Engulf and Devour
```

Of course we wouldn't allow a customer to shut down a real ATM. Only an employee of the bank would have that authority. But our simulation requires some way to tell our ATM we are done. Entering a zero for an account number is as good a way as any for now.

We will explain soon how you start this ATM program, so that you can duplicate the foregoing dialog rather than just read about it. If you want to do that before reading more about the program, read the "Compile/Run" section of this chapter now.

An Object Model for the Banking System

Now that we understand our application's user interface, we can study its implementation: the program that instructs our computer to behave like an ATM. We designed the implementation by thinking about the objects in the real world that the program must simulate.

Objects are constructs in programming languages that represent things in the real world. In general, anything that we can refer to with a noun, we can represent as an

---

[2] It's always wise to think before you start work about how you will stop. The brake pedal is more important than the accelerator. In an emergency, you can stop a running Java application by typing Ctrl+C (hold down the Control key as if it were a Shift key and type "C"). What's the best way to shut down your computer?

object in our program. This particular program uses four objects:

- Two **BankAccount** objects, one each for each of the two bank accounts being managed.
- One **Bank** object representing the bank that maintains the accounts.
- One **Terminal** object representing the ATM we use to communicate with the bank.

We begin by thinking about how a **BankAccount** object should behave. A real bank account's job is to keep track of how its balance changes as withdrawals and deposits are made. Figure 1-1 shows how we might draw a picture of a **BankAccount** object having a balance of 200.

In general, we refer to properties of an object that may change over time as its internal *state*. Each individual property is stored in a *field*, a place within the object that we can refer to by name. (These are words you will come to understand as you learn to program in Java. Don't take the time now to memorize the definitions.) The figure shows that each **BankAccount** object has a field we chose to call **balance** whose value at the moment happens to be 200. A more realistic model of a bank account would have more fields – for the user's name, address and PIN, and other information – and would maintain a balance in pennies.

Objects have *behavior* as well as state: They can do things as well as remember the values of their fields. To make an object behave, we send it a *message*; when the object receives the message, it takes some action. It might *return* some value based on its state, or it might change its state.

For example, Figure 1-2 shows a **BankAccount** object receiving a **getBalance** message and responding by returning the current balance, 200. (Don't worry now about who is sending the message, or what happens to the value 200 that's returned. We will address those questions in time.)

We can change the current balance by sending the **BankAccount** a **deposit** message, together with an *argument* indicating how much is to be deposited. Figure 1-3 illustrates depositing 40. In this case, the **BankAccount** object responds to the message by changing the value of its **balance** field from 200 to 240. No value is returned, but the object's internal state has changed.

BankAccount

Figure 1-1: A **BankAccount** object

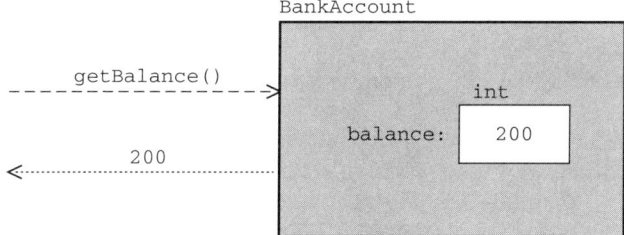

Figure 1-2: Sending a **getBalance** message

Figure 1-3: Sending a **deposit** message

Figure 1-4 depicts the **Bank** object in our program. A **Bank** has four fields:

- Field **bankName** stores the name of the bank – in this case, "Engulf and Devour".[3]
- The values of fields **account1** and **account2** are the two **BankAccount** objects that the bank maintains.
- Field **atm** stores a **Terminal** object.[4]

In Figure 1-4 the values of the bank's fields appear at the ends of arrows rather than inside the bank itself. That's because those values are other objects in the program.

The Simple Banking Program in Java

Now that we have designed the object structure for our banking system, we will see how to express that structure in Java. In Java, as in all object-oriented languages, each particular object is an ***instance*** of a ***class***. The two **BankAccount** objects are instances of class **BankAccount**, the one **Bank** object is an instance of class **Bank**, and the one **Terminal** object is an instance of class **Terminal**. The string **"Engulf**

---

[3] The name comes from the Mel Brooks film *Silent Movie*.
[4] In a more extensive example, where we had an ATM connected to a network of many banks, we might want to put the **Terminal** object elsewhere, because it would not belong to a single **Bank**.

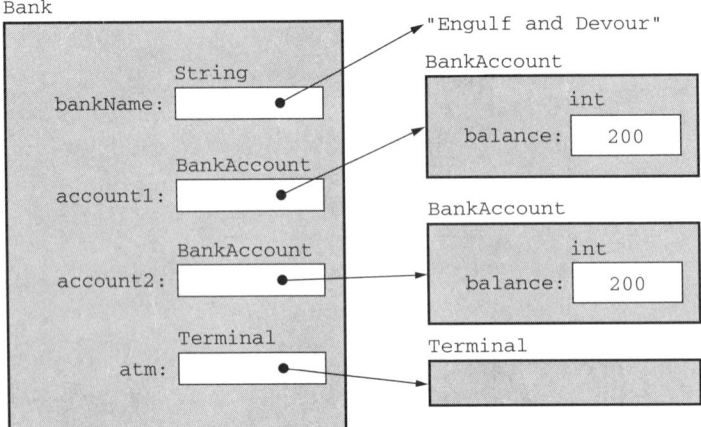

Figure 1-4: A **Bank** object and its fields

and Devour" is an instance of class **String**. The definition of the **BankAccount** class specifies the fields and the behavior of the objects that are instances of the class. This is just as it should be, because all instances of the class share the same properties. They have the same fields, though those fields may have different values in different instances – every **BankAccount** has a balance, but of course those **balance** fields have different values in different accounts.

Listing 1-1 is the Java *class definition* for the **BankAccount** class. In Java, each class definition is stored in a computer file whose name is the name of the class being defined with a **.java** suffix (called an *extension*) appended,[5] so that listing is just the contents of the file **BankAccount.java**.[6] Such a file is often referred to as a *source file;* the Java code in it is called *source code*.

Listing 1-1: BankAccount.java

```
1   // joi/1/bank/BankAccount.java
2   //
3   //
4   // Copyright 2003 Bill Campbell and Ethan Bolker
5
6   /**
```

---

[5] Usually. Later we will see a few situations in which a Java file contains the definition of several classes.
[6] In this and the other program listings in this book, the line numbers at the left are not part of the program; they are there so that we can easily refer to specific lines of code in our discussions. Listing 1-1 is displayed in full right here. Future listings will be longer. In order not to interrupt the flow of the narrative in the text, you will find all of them on the CD-ROM supplied with this text, and on the Web at www.cs.umb.edu/joi so that you can look at them online while reading the text.

```
 7    * A BankAccount object has a private field to keep
 8    * track of this account's current balance, and public
 9    * methods to return and change the balance.
10    *
11    * @see Bank
12    * @version 1
13    */
14
15  public class BankAccount
16  {
17      private int balance; // work only in whole dollars
18
19      /**
20        * A constructor for creating a new bank account.
21        *
22        * @param initialBalance the opening balance.
23        */
24
25      public BankAccount( int initialBalance )
26      {
27          this.deposit( initialBalance );
28      }
29
30      /**
31        * Withdraw the amount requested.
32        *
33        * @param amount the amount to be withdrawn.
34        */
35
36      public void withdraw( int amount )
37      {
38          balance = balance - amount;
39      }
40
41      /**
42        * Deposit the amount requested.
43        *
44        * @param amount the amount to be deposited.
45        */
46
47      public void deposit( int amount )
48      {
49          balance = balance + amount;
```

```
50      }
51
52      /**
53        * The current account balance.
54        *
55        * @return the current balance.
56        */
57
58      public int getBalance()
59      {
60            return balance;
61      }
62  }
```

BankAccount.java has two purposes. First, it describes the behavior of **BankAccount** objects in language that humans (computer programmers) can read and write. Second, it can be *compiled* – translated by a Java *compiler* into a form the computer can use when we run the bank simulation. We'll discuss compilation later.

Lines 1–13 in the listing are *comments* – text that is useful to the programmers who read and write the class definition but of no interest at all to the compiler. Any text from a **//** to the end of a line and any text between a **/*** and a ***/** is a comment. Every Java source file should begin with comments giving the program's name, the author's name, and a date. The body of the program should contain comments describing the class and its methods and comments at places where some explanation will help programmers understand how the program works.

The class definition proper begins on line 15, which says, naturally enough, that what follows is the definition of the **BankAccount** class. That definition extends through line 62. The curly brackets (**{** and **}**) on lines 16 and 62 serve to define the boundaries of the class definition.

Our class definition begins with a description of the field that will hold the account's balance:

```
private int balance;    // work only in whole dollars
```

Because it is labeled **private**, it is visible only within the boundaries of the class definition. The word **int** says that the field stores integer values.

The rest of the definition describes **BankAccount** behavior: three methods specifying how a **BankAccount** will respond to messages and **BankAccount** objects.

A *method* is a named sequence of instructions that specifies what an object does when it receives a message having that name. For example, here is the definition of

withdraw, which tells us what a **BankAccount** will do when it receives a **withdraw** message:

```
36      public void withdraw( int amount )
37      {
38          balance = balance - amount;
39      }
```

Line 36 is the *method header*. It names the method, makes it available to the **public**, tells us that it returns no value (**void**), and describes the arguments – the information the method needs in order to do its job. This method has one integer argument, **amount**, for the amount we wish to withdraw. The *method body*, enclosed between the curly braces (**{** and **}**), specifies the response to a **withdraw** message: We subtract the amount to be withdrawn from the balance. The definition of **deposit** is similar.

Here is the code for **getBalance**:

```
58      public int getBalance()
59      {
60          return balance;
61      }
```

The empty parentheses on line 58 tell us that **getBalance** needs no outside information to do its job. The **return balance** statement on line 60 makes the value of the **balance** field available to the object that sent the **getBalance** message.

A *constructor* is a special method whose purpose is to create a new object. In Java, the constructor method is the one whose name matches that of the class. Think of it as describing what happens when you place an order at an imaginary **BankAccount** factory.

```
25      public BankAccount( int initialBalance )
26      {
27          this.deposit( initialBalance );
28      }
```

The constructor is told (in its **initialBalance** argument) how much money the account will start with. The body of the constructor sends a **deposit** message to **this** object, the **BankAccount** under construction, asking it to deposit the proper amount in itself.

Our simulation has (one) **Bank** object that creates (two) **BankAccount** objects and sends messages to them to perform account transactions. To see how that is expressed in Java, we look at pieces of code from the description of the **Bank** class in file **Bank.java** (Listing 1-2).

Here is the **Bank** object constructor:

```
41      public Bank( String name )
42      {
43          bankName = name;
44          atm      = new Terminal();
45          account1 = new BankAccount( INITIAL_BALANCE );
46          account2 = new BankAccount( INITIAL_BALANCE );
47      }
```

This code shows that whenever we construct a **Bank** object we first set the **bankName** field in the **Bank** to the value passed as an argument. Then we use the Java keyword **new** to create the **Terminal** [7] object **atm** and the two **BankAccount** objects **account1** and **account2**, starting each out with 200, the value of **INITIAL_BALANCE** set on line 29:

```
29      private static final int INITIAL_BALANCE = 200;
```

In our simulation it's line 140 that actually creates the single **Bank** object we interact with. That line tells the new bank its name:

```
140     Bank javaBank = new Bank( "Engulf and Devour" );
```

Message Passing

We create objects in order to make them work for us. Right after we create the bank, we ask it to open itself:

```
141     javaBank.open();
```

That line illustrates message passing syntax: We name the object, then the method, then the information the object needs to do what we are asking – in this case there is no extra information, so the parentheses are empty.

There are many more examples in the code in the **Bank** class that processes transactions for an account:

```
107     String command = atm.readWord( "transaction: " );
108     if ( command.equals( "exit" ) ) {
109         moreTransactions = false;
110     }
111     else if ( command.equals( "help" ) ) {
112         atm.println( HELPSTRING );
113     }
```

---

[7] **Terminal** objects are described in the file **Terminal.java**, which is Listing 8-1. We won't study that code until Chapter 8. Until then, we will just use **Terminal** objects in our programs.

```
114        else if ( command.equals( "deposit" ) ) {
115             int amount = atm.readInt( "amount: " );
116             account.deposit( amount );
117        }
118        else if ( command.equals( "withdraw" ) ) {
119             int amount = atm.readInt( "amount: " );
120             account.withdraw( amount );
121        }
122        else if ( command.equals( "balance" ) ) {
123             atm.println( account.getBalance() );
124        }
125        else{
126             atm.println( "sorry, unknown transaction" );
127        }
```

Line 107 sends the **atm** (a **Terminal** object) a **readWord** message, telling it what prompt to use when it asks for input from the user. The **Terminal**'s **readWord** method collects the user's input and returns it to the **bank**, which stores the value in the variable **command**. The remaining code (lines 108–27) expresses the logic that examines the value of **command** in order to decide what to do. Read those lines this way:

- The statement **command.equals("exit")** sends the **command** string an **equals** message, asking it if its value (the string the user typed) is "exit". The **equals** method returns **true** or **false**, depending on the answer to the question. If the user did in fact type "exit", set the variable **moreTransactions** to **false** to indicate we're done with this particular bank account.

- Otherwise,[8] if the user typed "help", send the **atm** a message asking it to print out the value of **HELPSTRING**, the **String** listing all possible commands:

```
30     private static final String HELPSTRING =
31          "Transactions: exit, help, deposit, withdraw, balance";
```

- Otherwise, if the user typed "deposit", send the **atm** a **readInt** message, asking it to prompt for, read, and return an integer amount. Then send a **deposit** message to the **BankAccount** object **account**, with that amount as an argument.

- Otherwise, if the user typed "withdraw", send the **atm** a **readInt** message, asking it to prompt for, read, and return an integer amount. Then send a **withdraw** message to the **BankAccount** object **account**, with that amount as an argument.

- Otherwise, if the user typed "balance", send the **atm** a **println** message, asking that it display the current balance. To get that value we first send the account a

---

[8] In Java, **else** can always be read as "otherwise."

getBalance message. The value returned by **account.getBalance()** is in turn the argument to the **println** message sent to the **atm**.

- Otherwise, the command is not one of the available transactions. Send the **atm** a **println** message, asking it to inform the user.

Compile/Run

In order to run the bank simulation application, we must first *compile* all of the files to translate the Java source code into a form the computer can understand. How you tell your computer to compile a file depends on your local programming environment. In this book we assume that environment provides you with a command-line interface that prompts you for what you want do next. Windows usually uses a > as its command prompt; Unix and Linux use a % unless someone has programmed a different prompt. To avoid taking sides in a political controversy, we will use both, writing

```
%> javac BankAccount.java
```

when you are to type "javac BankAccount.java" at the command prompt. This particular command causes the Java compiler to produce a *class file* **BankAccount.class**. In general, the class file's name is the same as the class name with a **.class** extension replacing the **.java** extension.

You can compile both files at once with the command

```
%> javac BankAccount.java Bank.java
```

Our banking system requires several more class files in addition to **Bank.class** and **BankAccount.class**. One is **Terminal.class**, containing the description of **Terminal** objects. Another is **String.class**, containing the description of **String** objects. You do not need to do anything special to use the **String** class, which comes along with Java. The **Terminal** class is particular to *Java Outside In*.[9]

When you have created class files by compiling Java source code with the javac compiler you are ready to run the bank simulation. The *Java Virtual Machine (JVM)* is a computer program that reads class files and executes their contents. To start the JVM and ask it to start the bank application, we execute the command

```
%> java Bank
```

This produces the behavior we have sketched previously, allowing a user to interact with the program.

---

[9] If you are using *Java Outside In* as a text in a programming course your instructor will have made the **Terminal** class available to you. If you are studying on your own, consult the section on the *Java Outside In* CD-ROM or Web page www.cs.umb.edu/joi to find out how to configure your environment so that your programs can see the **Terminal** class.

We encourage you to look through **Bank.java** and **BankAccount.java** now, even though this banking application is a larger program (almost 200 lines) than you will usually find in the first chapter of an introductory text. We think it is valuable to encounter a program of this size right at the start of your studies: It's large enough to be genuinely interesting. Just understand that you need not understand it all right now.[10]

A Traffic Light Program

Our second example is an application that simulates the behavior of a traffic light. Following the pattern we have just introduced, we consider first our program's behavior (its user interface), then the objects that model an implementation of that behavior, then part of the Java program that gives life to our light.

Traffic lights at an intersection change color from time to time in order to guarantee a smooth and safe flow of traffic. In the real world, traffic lights are controlled by sophisticated software that responds to input from timers and sensors and buttons. Our program models an unrealistically simple situation – just one light, whose color changes when the user presses just one button.

The Behavior of the Traffic Light Program

We communicated with the bank application using a ***command-line interface***: a sequence of typed commands and typed responses. The traffic light application has a ***graphical user interface*** (GUI): We use the mouse to talk to the program. In response, the program changes the pictures on the screen. GUI programming is more difficult than command-line interface programming. Because we don't think mastering those difficulties is the best way to learn to program, we won't do much of it in this text, but we want to give you a taste of it here in the first chapter.

To run the traffic light application, we compile its source code to build class files:

```
%> javac TrafficLight.java Lens.java Sequencer.java
%> javac NextButtonListener.java
```

and then start the JVM:

```
%> java TrafficLight
```

Figure 1-5 shows a black and white rendering of what you will see on your computer screen: a traffic light showing a green lens lit (the red and yellow lenses are there but invisible), and, beneath the light, a single button marked "Next". When you move your mouse to that button and click it, the light responds by advancing to its next state, from green to yellow, from yellow to red, from red back to green, and so on.

---

[10] It won't be on the test . . .

Figure 1-5: A traffic light system (green)

How you shut the program down depends on the particular window system your computer is using. You should find both a button to click on and a Close choice on a menu. Either will do.[11]

An Object Model for the TrafficLight Program

The design we have chosen for our application uses several objects. Some of them are visible:

- A **TrafficLight** object, with three **Lens** objects
- A **Button** object to push

Some of them are invisible, but necessary:

- A listener object to respond to clicks on the button
- A **Sequencer** object to control the light in response to messages from the button listener.

Figure 1-6 shows the object model for our traffic light application. We can view that picture as a hardware diagram, in which the arrows represent wires that carry electrical signals from one component to the next. We can also see it as an object diagram like Figure 1-4, in which the arrows represent the values of the various objects' fields by pointing to the objects they contain. Some (unspecified) field in the **Button** has as its value a **NextButtonListener**. The **sequencer** field in the **NextButtonListener** has as its value a **Sequencer**. The **Sequencer**'s **light** field has as its value a **TrafficLight**. The **TrafficLight** has three fields named **red**, **yellow**, and

---

[11] Recall that whenever you begin working with a new user interface one of your first tasks should be to learn how to shut it down.

Figure 1-6: Object model for the traffic light application

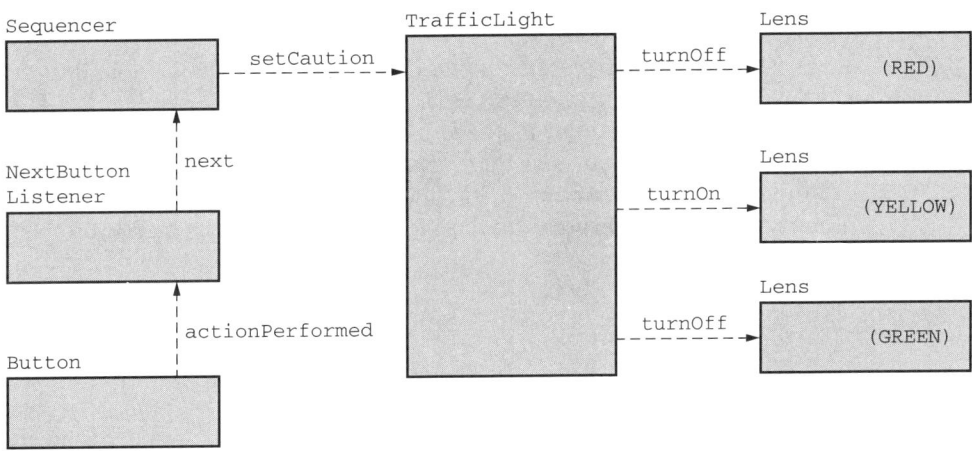

Figure 1-7: Message passing diagram for the traffic light application

green, each of which holds a distinct **Lens**. Each **Lens** has a field that holds its **color**.

Recall that in object-oriented programs, work is done when objects send messages to one another. Figure 1-7 represents the messages that will be sent when the light is green and the user presses the "Next" button, represented by the **Button** object in our model. The **Button** object sends an **actionPerformed** message to the **NextButtonListener**, which in turn sends a **next** message to the **Sequencer** object. The **Sequencer** responds by shifting itself to the next state and sending the appropriate message, **setCaution**, to the **TrafficLight**. The **TrafficLight** in turn interprets the **setCaution** message from the **Sequencer** by sending messages to the three lenses: **turnOff** to **red**,[12] **turnOn** to **yellow**, and **turnOff** to **green**.

That changes the light from green to yellow; Figure 1-8 shows the result.

The Traffic Light Application in Java

You will find the source code for the four classes we have written in Listings 1-3, 1-4, 1-5, and 1-6: **TrafficLight.java**, **NextButtonListener.java**, **Sequencer.java**, and **Lens.java**, respectively. We don't need source code for **Button** because **Button.class** (like **String.class**) comes with Java.

Let's take a look at the **Sequencer** class, defined in **Sequencer.java** (Listing 1-5). A **Sequencer** object controls the sequence of states that the traffic light passes through.

A **Sequencer** object has two fields. The **TrafficLight** field, **light**, declared on line 19 refers to the light that this **Sequencer** is controlling. The integer field **currentState**, declared on line 26, holds the state that the traffic light is currently in: **GO, CAUTION**, or **STOP.** The integer constants declared and initialized on lines 22, 23, and 24 represent these states.

A **Sequencer** has just two methods: a constructor, defined on lines 34–9, and the method **next**, defined on lines 47–69.

The constructor initializes the value of the **light** field with the **TrafficLight** passed as its argument and then sets the initial state of the **Sequencer** to **GO** by setting the **currentState** field (line 37) and sending the light a **setGo** message (line 38). (The light responds to this message by running its **setGo** method. If you look

Figure 1-8: A traffic light system (yellow)

---

[12] The red lens is actually already off at this moment, but this defensive program makes sure by sending the redundant message.

at **TrafficLight.java** you can see how that method sends messages to turn the light's **green** lens on and its **red** and **yellow** lenses off.)

Figure 1-7 shows that the method **next** is invoked in response to **next** messages sent from the **NextButtonListener** object. It uses a **switch** statement to examine the value of the **currentState** field and act appropriately, changing the value of that field and sending the light the right message.

For example, when **currentState** is **GO**, execution of the program branches to the code

```
51      case GO:
52          this.currentState = CAUTION;
53          this.light.setCaution();
54          break;
```

The state is changed to **CAUTION**, and a **setCaution** message is sent to the light (causing it to send appropriate messages to its lenses). The **break** statement on line 54 tells Java that the **switch** on line 49 is done, completing the method at line 69.

Control branches to the **default** clause on line 66 only if **currentState** matches none of the intervening cases. This will not happen in our program.[13]

Thus the **Sequencer** object contains all of the logic necessary for maintaining state and shifting through the states **GO, CAUTION**, and **STOP**, and back to **GO** upon receiving successive **next** messages. We leave the provision of an additional **WALK** state as an exercise.

The Software Development Cycle

In the two examples we have studied, one application turned our computer into an ATM connected to a bank, the other into a traffic light. The process that produced these examples is typical of the way software is developed. That process has several identifiable stages:

1. *Imagine.* You have an idea – an image of the application you wish existed, the special-purpose machine you want to run on your general-purpose computer.
2. *Design.* Think about your application's user interface – how it will behave – and then think about the software objects you will build to implement that behavior.
3. *Edit.* Write the Java code that constructs the objects you have designed.
4. *Compile.* Invoke the Java compiler to construct class files from your source files. If there are any errors, return to Step 3.

---

[13] A programmer's last words . . . . Note that our program is designed to print an error message even in a situation we are sure can never occur. That's defensive programming.

5. *Run/test*. Invoke the JVM to execute your program. If you find errors, return to Step 3 (or perhaps Step 2).

6. *Release*. Declare your program ready for public access – sell it, or give it away, or submit it to your instructor. When you get feedback, return to Step 1 to imagine improvements.

In the examples in this text we have done most of the work of Steps 1 and 2; you will spend your time mastering Steps 3, 4, and 5. As you read through the text, you will see Step 6 and the return to Step 1 as we study increasingly more sophisticated versions of the examples. But we will not neglect imagination and design. The exercises will ask you to write about them as well as to write and modify programs.

In order to do that work, you will need a ***development environment***: a set of software tools on your computer that makes it possible for you to edit files and compile and run Java programs. Because most of the programs you write will modify parts of programs we discuss in this book, you will need access to those programs. If you are reading this book for a course in which you are enrolled, your instructor will provide an environment for you. If you are studying it on your own, you may find the discussions in the development environment section on the CD-ROM and the *Java Outside In* Web page useful.

Summary

In this chapter we introduced computer programming by studying two sample applications – one creating a banking system, one a traffic control system. In each case we looked first at the system's behavior, then at its structure (what objects and what messages between them make it behave as it does), and then at (part of) its implementation in Java (how we create those objects in the Java programming language).

Although one of our programs has a command-line interface and the other a graphical user interface, they share a common architecture: Both are object oriented. Objects represent banks, bank accounts, terminals, traffic lights, lenses, and buttons. Indeed, even the sequential logic of a traffic light is encapsulated in a **Sequencer** object. In all cases, programs work because objects send messages to other objects.

It is software that makes our general-purpose computer look like a variety of special-purpose machines. You can think of the Java compiler (which we invoke with the **javac** command) and the Java Virtual Machine (which we invoke with the **java** command) as programs that together serve to make our computer act like a special-purpose Java machine that can read and understand Java programs. Then Java programs (for example, our traffic light) in turn make our "Java machines" look like more specialized machines (for example, a traffic light). Little magic is as much fun as this reality!

In the chapters that follow, we study object-oriented programming, particularly Java programming, in a more orderly fashion. In Chapter 2 we start by systematically examining some of the primitive linguistic elements in Java. We will also see how Java does arithmetic, how a **main** method gets things started, and how we can test our Java classes. These concepts will be useful to us in succeeding chapters.

Exercises

The exercises in this chapter ask you to explore the two programs we have studied and then to make small (and sometimes not-so-small) changes so that they behave a little differently. Some of the changes affect code we've discussed in the chapter; others affect files you will have read on your own. The exercises should reinforce your understanding of how the programs work and give you a chance to become familiar with your computing environment.

1-1   Start a journal for recording your experiences while working on the exercises. You will find that writing about your work makes it easier to understand what you have been doing. When we teach this or any other programming course, we require our students to submit some version of a journal with each assignment.

1-2   Compile and run the banking application. Play with the simulation and write about its behavior. In particular, record what happens when an account is overdrawn (more is withdrawn than has been deposited), or when you type in silly responses to the prompts. Describe how the program's interaction with the user (that is, the *user interface*) might be improved. You don't have to make the improvements; just discuss what they should be.

1-3   Make a copy of **Bank.java**. Then make the following changes. (You should not alter **BankAccount.java**.) Complete each part of the exercise by compiling, running, and testing your program before proceeding to the next part. Record your progress in your journal. What mistakes (if any) did you make? How did you fix them? What was confusing? How did you clear up the confusion? Be sure to insert a comment in the program documenting each change as you make it. Be sure also to preserve the way the program source looks to the reader: the indentations, the use of white space, and the conventions for when to use uppercase letters.

    a. Change the name of the bank from "Engulf and Devour" to one of your own choosing in the welcoming and departing messages. Notice that the change need be made in only one place in the source code.

    b. Add a third **BankAccount**, **account3**, and make all necessary changes so that the user can perform transactions on it.

c. Have the program print out the balances of all accounts, just before saying goodbye. For example:

```
account1 balance: $1000
account2 balance: $2000
account3 balance: $3000
Goodbye from Engulf and Devour
```

d. Have the program print out the total of all the account balances just before saying goodbye. For example:

```
account1 balance: $1000
account2 balance: $2000
account3 balance: $3000
total of all balances: $6000
Goodbye from Engulf and Devour
```

Make that computation at the last minute – do not try to keep track of the total as the balances change.

1-4   Make a copy of **BankAccount.java**. Modify the methods **getBalance**, **deposit**, and **withdraw** so as to charge a fixed fee of one dollar for each transaction by subtracting 1 from **balance** in each method. Recompile **BankAccount.java** and rerun the banking program to see how it behaves now. Write about any problems you encountered along the way and how you solved them. Write about how you made sure you adequately tested all of your changes.

1-5   Modify the **Bank** class so that a customer can transfer money between accounts:

```
Welcome to Engulf and Devour
Account number (1,2 or 3), 0 to shut down: 1
Transactions: exit, help, deposit, withdraw, transfer, balance
transaction: balance
200
transaction: transfer
account you want to transfer to: 2
amount: 50
transaction: balance
150
transaction: exit
Account number (1, 2 or 3), 0 to shut down: 2
transaction: balance
250
transaction: exit
Account number (1, 2 or 3), 0 to shut down:
```

Implement this by defining method **transfer** in **Bank.java**:

```
public void transfer( BankAccount from, BankAccount to )
{
        // write the Java code here to do the work
}
```

and making "transfer" one of the choices in **processTransactionsForAccount**.

1-6   Compile and run the traffic light simulation. Try clicking on the button labeled "Next" several times. Write about any improvements that you'd like made to the graphical user interface.

1-7   Modify **Sequencer.java** so that the traffic light goes through a **WALK** state. Notice that **TrafficLight** already has a **setWalk** method. You will have to introduce a new constant, **WALK**, to represent the additional state, as well as a new **case** clause in the **switch** statement. Be sure to comment your modified program appropriately.

1-8   When you have completed the previous exercise and run the program, you should see that a "Walk" light is a red and yellow displayed simultaneously. This is how it is in Boston, our (the authors') home town. Perhaps it is different in yours. If so, modify the program so that it simulates your local "Walk" light. Otherwise, modify the program so that the "Walk" light is red and green displayed simultaneously.

1-9   This is harder: Modify the traffic light simulation so that a traffic light has a "Walk" button below the "Next" button in the GUI. When the user presses the "Walk" button, the light should pass through a **WALK** state *when it next leaves the* **STOP** *state*. For example, if the light is yellow when "Walk" is pressed then when "Next" is pressed once, the light turns red as usual. When "Next" is pressed again, the light shows "Walk."

You will have to add an extra **Button** in **TrafficLight** and write another listener class, **WalkButtonListener**.

Here is one plan of attack. First, make changes to **Sequencer**:

a. Write out the list of states that the light should pass through. Note the special conditional in the **STOP** state. If the "Walk" button has been pressed, we must shift to the **WALK** state; otherwise, we shift to the **GO** state. Think about how you might keep track of whether or not the "Walk" button has been pressed.

b. Modify **Sequencer** to add the new state constant **WALK**. Declare the **boolean** field **walkPressed** for keeping track of when the "Walk" button has been pressed. This field should be initialized to **false** to reflect the initial condition that the button has not yet been pressed.

c. Add a new method to **Sequencer** named **pressWalk**, which sets the field **walkPressed** to true.

d. Modify **Sequencer**'s method **next**, to reflect the new sequence of states you've outlined in step a. Don't forget to reset the **walkPressed** field to **false** when moving from the **WALK** state back to the **GO** state.

Second, define a new class, **WalkButtonListener**, in the file **WalkButtonListener.java**. This class will be very much like **NextButtonListener**, but the **actionPerformed** method will send the **Sequencer** a **setWalk** message instead of a **next** message. To save having to type the whole thing from scratch, you can start with a copy of **NextButtonListener.java** and change it.

Finally, modify the **main** method in **TrafficLight** as follows:

a. Introduce a new **Button**, labeled "Walk," and a new **WalkButtonListener**. Follow the pattern used for the "Next" **Button** and its **NextButtonListener**. Don't forget to associate **WalkButtonListener** with the new **Button**, using an **addListener** message. This completes the object structure.

b. Then add the new "Walk" **Button** to the **Frame**, placing it in the **SOUTH** position, just beneath the "Next" **Button**.

1-10   This is also harder: Add a second light and modify the **Sequencer** so that the two lights are synchronized as if they were controlling two intersecting lanes of traffic.

1-11   Play with the values of **SIZE** and **OFFSET** in **Lens.java** to see how they affect the display.

EStore exercises

The following exercises deal with what we call the EStore. We have written an application that simulates online shopping. The design uses objects to represent an **EStore**, **Item**s to purchase, and a **ShoppingCart** to put them in. The source code is in Listings 1-7, 1-8, and 1-9. We will not discuss the EStore application in the text but will provide exercises based on that application in this and succeeding chapters.

1-12   Before you look at the **EStore** simulation, you should try the real thing (up to the point at which you actually enter your credit card number). Point your Web browser at an online store and think about the user interface you encounter. Try a nonprofit site like http://store.massaudubon.org (the Massachusetts Audubon Society).

Now compile the **EStore** source with the command

```
%> javac EStore.java ShoppingCart.java Item.java
```

and run the shopping simulation with the command

```
%> java EStore
```

After you have played with the **EStore** application, write several paragraphs describing how the store behaves. In particular, record what happens when you type in silly responses at the prompt. Describe how the store's user interface might be improved. What features would you like to see in the store? How does it compare to your real (fake) shopping experience?

You might want to explore a Web site that a small business might use to design and build its online store.

1-13   Change the name of the **EStore** from "Virtual Minimal Minimall" to whatever name you choose. To do that,

    a. Edit a copy of **EStore.java**. Find the place in the file where the name is set. Change it. Save the file.

    b. Recompile **EStore.java**.

    c. Run the simulation.

    d. Check that the change you made to the program produces the correct output.

    e. Write yourself a congratulatory note in your journal.

1-14   Add another **Item** to the **EStore** inventory. You choose its name and its cost. Follow the same software development cycle steps outlined in the previous exercise.

1-15   Figure out how to have the **EStore** keep track of the number of customers who have visited it, the total amount of money they have spent, and the total number of **Item**s purchased. Have the program print out that information just before the store closes.

Chapter 2

First Things Second

In Chapter 1 we studied two programs that work by having objects communicate with one another. In this chapter we introduce some of the more primitive elements we need to build objects in Java – identifiers, keywords, literals, types, values, and variables – and the order in which statements in source code are executed. We study two examples, a simple change-making program and a program that uses objects to model linear equations. Those examples demonstrate how Java does arithmetic, how to start a Java program with a **main** method, how conventions make programs easier to read, and how to test programs. We start where Java programs start, with **main**; we finish with an introduction to flow control in programs.

The main Method

In Chapter 1 we asked the JVM to start the banking and traffic light applications with the commands **java Bank** and **java TrafficLight**, respectively. Those commands work because each of the classes **Bank** and **TrafficLight** contains a **main** method: Java programs start at a **main**[1] method that looks like this:

```
public static void main (String[] args)
{
    // code to execute goes here
}
```

We will discuss the meaning of all the words on that line in time. For now, just copy them when you need to write **main**. For example, consider the change-making application defined in class **Change** and shown in Listing 2-1.

Listing 2-1: A change-making program
```
1   // joi/2/change/Change.java
2   //
3   //
4   // Copyright 2003 Bill Campbell and Ethan Bolker
5
```

---

[1] Applets, programs meant to run under the control of a Web browser, work differently. Applets have no **main** method because the browser itself is the "main program." We address applets in Chapter 10.

```
 6  /**
 7   * Program to make change.
 8   * Prompts for input using Terminal method readInt().
 9   *
10   * @version 2
11   */
12
13  public class Change
14  {
15     /**
16      * Illustrate simple arithmetic.
17      */
18
19     public static void main (String[] args)
20     {
21        Terminal terminal = new Terminal();
22        int amount;
23
24        amount      = terminal.readInt("Amount, in cents: ");
25        int dimes   = amount/10;
26        amount      = amount %  10;
27        int nickels = amount / 5;
28        amount      = amount % 5;
29        terminal.println(dimes   + " dimes");
30        terminal.println(nickels + " nickels");
31        terminal.println(amount  + " pennies");
32     }
33  }
```

main is the only method in the **Change** class. The code in **main** creates a **Terminal** object for reading and writing, prompts the user for an amount (in cents), and then prints out the number of dimes, nickels, and pennies needed to express that amount as change. For example, if the user were to choose 133 as an amount, the entire interaction would look like this:

```
%> java Change
Amount, in cents: 133
13 dimes
0 nickels
3 pennies
```

Because this program is much shorter and simpler than the ones we looked at in Chapter 1, we can study it in more detail. We use it to explain some of the *syntax* of

Java – the rules you must follow in order to construct a program that the Java compiler can process.

Tokens

When you read English you naturally pay attention to the words and the punctuation, because they convey the meaning. You rarely focus on the individual letters that make up the words. You read Java the same way, breaking the text into tokens, the official Java term for the pieces you pay attention to when you read a program. A *token* is the smallest part of a program that has meaning in its own right. The tokens on line 25 of **Change.java** are **int**, **dimes**, **=**, **amount**, **/**, **10**, and**;**. On line 29, **terminal.println** is not a token (it's three tokens), nor is **print** (it's part of the token **println**). What the tokens are in any given Java statement will become clear with experience.

Identifiers

An *identifier* is a token we use to name something in a program. For example, in the change-making program the identifiers **Change**, **String**, and **Terminal** are the names of classes; the identifiers **main**, **readInt**, and **println** are the names of methods; the identifier **args** is the name of a parameter to the **main** method; and the identifiers **terminal**, **amount**, **dimes**, and **nickels** are the names of variables. In the **BankAccount** class we studied in Chapter 1, **balance** is a field (there are no fields in the **Change** class).

A token used as an identifier must be a sequence of letters and digits the first of which must be a letter. The underscore character (_) and the dollar sign (**$**) are considered letters in identifiers.[2] **account1** and **an_account** are legal identifiers. **1account an-account** and **account*** are not.[3] Case does matter: on line 21 in **Change.java**, **Terminal** and **terminal** are different identifiers.

Some identifiers in a program name things that have been defined elsewhere for our use. For example, in the change-making program, the class **String** comes from the Java library. We wrote class **Terminal** and its methods **readInt** and **println** for this text in order to simplify input and output.

We choose the names for things that we introduce ourselves. In the change-making program, we are responsible for, and so name, the class **Change** and the variables **terminal**, **amount**, **dimes**, and **nickels.** The particular names are not important to the Java compiler. If we change the identifier **amount** to the identifier **uncle** everywhere in the source code, we will not change how the program behaves.

---

[2] Java even allows one to *start* an identifier with one of these special characters, but please don't.
[3] The legal characters in identifiers are not limited to those familiar to writers of English. Both **café** and **mañana** are acceptable identifiers.

But the names we choose are extremely important to someone reading our program. Recall that a program has *two* audiences. The first is the Java compiler. The second is the other programmers who must be able to read and understand our code. For each of these audiences there corresponds a body of rules that we must follow if our programs are to be meaningful. The compiler requires that we follow official Java syntax so that it can create the class files for the JVM to execute. Other programmers expect that we will honor some programming ***conventions*** – rules governing the style in which we write.

Both audiences are equally important. A program that doesn't compile can't be executed. A program that's poorly written can't be read and thus can't be maintained. In the software industry, maintenance can account for as much as 85 percent of a program's development costs over the course of its lifetime. Moreover, we learn how to program from reading other people's programs. If we can't read them, we won't learn much!

We will learn many programming conventions as we learn Java. We start with those that govern how we choose identifiers:

- Every name should provide a good, compact description of the thing it names. So `amount` really is better than `uncle` in the change-making program.
- Class names should be nouns and begin with uppercase letters. When the name consists of several words, the internal words should also start with uppercase letters. For example:

```
Terminal
BankAccount
String
```

- Field names and variable names should be nouns and begin with lowercase letters. Internal words should start with uppercase letters. For example:

```
terminal
amount
account1
balance
bankName
```

- Method names should be verbs and begin with lowercase letters. Internal words should start with uppercase letters. For example:

```
readInt
getBalance
deposit[4]
```

---

[4] In English, some words may serve as both a noun and a verb – for example, "deposit". Even in the face of that ambiguity, we thought it was the best word for the `BankAccount` method that adds an amount to the balance.

- Names of things that remain constant[5] should be uppercase, and internal words should be separated by underscores. For example:

```
int INITIAL_DEPOSIT = 200
int OFFSET = 20
int MAX_VALUE = 2147483647
double PI = 3.14159265358979323846
```

Following these naming conventions makes a program easier to read, because the *form* of an identifier tells us something about its purpose. We can tell immediately that in line 21 of **Change.java**

```
21        Terminal terminal =
```

the identifier **Terminal** names a class, whereas the identifier **terminal** names a variable.

Keywords

Some tokens are *reserved words*. Each has a special meaning in Java and so cannot be used as an identifier. Some reserved words are *keywords*. Here are the Java keywords[6] – each is described in the glossary. Most we will discuss in the text.

abstract	double	interface	switch
assert	else	long	synchronized
boolean	extends	native	this
break	final	new	throw
byte	finally	package	throws
case	float	private	transient
catch	for	protected	try
char	goto	public	void
class	if	return	volatile
const	implements	short	while
continue	import	static	
default	instanceof	strictfp	
do	int	super	

The tokens **true**, **false**, and **null** are reserved words even though they are not keywords.

---

[5] In Chapter 9 we will learn how to use the Java keyword **final** to declare things that can't be changed.
[6] These are the keywords for the version of Java current at this writing. More may be added in later versions.

Literals

A *literal* is a token that denotes a value. The tokens **5**, **10**, and
"Amount, in cents: " are literals in our change-making program.

The tokens **5** and **10** are integer literals expressed in familiar decimal (base 10) notation.

"Amount, in cents: " is a **String** literal. Note that it's all one token even though the English text inside the quotation marks consists of several words and punctuation marks.

The tokens **'a'** and **'\n'** are character literals. The first represents the lowercase character **a**, and the second is a special construct representing the newline or carriage return character.[7] We will learn more about characters in Chapter 8.

The tokens **2.718** and **6.02e23** (or **6.02E23**) are literals representing decimal fractions. The second illustrates Java's syntax for numbers expressed in scientific notation. It is how we write 6.02×10^{23}.

The reserved words **true** and **false** are **boolean** literals. **null** is an object literal.

White Space

Spaces, tabs, and carriage returns are ***white space***. White space is one way the Java compiler can tell where tokens start and end. For example, in line 13

```
public class Change
```

white space separates the keywords **public** and **class** and the identifier **Change**. In line 25

```
int dimes   = amount/10;
```

white space separates the keyword **int** from the identifier **dimes**. No white space is needed around the division operator, **/**, because the compiler knows that **/** is not part of an identifier and can't start a literal, so the compiler can separate the tokens for the identifier **amount**, the operator **/**, and the integer literal **10**. Even the white space surrounding the **=** operator is unnecessary. The Java compiler will accept

```
int dimes=amount/10;
```

But extra white space can make the program easier to read. We used several extra blanks in order to line up the equals signs on lines 24–8.

The use of white space above and beyond what the compiler requires is called ***prettyprinting***. When you modify a program, try to follow the prettyprinting style you

---

[7] This special newline character works well for Java programs in Windows and Unix systems but may fail on a Macintosh. There are tools in the Java library that will work on all three, but they are not easy for beginners to use, so we have not introduced them here.

find there.[8] Many software companies prescribe the prettyprinting conventions their programmers should use. When you write programs yourself, establish conventions that please you and are likely to please your readers. Some text editors can help prettyprint your programs for you. Here are a few of the prettyprinting conventions we follow in this book. We will encounter more later.

- In general, we put just one statement (often ending with a semicolon) on each line.
- We put the curly braces (**{** and **}**) that enclose class bodies and method bodies on separate lines, with the closing brace in the same column as the opening brace.
- We use indentation to clarify the logical structure of our programs. In particular, when curly braces enclose code, we indent the enclosed code four spaces.
- We use one or more completely blank lines to separate the definitions of methods in a class. We rarely use blank lines within a method.

Comments

We have already seen **comments** in programs. To the Java compiler, comments are a form of white space. It acts as if they weren't there. But the human reader needs good comments that document both how a program is to be used and how it is implemented. Java supports three kinds of comments:

- Text extending from the characters **//** to the end of the line forms a **line comment**. For example:

```
// I am a line comment; I extend to the end of the line.
```

- Text between the characters **/**** and ***/** forms a **javadoc comment**. For example:

```
/**
 * I am a
 * javadoc comment.
 */
```

Javadoc comments describe classes, fields, and methods. The **javadoc** program, which we discuss later, converts javadoc comments to Web pages you can use to study how a class is constructed. The *****'s on the middle lines of this javadoc comment are not necessary. But you will always see them in our code; they are one of our programming conventions.

- Text between the characters **/*** and ***/** forms a **traditional comment**. For example:

```
/* I am a
traditional comment. */
```

---

[8] When we grade our students' programs, we deduct points for poorly formatted code, even when the programs run perfectly.

Traditional comments are a legacy from the C language. We rarely use them in our programs.

Variables, Types, and Values

Now that we know some of the rules for constructing the tokens in Java programs (the *syntax*), we can start to think about what those tokens mean (the *semantics*). We'll start with variables.

A *variable* is a place in a program to store a *value*. In the change-making program, **terminal**, **amount**, **dimes**, and **nickels** are variables. Fields like the **balance** in a **BankAccount** object are variables too.

Each variable has a *name*, which is an identifier.

Each variable has a *type* that specifies what kind of value it can store. The variables **amount**, **nickels**, **dimes**, and **balance** are of type **int**; they hold integer values. The variable **terminal** is of type **Terminal**; it refers to a **Terminal** object.

Every variable must be *declared* before it can be used. The declaration tells the compiler the variable's type and name. In the change-making program, the statements

```
Terminal terminal = ... ;
int amount;
```

declare the variables **terminal** of type **Terminal** and **amount** of type **int**, illustrating the general form of the declaration statement:

```
type variableName;
```

Note that when the type is a class, like **Terminal**, it begins with an uppercase letter.

Assignment

Once a variable has been declared, it can be given a value in an *assignment statement*, using the token **=**. On lines 24, 26, and 28 of **Change.java**, several different values are assigned in turn to the **amount** variable.

It is possible (and common) to declare a variable and initialize it with an assignment statement all in one line rather than in two. An experienced programmer would probably replace the lines

```
22      int amount;
23
24      amount   = terminal.readInt("Amount, in cents: ");
```

with the single line

```
int amount = terminal.readInt("Amount, in cents: ");
```

If we attempt to assign a **String** value to **amount**, with code like

```
amount = "150";
```

the Java compiler will detect the type mismatch, generate an error message, and refuse to produce a class file. As a beginning programmer you may find the compiler annoyingly picky and wish it would just do what you mean, whatever you say. As you gain programming experience, you will bless a compiler that checks so much at compile time.

Arithmetic

Our change-making program provides an opportunity to learn how Java handles integer arithmetic.

The Standard Binary Operators

Java, like most programming languages, supports the usual arithmetic operators **+**, **-**, *****, and **/**. (The asterisk (*****) is the multiplication operator.) These are called binary operators because each combines two numbers (operands). Java honors the usual rules of operator precedence. For example, in the expression

```
a + b * c
```

the multiplication **b * c** is done before the addition of **a**. The binary operators ***** and **/** are said to have greater precedence than the binary operators **+** and **-**. These operators are *left associative* – that is, a sequence of computations using operators of the same precedence is evaluated from left to right. For example, the expression

```
a / b / c * d
```

is the same as

```
((a / b) / c) * d
```

Fortunately, Java supports the use of parentheses to force any particular order of operations we wish. For example,

```
(a + b) * c
```

guarantees that the addition is done before the multiplication. When you write a complicated arithmetic expression, always insert enough parentheses to make the meaning clear. Do not rely on the possibly arcane precedence rules of the particular language you are using.

+ and − as Unary Operators

Java supports the use of **+** and **−** as unary operators, written as a prefix to the single operand. When used that way they have the greatest precedence of all. Thus, the expression

```
- a * b + - c / d
```

is equivalent to

```
((- a) * b) + ((- c) / d)
```

Unary operators are right associative. For example,

```
- - - a
```

is the same as

```
- (- (- a))
```

but you would *never* use either expression in a real program.

You will find a table summarizing the precedence and associativity for *all* Java operators in the glossary under ***operators***.

Integer Division and Remainders

All our arithmetic so far has been with integers. What Java does when you divide two integers may surprise you. It *truncates* the quotient – that is, it computes the integer part of the quotient. So **49/10** is **4**, not the **4.9** you might expect. In fact, our change-making program relies on this feature in lines 25 and 27 to compute the number of dimes and nickels.

To find the integer remainder when you divide two integers, use the modulus operator **%**.

```
49 % 10
```

yields the value **9**, the remainder obtained when you divide **49** by **10**. Our change-making program uses this operator on lines 26 and 28 to compute what would be left after subtracting the value of the dimes and nickels.

+ for Strings

When the operands for **+** in a Java program are **String**s (rather than the numbers you would expect), the operator stands for string concatenation. ("Concatenate" is a fancy way to say "glue together.") When Java evaluates the expression

```
"hound" + "dog"
```

it produces a new **String "hounddog"**. If only one of the operands is a **String**, and if Java knows how to convert the other operand to a **String**, then it makes the conversion and does the concatenation. Thus, if the integer variable **dimes** has the value 2,

```
dimes + " dimes"
```

evaluates to produce the **String "2 dimes".** Note the space in the **String** literal **" dimes"**. Without it you would get the ugly and wrong **"2dimes"**.

Testing the Limits

In an ideal universe, there are infinitely many integers and no one even dreams of dividing by zero. In Java, integers do not go on forever, and division by zero sometimes happens and must be dealt with. In the exercises, you will study these phenomena by playing with the program **IntArithmetic** (Listing 2-4).

Example: Linear Equations

To continue our study of arithmetic in Java, consider the problem of converting temperature measured on the Celsius scale to degrees Fahrenheit. If **c** is the Celsius temperature, the Fahrenheit temperature **f** can be calculated with the formula

```
f = (9/5)c + 32
```

If we solve this equation for **c** in terms of **f**, we discover how to convert from Fahrenheit to Celsius:

```
c = (5/9)(f - 32)
```

These formulae are almost Java. Before we turn them into Java, we observe that we can do considerably more than these simple conversions without doing much more work. Rather than focus on temperatures, we will study the more general linear equation

```
y = mx + b
```

whose graph is the line with slope **m** and y-intercept **b**.

Integers will not be good enough to represent the slopes and intercepts of our linear equations; we need 9/5, which is 1.8, for Celsius-to-Fahrenheit conversion. We use type **double** to store double precision floating point numbers. These numbers model the decimals we compute with in everyday life.

Class **LinearEquation** defines a class of objects that represent linear equations. It has no **main** method and can't be run. Like the **BankAccount** class, it exists to provide services for other programs that need what it has to offer. Class **Temperatures** is an application that uses **LinearEquation** objects to solve the temperature-conversion problem and, at the same time, acts as a test program for those objects. We will look first at **Temperatures.java** (Listing 2-2), then at **LinearEquation.java** (Listing 2-3).

In **Temperatures.java**, we construct a **LinearEquation** object for capturing Celsius-to-Fahrenheit conversion by supplying a slope (9/5) and an intercept (32):

```
25 LinearEquation c2f = new LinearEquation( 9.0/5.0, 32.0 );
```

This line of code first declares variable **c2f** of type **LinearEquation** and then creates a **new LinearEquation** object for that variable to refer to. The decimal points in the argument **9.0/5.0** are very important. To human eyes they seem unnecessary. But if we had written simply **9/5**, truncated division for integers would have taken effect and the argument passed would be 1 (converted by default to 1.0). The decimal point and trailing 0 in **32.0** are not necessary but do help the reader.

To use a **LinearEquation** object, once we have constructed it, we can send it a **compute** message. For example, to convert 20.0 degrees Celsius to degrees Fahrenheit, we would invoke **c2f**'s **compute** method with 20.0 as its argument by sending the message

```
c2f.compute( 20.0 )
```

The **compute** method will return the (Fahrenheit) result 78.0. In **Temperatures**.java we use **compute** this way:

```
35    terminal.print( "c2f.compute( 0.0 ), should see 32.0: ");
36    terminal.println( c2f.compute( 0.0 ) );
```

Line 35 just prints the string **"c2f.compute(0.0), should see 32.0: "**, telling the user what to expect. Line 36 prints the result of sending a **compute(0.0)** message to the **LinearEquation** object **c2f**. If 32.0 is *not* what you see, then there is an error somewhere in the program.

Testing Programs

When you have designed and written a program that compiles successfully, you are ready to begin testing. Testing is a central part of software construction. A program isn't necessarily correct just because it compiles and runs. Someone must check that it does exactly what it was designed to do. There are entire books (from Cambridge University Press and other publishers) that address the problems of testing large programs. As a beginning programmer, you need to learn how to test the relatively small programs you write.

We have just seen how to begin testing the constructors and methods in the **LinearEquation** class by writing a *test driver*: an application like **Temperatures** that tries them out. That application resembles the change-making application in one respect: All it has in it is a **main** method to start things off. There are no **Temperatures** objects, just as there are no **Change** objects. **Temperatures** exists only in order to exercise the **LinearEquation** class – we don't really have any immediate need for a temperature-conversion program.[9]

There is more to **Temperatures.java** than what we have seen so far. **LinearEquation** has a public method, **getInverse**, that returns the new **LinearEquation** object you would get by "solving for x in terms of y" as in our temperature-conversion discussion above. We test that in **Temperatures** by declaring another **LinearEquation** variable **f2c** and initializing it with the result of sending **c2f** a **getInverse** message:

```
28     LinearEquation f2c = c2f.getInverse();
```

Then we test **f2c** as we did **c2f**:

```
37 terminal.print("f2c.compute(212.0), should see 100.0: ");
38 terminal.println( f2c.compute( 212.0 ) );
```

These tests in the first part of **main** (lines 34–8) are ***self-documenting***. Each tells the user first what to expect and then what has been computed so that it is easy to see whether the answers returned by the **LinearEquation** methods produce what we know to be correct answers. Programmers can write self-documenting tests when they know just what their code should do.

But it is not reasonable to rely exclusively on programmers to test their work. They may not think of all the cases that need testing. They may not imagine how careless the user of the program may be. Software companies have quality-assurance engineers whose task is to try to break programs by testing them with all kinds of strange input values. To help them do their job, programmers write ***interactive*** tests. These more closely resemble the way the program will be used, because the programmer does not know the input values. Lines 45–56 in **Temperatures.java** provide an interactive test for **LinearEquation** objects:

```
45     terminal.println( "Interactive tests:" );
46     while ( terminal.readYesOrNo("more?") ) {
47         double degreesCelsius =
48             terminal.readDouble( "degrees Celsius: " );
49         terminal.println(" = " +
50                           c2f.compute( degreesCelsius ) +
51                           " degrees Fahrenheit" );
52         double degreesFahrenheit =
53             terminal.readDouble( "degrees Fahrenheit: " );
```

---

[9] In fact, in an early draft of *Java Outside In* this program was called **TestLinearEquation**.

```
54          terminal.println(" = " +
55                          f2c.compute( degreesFahrenheit ) +
56                          " degrees Celsius" );
57    }
```

The **while** loop sends the **terminal** a **readYesOrNo** message. The code there prompts the user to enter "y" if she wishes to continue, "n" if not. If yes, she is asked first for a Celsius temperature to convert to Fahrenheit, then for a Fahrenheit temperature to convert to Celsius. In this interactive test the program cannot know what the correct value should be. It can report only what the **LinearEquation** objects tell it. The tester must work the answers out with a calculator (or on scratch paper) in order to check that the program is behaving correctly.

Flow Control

We close this chapter by making explicit something we have been taking for granted so far. How does the JVM decide which line of code to execute? The answer is straightforward. Execution begins at the first statement of the **main** method and then continues with the statements in the order in which they appear in the source code, with a few simple exceptions:

- When a statement sends a message to an object, the JVM looks in that object's description for the body of the method with the corresponding name. The statements there are executed in order. When the method returns, execution resumes just where it left off. Line 45 in the code fragment above from **Temperatures.java** provides an example. When this line executes, the JVM looks in **Terminal.java** for the **println** method, runs the code it finds there (printing **"Interactive tests: "**), and then returns to execute line 46.
- "**while** loop" logic can change the order of execution. Line 46 provides an example. If the user types "y" in response to the prompt, then the **terminal**'s **readYesOrNo** method returns the value **true**, and the body of the **while** loop (lines 47–55, governed by the braces **{** and **}** on lines 46 and 56) executes. Then control returns to the top of the loop, and line 46 executes again. If this time the user types "n", then control passes to the first line after the loop body. That would be line 57 in **Temperatures.java**.

  Programs **While1Demo.java** and **While2Demo.java** (Examples 2-1 and 2-2) explore the syntax and semantics of **while** in more detail.

- "**if else**" logic can change the order of execution. The code

```
1     if (x == 1) {
2         terminal.println("x is 1");
3     }
```

```
4        else {
5            terminal.println("x is not 1");
6        }
7        terminal.println("after the if-else: x is " + x );
```

produces the following output when the value of the integer variable **x** happens to be 1:

```
x is 1
after the if-else: x is 1
```

The test on line 1 is true, so line 2 executes. The **else** clause is not examined and control passes to line 7 – the first line after the **if-else** statement. This follows from the ordinary meanings of the words "if" and "else" in English, and from the fact that Java uses the **==** operator to test whether two **int**s are the same. If the value of **x** were 2, we would see

```
x is not 1
after the if-else: x is 2
```

Here is a somewhat more complicated example from **Bank.java** (Listing 1-1):

```
84       if ( accountNumber == 1 ) {
85            return account1;
86       }
87       else if ( accountNumber == 2 ) {
88            return account2;
89       }
90       else if ( accountNumber == 0 ) {
91           return null;
92       }
93       else {
94           atm.println( "No account numbered " +
95                        accountNumber + "; try  again" );
96           return this.whichAccount();
97       }
```

IfDemo.java (Example 2-3) explores the syntax and semantics of **if** in more detail.

Summary

This chapter has spelled out some of the nitty-gritty details you need to know to read, write, and run Java programs. You should now understand

- that the JVM looks for a **main** method to start an application
- how to break Java source code into tokens

- keywords, literals, and identifiers
- how to do arithmetic in Java
- flow control (what happens next in a running program)

While learning this material, we also learned about programming conventions[10] and program testing in the context of an application modeling linear equations.

In the next chapter we will look in more detail at how Java manages objects.

Exercises

2-1   Create a text file for your journal for this chapter. You can use this journal to record any observations about your work on these exercises. Among other things, discuss

- Which parts were easy?
- Which parts were hard?
- Which parts were interesting?
- Which parts were boring? (Interesting/boring may or may not correlate with hard/easy!)
- Where did you get stuck and what did you do about it?
- How might the instructions be improved?

2-2   Explain why you cannot run the **BankAccount** program with the command

```
%> java BankAccount
```

You might want to try this and interpret the error message.

2-3   Practice your understanding of the words "token," "identifier," "literal," "variable," "type," and "prettyprint" and the phrase "programming convention" by using them to describe the structure of some interesting lines from **BankAccount.java**.

2-4   Which of the Java keywords listed in this chapter appear in programs we have studied so far? (Your text editor or operating system probably has a command that will search for a word in a file or a set of files quickly and easily. Now would be a good time to learn that command.)

2-5   Make a copy of the file **Change.java** in your own workspace. Compile it, run it, read it, and understand it. What happens when you ask it to make change for 123.45 cents? For 100 cents? For a negative amount? For xyz cents?

---

[10] For more information, see Sun's Java conventions at http://java.sun.com/docs/codeconv/ and consult *The Elements of Java Style* (Allan Vermeulen et al., Cambridge University Press, 2000).

2-6   Modify your copy of **Change.java** in several ways that the Java compiler might not like. List and discuss the error messages you see. When a change is acceptable to the compiler but violates a programming convention, say so. Here are some things you might try:

- Omit a semicolon
- Omit a closing parenthesis, curly brace, or quotation mark
- Misspell "amount" somewhere in the program
- Change "amount" to "uncle" everywhere in the program. (Your text editor probably has a command that will do this for you quickly and easily. Now would be a good time to learn that command.)
- Change the indentation of some lines. Put several statements together on a line. Split a statement over two lines.

2-7   Modify a fresh copy of **Change.java** so that it makes change using dollar bills, half dollars, and quarters, as well as nickels, dimes, and pennies. While you are making those changes, also have it report the total, this way:

```
%> java Change
Make change.
Amount in cents: 123
1 dollars
0 half dollars
0 quarters
2 dimes
0 nickels
3 pennies
total: 123 cents
```

There are at least two ways you might report the total:

- Use another variable to remember the input amount so that you can print its value at the end.
- After the change has been made, use the values of the variables for each kind of coin to compute the total amount of money those coins represent, and print that value.

What do you see as the advantages and disadvantages of each method? Which will you choose, and why?

Remember to follow good software engineering practices:

- Edit the header comment in **Change.java** to indicate that you have changed the original.
- Be sure your modified program honors the prettyprinting conventions of the original.

- Be sure to test your program for all kinds of input, to make sure it's working properly. Your journal should describe the tests you tried.

2-8   Modify your **Change.java** so that if no coins of a particular type are used to make change, then the line corresponding to that coin is not reported:

```
%> java Change
Make change.
Amount in cents: 123
1 dollars
2 dimes
3 pennies
total: 123 cents
```

2-9   Modify your **Change.java** further to leave off the plural "s" when there is only one of a particular kind of coin or bill. Remember that the singular for "pennies" is "penny", not "pennie". In our example, you should see:

```
%> java Change
Make change.
Amount in cents: 121
1 dollar
2 dimes
1 penny
total: 121 cents
```

2-10   Imagine a country with only two kinds of coins: nickels, worth five cents, and doubloons, worth two cents. Write class **Doubloons** (in file **Doubloons.java**) to make change in that country. This is tricky. For example, to make change for 1 cent you might offer a nickel and (-2) doubloons, or 3 doubloons and (-1) nickels. Be sure to test your program thoroughly. Write about your design and testing in your programmer's diary.

2-11   Write program **HelloWorld** (in file **HelloWorld.java**) that just prints the **String** "hello, world". You can start with a copy of **Change.java** and remove most of what's there. This short program is commonly the first one you write when you learn a new programming language. Our Java teaching philosophy relegates it to an exercise in Chapter 2. You can write this traditional program without using a **Terminal** for output by sending a **println** message to **System.out** instead:

```
System.out.println("hello, world");
```

2-12   Compile the program **IntArithmetic.java** (Listing 2-4) and run it, observing its behavior. Experiment to find the largest integer the program will accept. What happens when you when you add 1 to it? What happens when you add it to itself? What happens when you divide by 0 (zero)?

2-13   Write class **DoubleArithmetic** so that you can answer the preceding questions about Java operations on values of type **double**. You will want to start with a copy of **IntArithmetic.java** for your **DoubleArithmetic.java** and change **int** to **double** everywhere. Your text editor probably provides a command for that job to save you the searching and typing it would take to make those changes one at a time.

2-14   Write a program modeled on **IntArithmetic.java** that you can use to discover the largest allowable values for the primitive integer types **short** and **long**.

2-15   Write **main** in class **Statistics** to prompt for an integer **n** and then read **n** more integers. After those integers have been entered, the program prints their maximum, minimum, sum, and average. Use the **Terminal** method **readInt** to collect input. Here is a sample program run:

```
%> java Statistics
Integers to read? 3
> 4
> 100
> -4
maximum: 100
minimum: -4
sum: 100
average: 33.333333333333336[11]
```

2-16   One improvement we might make to the bank simulation is to model bank accounts better. What fields besides the integer **balance** do you think a **BankAccount** object needs? Your answer should provide valid declarations for those fields, with comments. For example, you may want

```
private String name; // the account owner
```

Feel free to imagine other objects that will improve your design. For example, you may require

```
private Address address; // the account owner's address
```

even though you know of no **Address** class. If there were such a class, it would have fields for street, city, ZIP code, and so on. You can be as ambitious as you like as long as you explain yourself. What else might the **Bank** want to know about its customers?

If you declare a field of type **Address** in **BankAccount.java**, you must create and compile **Address.java** too. Otherwise **BankAccount.java** will not compile. But an essentially empty **Address.java** will do. You need not specify any fields or methods there.

---

[11] The way Java rounds infinite decimals is not specified.

2-17   Compile and run **Temperatures.java**. Try all sorts of interactive input, including doubles like 32.0 and integers like 12. Try very large numbers and very small numbers. Try doubles written in scientific notation. Experiment to discover what temperature is the same in both degrees Celsius and degrees Fahrenheit. Write about your findings.

2-18   You may recall from your study of algebra that you can find the slope and intercept of a line if you know two points (x_1, y_1) and (x_2, y_2) each of which lies on the line, because then

```
m = (y2 - y1) / (x2 - x1)
b = y1  - x1 m;
```

We have built this algebra into our **LinearEquation** class; we can also construct a **LinearEquation** object by supplying two points (x_1, y_1) and (x_2, y_2) to the alternative version of the constructor:

```
39     public LinearEquation( double x1, double y1,
40                            double x2, double y2 )
```

Nothing in **Temperatures.java** tests this code. Write a test driver for this part of **LinearEquation** by creating class **Interpolate.java** that uses a **LinearEquation** object to find new points on the line joining two given points. Model your program on **Temperatures.java**. First provide some hard-coded self-documenting tests to which you know the answers. Then provide a loop that repeatedly prompts (using the **Terminal readDouble** method) for the coordinates of two points on a line and a value of x for which to compute y. Here is how your application should behave:

```
%> java Interpolate
Hard coded self documenting tests:
study line joining (1,2) and (3,7).
y when x is -1 should be -3: ???
y at midpoint should be 4.5: ???

Interactive tests:
more (y or n): y
x1: 1.5
y1: 2.3
x2: 3.7
y2: 5.3
input x: 4.4
computed value of y: ???
more (y or n):
```

Of course it should produce the right answers instead of **???**.

Consider the sample output above as a precise specification for how your program should behave. Make sure the text and prompts you write match the ones you see here.

Be sure to create **LinearEquation** objects to do the arithmetic. There should be none in your **Interpolate** code!

2-19   Create class **RentalCosts** in file **RentalCosts.java** that uses a **LinearEquation** object to help a customer answer questions about the cost of renting a truck. Your program should prompt the user for the flat fee and the cost per mile and then prompt for the length of the trip and the maximum amount she is willing to spend. Here is how your program should behave:

```
%> java RentalCosts
Flat fee (in dollars): 100
Cost per mile (in dollars): .30
Mileage: 100
Rental cost: $130.0
Amount willing to spend (in dollars): 160
Maximum distance (in miles): 200.0
```

Be sure to create **LinearEquation** objects to do the arithmetic. There should be none in your **RentalCosts** code!

2-20   Create class **PhoneBill** in file **PhoneBill.java** that uses a **LinearEquation** object to help a customer answer questions about the cost of telephone service. Your program should prompt for the monthly basic rate and the cost per message unit and then prompt for the number of message units and the maximum amount she is willing to spend. Here is how your program should behave:

```
%> java PhoneBill
Basic rate (in dollars): 30
Cost per message unit (in cents): 5
Number of message units: 101
Phone bill is: $35.05
Amount willing to spend (in dollars): 40
Maximum number of message units: ???
```

Be sure to create a **LinearEquation** object to do the arithmetic. There should be none in your **PhoneBill** code!

2-21   Think of a real-world system that can be modeled by a linear equation. Design and implement a Java application for that system. Use the previous two exercises as a guide.

2-22   If f(x) = ax + b and g(x) = cx + d are two linear equations, then we can create another linear equation by composing f and g to get the linear equation whose value at
x is computed as f(g(x)) = a(cx+d)+b. Modify **LinearEquation.java** to define
method **compose** such that when **f** and **g** are **LinearEquations**, **f.compose(g)**
returns the **LinearEquation** object that is that composition. Add code like
this:

```
/**
 * (javadoc here describing your method.)
 *
 * @param g (fill in description.)
 * @return (fill in description.)
 */

public LinearEquation compose( LinearEquation g )
{
        // algebra here to create a new LinearEquation from
        // m and b (slope and intercept of this LinearEquation)
        // and g.m and g.b (slope and intercept of g).
        return ???; // the LinearEquation you created
}
```

You will have to work out the algebra to get the slope and intercept of the composition.

To test the **compose** method, modify the **main** method in **Temperatures.java**:

a. Create a new **LinearEquation** object **c2k** converting temperatures from degrees
Celsius to the absolute Kelvin scale, for which the formula is k = c + 273.15.

b. Create a new **LinearEquation** object **f2k** for converting Fahrenheit temperatures
to the Kelvin scale by composing **c2k** and **f2c** in the proper order.

c. Add hard coded self-documenting tests to demonstrate that **c2k** and **f2k** behave as
they should.

d. Add interactive tests for **f2k** and its inverse **k2f**.

2-23   One improvement we might make to the **EStore** simulation (introduced in the exercises in the previous chapter) is to model **Item**s better. What fields besides the
integer **cost** do you think an **Item** object needs? Your answer should provide valid
declarations for those fields, with comments. For example, you may want

```
private String description; // a description of the Item
```

Feel free to imagine other objects that will improve your design. For example:

```
private Manufacturer manufacturer; // who makes this Item?
```

even though you know of no **Manufacturer** class. If there were such a class, it would have fields for an address, a phone number, and so on. You can be as ambitious as you like as long as you explain yourself. What else might the **EStore** want to know about the **Item**s it stocks?

If you declare a field of type **Manufacturer** in **Item.java**, you must create and compile **Manufacturer.java** too. Otherwise **Item.java** will not compile. But an essentially empty **Manufacturer.java** will do. You need not specify any fields or methods there.

Chapter 3

Classes and Objects

In Chapter 1 we looked at two moderately large applications, simulating bank accounts and traffic lights. In Chapter 2 we learned about tokens, keywords, identifiers, arithmetic, flow control, and some Java conventions by studying the linear equation and change-making applications. In this chapter we look more systematically at classes and objects, introducing two new examples – one modeling text files, the other modeling shapes on a computer screen.

Text Files

We want to model the text files on a computer as objects in a Java program. To do that, we will write class **TextFile**. Just as a **BankAccount** object has a **balance** field and a **LinearEquation** object has fields for its **slope** and **intercept**, each **TextFile** attribute will be stored in a field in a **TextFile** object. The most important attribute is the file's contents: the text it contains. Our **TextFile**s will also have an owner, the name of the user who created the file; a creation date, identifying when the file was created; and a modification date, indicating when the file was last modified. Just as a **BankAccount** needs methods for changing and querying its **balance**, a **TextFile** needs methods for modifying its contents and for returning the values of its several attributes.

In our work so far we have started from examples showing the application's behavior. But now we are not thinking about a complete application with a user interface, just about the **TextFile** objects that might be used in some program someday. So we will read the code in file **TextFile.java** (Listing 3-1) first, and demonstrate its use later. Unfortunately, reading the code a line at a time from beginning to end is not the best way to learn what's there. We will look at almost all the lines, but in a more rational order.

Declarations

Java requires the programmer to tell the compiler (and the reader) in advance about each entity it will use. The code that does that is a ***declaration***. Classes, methods, fields, and variables must all be declared before they can be referred to elsewhere in the program.[1]

---

[1] Some programming languages, such as the original BASIC, LISP, and today's scripting languages like Perl, do not require explicit declarations.

Class Declarations

Line 18 in **TextFile.java** declares class **TextFile**:

```
18    public class TextFile
```

The keyword **class** tells the Java compiler that we are declaring a class. The identifier **TextFile** is the name we have chosen for that class. The keyword **public** tells the compiler that this class may be used by any other class. The braces (**{}**) on lines 19 and 179 surround the *body* of the **TextFile** class declaration. The code between those braces provides the blueprint for constructing and using **TextFile** objects (instances of the **TextFile** class). It contains declarations for the fields (instance variables) that belong to **TextFile** objects and declarations for the methods that are invoked when messages are sent to those objects.

A class declaration establishes a new *reference type* that may be used in other parts of the program in the declarations of variables, fields, and method parameters. Thus in the banking example in Chapter 1, the declaration of class **BankAccount** in **BankAccount.java** allows the **Bank** object described in **Bank.java** to use objects of type **BankAccount**.

Instance Variable Declarations

Lines 22–5 declare the four instance variables (fields) that every **TextFile** object maintains in order to remember what we have decided it must know about itself.

```
22 private String owner;    // Who owns the file.
23 private Date createDate; // When the file was created.
24 private Date modDate;     // When the file was last modified.
25 private String contents; // The text stored in the file.
```

Each of these declarations provides the type and the name of the field being declared. The name is an identifier we choose. The type must be one of the primitive types (like **int** or **double** or **boolean**) or a reference type: the name of a defined class. The **TextFile** fields **contents** and **owner** refer to objects of type **String**. The fields **createDate** and **modDate** refer to objects of type **Date**. We can use those reference types here because the library of classes that comes with Java provides definitions of class **String** and class **Date**.[2]

The adjective **private** in these declarations means that only the methods in the **TextFile** class may refer to these fields.

---

[2] The Java compiler knows where to find class **String**. We need to tell it where to find class **Date** with the import statement on line 6:
```
6    import java.util.Date;
```

These instance variables are visible only in the body of the class declaration – that is, between the outermost curly braces on lines 19 and 179. We refer to that area of the program in which a name will be recognized as its ***scope***. If you try to refer to a variable outside its scope, the Java compiler will complain.

Declarations of instance variables may appear anywhere in the body of the class declaration. But it's a common convention (and one that we will follow) to put them first.

Instance Method Declarations, Local Variables, and Parameters

We know from our study of the banking system and the linear equation programs that, in object-oriented programming, work is done when an object is sent a message. The code that runs when an object receives a message is specified in an ***instance method*** in that object's class. For example, in the statement on lines 174 and 175,

```
174     terminal.println ("TextFile myTextFile contains " +
175                    myTextFile.getSize() + " characters.");
```

the expression **myTextFile.getSize()** sends a **getSize** message to **myTextFile**, an instance of the **TextFile** class. The **myTextFile** object receives that message and in response runs the code in its **getSize** method declared on line 97:

```
97      public int getSize()
98      {
99          int charCount;
100         charCount = contents.length();
101         return charCount;
102     }
```

Each method declaration has a header (the first line here) and a body (between the curly braces). Most of the header resembles the header for the declaration of an instance variable: It prescribes the access restrictions (**public** here), then the type of the value returned by the method (**int** here), then the identifier for the name the programmer has chosen for the method (**getSize**). The new feature is the list of formal parameters, represented here by the empty parentheses because there are no parameters for the **getSize** method.

To see how the **getSize** method does its job, we read the code in its body.

Line 99 is another declaration, this time for a ***local variable*** we have chosen to name with the identifier **charCount**. It will hold a value of type **int**. This local variable declaration is like a field declaration, but there is no need for an access modifier. A local variable is neither **public** nor **private**. Its scope is the rest of the block of code (surrounded by curly braces) in which it is declared. In this case, that's until line 102.

Line 100 assigns to the **charCount** variable the value returned when we send a **length** message to **contents**, the field of type **String** declared on line 25 representing the text, asking it to return its length.

Line 101 uses the Java keyword **return** to provide the requested information to whoever sent this **TextFile** a **getSize** message. The type of the value returned, in this case **int**, must match the return type in the declaration header for the method on line 97.

An experienced Java programmer would write the body of the **getSize** method as a single line of code:

```
return contents.length();
```

asking the **String contents** for its length and simply passing the answer on to whoever requested the information. Often one object's method just passes a request along to another object. That is known as **delegation**. In this case, delegation saves the cost (to the programmer and the computer) of declaring and using the **charCount** variable. We wrote it the long-winded way so we could more easily study its pieces.

For a second example, consider line 172, which sends an **appendLine** message to **myTextFile:**

```
172     myTextFile.appendLine( "How are you today?" );
```

That message causes the **appendLine** method declared on lines 85–8 to respond

```
85      public void appendLine( String text )
86      {
87          this.setContents(contents + '\n' + text);
88      }
```

In the declaration header on line 85, the keyword **void** indicates that the **appendLine** method does not return any value. The code inside the parentheses, **String text**, is itself another declaration, this time of a **formal parameter**. This declaration looks just like the declaration of a local variable: It specifies the type (here **String**) and the identifier we have chosen as the parameter name (here **text**). In the body of the **appendLine** method, **text** acts like a local variable of type **String**. The value of that variable is set when the method is invoked, at which time the text to be appended is known. In the call to **appendLine** on line 172, the value of **text** is the **String** **"How are you today?".** The value supplied for the formal parameter when the method is invoked is the **actual argument**.

The single line in the body of the **appendLine** method delegates the work by sending a **setContents** message to **this** object. **this** is the Java keyword for "the object we are working on right now" – the **TextFile** to which we are appending a line. The actual argument passed to the **setContents** method is the **String** that results when we use the **+** operator on **String**s to concatenate the current contents of this **TextFile**, a carriage return (the special character literal **'\n'**), and the text that is to appear on the new line. We will read the **setContents** method soon.

Constructor Declarations

Lines 37–43 declare a ***constructor*** for **TextFile** objects. A constructor declaration looks like a method declaration with two changes: There is no return type, and the name of the method is the name of the class, in this case **TextFile**.

```
37   public TextFile( String owner, String contents )
38   {
39       this.owner    = owner;
40       this.contents = contents;
41       createDate    = new Date(); // date and time now
42       modDate       = createDate;
43   }
```

Ordinary methods are invoked when an object receives a message. The constructor is the method invoked when an object is first created. In this example that happens on line 161:

```
161  TextFile myTextFile = new TextFile("bill", "Hello, world.");
```

Let's see how the **TextFile** constructor responds to this message. The code between the parentheses on line 37 declares two formal parameters, **owner** and **contents**. Line 161 tells us that their values (the actual arguments) are the **String**s **"bill"** and **"Hello, world."**.

The body of the constructor starts on line 39, initializing the owner field declared on line 22 by giving it the value of the owner parameter declared on line 37 (in this example it's **"bill"**). Because we have used the identifier **owner** for two different variables, we can't just write

```
owner = owner;
```

We need a way to distinguish between the formal parameter **owner** and the field **owner** in order to say

```
/* field */ owner = /* argument */ owner;
```

The Java keyword **this** comes to the rescue. Recall that **this** always denotes *the object at hand*. So **this.owner** is the **owner** field in the **TextFile** object being constructed, while **owner** by itself refers to the constructor's formal parameter because, within the body, the formal parameter declaration for **owner** hides the instance variable declaration for **owner**. So

```
39  this.owner = owner;
```

does the job.

Using **this** allowed us to reuse the identifier **owner**. That's not the only way to accomplish the task. We could have avoided the need for **this** by choosing different names for the formal parameters, perhaps **newOwner** and **newContents**. But to do that we would have had to think up new names for things we already thought carefully about naming well. In the code as we wrote it, it's clear that the **owner** parameter holds the initial value for the **owner** field, and the **contents** parameter holds the initial value for the **contents** field. We always follow the convention that when a constructor's parameter holds the initial value for a field, we use the field's name for the parameter and **this** to disambiguate them.

Line 41

```
41    createDate = new Date(); // date and time now
```

uses the Java keyword **new** to invoke the constructor in the definition of the **Date** class, creating a new **Date** object that holds the exact date and time at which it was constructed, and assigns that **Date** object to the **createDate** field. The next line assigns the same **Date** object to the **modDate** field.[3]

Box-and-Arrow Pictures

Often a picture can help us understand the structure of an object. We drew pictures of **Bank**s and **BankAccount**s in Chapter 1. Figure 3-1 shows the **TextFile** we have just constructed.

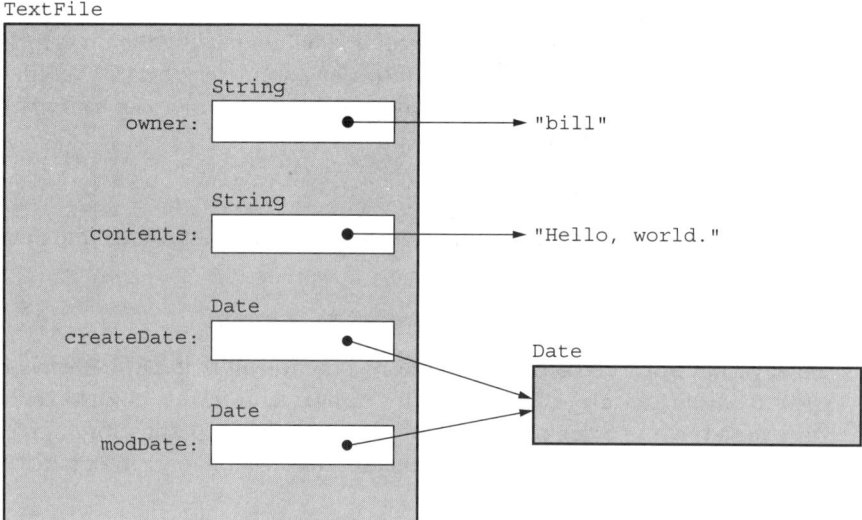

Figure 3-1: A **TextFile** Object

---

[3] These two lines could have been expressed more compactly using the *multiple assignment*:
```
createDate = modDate = new Date();
```

That figure illustrates some of the conventions we will use to draw objects:

- An object itself is drawn as a rectangular box with a shaded interior and a heavy border.
- The type of the object represented appears above the box. In this case the label is **TextFile**.
- Each field is represented by a small blank box inside the object's box. The name of the field, followed by a colon, appears to the left of the field's box. Its type is above its box.
- When a field refers to an object, its value is indicated by an arrow from the field's box to a box representing that object. That is illustrated here by the arrows from the **createDate** and **modDate** fields to a **Date** instance. Note how the picture shows clearly that when a new **TextFile** is constructed, its **createDate** and **modDate** are the same **Date**.[4]
- When we do not know (or do not care about) the internal structure of an object, we darken the interior of the box that represents it. In this example that is illustrated by the picture of the **Date** object.
- We use a Java string literal to represent a **String** object.

From time to time we will follow these conventions to draw box-and-arrow pictures to help illustrate how Java works. In the programming literature you will find many different kinds of pictures that resemble these, with conventions that differ. We have chosen some that we think are best for beginners rather than use an established set.

Access, Getters, and Setters

We have seen that each declaration of a field, a constructor, or a method is preceded by one of the keywords **private** or **public**. These *access modifiers* govern the accessibility of the entity being declared.

A **private** access modifier says that the entity is accessible only within the body of the class declaration. In **TextFile.java**, all four fields are declared to be **private**. Inside the **TextFile** class we can refer to **this.contents**, but the Java compiler will object if we try to refer to that field in any other class. The same is true of the **balance** field in a **BankAccount**, declared this way in **BankAccount.java**:

```
16  private int balance; // work only in whole dollars
```

When the **Bank** wants to know about an **account**'s balance, it must ask this way:

```
129  atm.println( account.getBalance() );
```

---

[4] That the type label (here **Date**) appears twice, once above the variable's box and once above the object's box, may seem redundant. In Chapter 4 we will see why we need the label in both places.

using the **public getBalance** method. If **balance** itself had been declared **public**, then

```
atm.println( account.balance );
```

in **Bank.java** would work, and so would

```
account.balance = 1000000;
```

allowing for massive fraud. But when the **balance** field is **private**, the Java compiler will object to both these statements.

Although the fields in the **BankAccount** and **TextFile** classes are **private**, we declared the methods **public**, because we want to work with those objects by sending them messages. **TextFile**'s **getContents** is straightforward and unsurprising:

```
63      public String getContents()
64      {
65          return contents;
66      }
```

Its header declares it **public** and tells the Java compiler that it returns a **String** value. The empty parameter list tells us it is invoked with no arguments. The name we have chosen for the method suggests (correctly) that invoking it will tell us the contents of the **TextFile**. Line 65 does just that. Because **getContents** is public, we can use it outside the **TextFile** class to access the contents of a **TextFile** object:

```
terminal.println(myTextFile.getContents());
```

Method **setContents** is more subtle:

```
51      public void setContents( String contents )
52      {
53          this.contents = contents;
54          modDate = new Date();
55      }
```

Its header declares it **public** and tells the Java compiler that it returns **void** – that is, it returns no value. The parameter list tells us it must be invoked with a single **String** argument. The name we have chosen for the formal parameter suggests (correctly) that its value is the **String** that should become the contents of the **TextFile**. So line 53 in the body uses **this** to assign to the **contents** field the value of the **contents** parameter. That is no surprise. It's what we expect when we send a **setContents** message this way:

```
myTextFile.setContents( "Goodbye, world." );
```

Line 54 changes the value of the **modDate** field so that it stores the date of this change.[5]

The **getCreateDate** method is subtle in another way:

```
110     public String getCreateDate()
111     {
112         return createDate.toString();
113     }
```

It does not return the value of the **createDate** field. Instead, it sends that **Date** object a **toString** message asking it how it represents itself as a **String**, and returns that **String**.

Data Abstraction

Wise use of the **public** and **private** access modifiers allows the programmer to control what information in a class's implementation is hidden from the outside world and what is made public. When we use getters and setters, we are practicing *data abstraction*, hiding a class's implementation details and making public only the *interface*, the methods necessary to use it. There are several reasons for declaring fields private and writing public getters and setters rather than relying on public fields:

- The class can be offered for general use by other programmers or on other projects. Those programmers need know only the headers of the public methods of the class, not how they are implemented. The implementation can be changed without notifying the users, as long as the headers of the public methods (that is, the class's public interface) do not change. Throughout this text we use **Terminal** objects that way, sending them messages that invoke public methods. Even though we changed the implementation in **Terminal.java** several times while writing *Java Outside In*, we never had to change the programs that use a **Terminal**.

  TextFile's **getSize** method offers another example. There we send a **length** message to the **String contents** field of the **TextFile** without knowing anything about how the **String** class manages its internal data. A **String** might maintain a private instance field for tracking its length, or it might compute its length by counting its characters (trading time for space). As users of the **String** class, we don't care. Moreover, we wouldn't care if the implementation changed, so long as **length** always returned an **int** – presumably, the correct **int**.

- Setters and getters allow us to control the *kind* of access other classes have to an object's instance fields. Getters grant only read access; setters grant only write

---

[5] We could have written the second line as

```
54          this.modDate = new Date();
```

in order to remind ourselves that the **modDate** that's changing is a field. But we don't have to use **this** because there is no other **modDate** variable or parameter that might be mistaken for the field.

access. For example, **TextFile** supports a getter, **getCreateDate**, granting read access to the **createDate** field. But there is no corresponding setter, nor should there be. The creation date of a file can't be changed after the file was created!

In fact, that consideration influenced the design of **getCreateDate**. If we had written

```
110    public Date getCreateDate()
```

instead of

```
110    public String getCreateDate()
```

then a program that sent a **TextFile** a **getCreateDate** message would be told the actual **Date** object stored in the **TextFile** instance. Then it could send that **Date** a message asking it to change itself. By converting the **Date** to a **String** and returning just that **String**, we prevent that unwanted possibility.

- When all instance variables are accessible only through the getters and setters, it is much easier to associate extra behavior with access. For example, each invocation of a **TextFile**'s **setContents** method updates the **modDate** field as well as the **contents** field. If the **contents** field were public, it could be set directly by another object. Then the **modDate** field would no longer reflect the date of the last change to the **contents**. The **setContents** method nicely encapsulates both the setting of **contents** and the recomputation of the modification date. That is why in the **appendLine** method we studied, the change to the **contents** is made by a call to **setContents** rather than by the simple assignment statement **contents = contents + text**.

As another example, consider the **BankAccount** class from Chapter 1. It provides the public methods **getBalance**, **deposit**, and **withdraw**. This design makes it easy to charge a transaction fee simply by editing **BankAccount.java**, subtracting the fee from the **balance** in **deposit** and **withdraw**.[6] If the **balance** field were public, you could not reliably make that change by changing just the **BankAccount** code because **Bank.java** might make a deposit simply by increasing the **BankAccount**'s **balance** field.

- Getters may seem to return the value of a field when in fact they are returning the result of a computation. **getInverse** in class **LinearEquation** provides an example:

```
64     public LinearEquation getInverse()
65     {
66         return new LinearEquation( 1.0/m, -b/m );
67     }
```

---

[6] This is Exercise 1-4 in Chapter 1.

- Finally, allowing unrestricted access to the instance fields breaks the object model in which objects get things done only by sending messages to other objects. The simplicity of the object model makes it easier to organize programs, particularly large programs. It's not something we want to toss out.

For these reasons, we honor the following programming conventions and accompanying naming conventions:

- Always declare fields private.

```
private Type aField;
```

Then, only methods defined within the class may access those fields directly. Allow other objects access to the fields only through public getter and setter methods.

- Name and declare getters and setters this way:

```
public void setAField( Type newValue )
{
    /* method body */
}

public Type getAField()
{
    /* method body */
}
```

- Organize the class declaration in this sequence:
  a. Field declarations.
  b. Constructors.
  c. Methods other than **main**. Group together methods having like functionality, or methods that support one another.
  d. A **main** method, if any.

Application Programming Interfaces: Javadoc

The behavior of the public methods in a class is known as the class's ***application programming interface (API)***. When we want to use a class, we need documentation for the public methods: a description of *what they do*, not *how they do it*. Sometimes the abbreviation API is used to describe that documentation as well as the behavior itself.

Java comes with a rich library of classes that make programming easier, and a detailed API documents that library. That documentation is available online at `http://java.sun.com/j2se/1.4/docs/api/index.html` and other places.

The documentation for classes defined in *Java Outside In* is available on the JOI CD-ROM and online on the JOI Web site `www.cs.umb.edu/joi`.

Java provides the *javadoc* tool to generate API documentation automatically from the declarations and the javadoc comments in the class declaration. The command

```
%> javadoc TextFile.java
```

produces several new files that contain text that can be understood by a Web browser. One of those files is **TextFile.html**. Figure 3-2 shows how our browser displays the beginning of that file.

The javadoc program builds these Web pages from the declaration headers and the javadoc comments in the source code. You can see how Figure 3-2 represents this code from **TextFile.java**:

```
 8    /**
 9     * A TextFile mimics the sort of text file that one finds
10     * on a computer's file system. It has an owner,
11     * a create date (when the file was created),
12     * a modification date (when the file was last modified),
13     * and String contents.
```

Figure 3-2: A javadoc fragment for `TextFile`

```
14    *
15    * @version 3
16    */
17
18    public class TextFile
19    {
```

The **@version** on line 15 is a *javadoc tag*, which earns special treatment from the javadoc program. We will see other javadoc tags from time to time.

Similarly, javadoc reads the declaration header and the documentation comment for the **appendLine** method

```
79    /**
80     * Append a new line of text to the end of the file.
81     *
82     * @param text the text to be appended.
83     */
84
85    public void appendLine( String text )
```

in order to produce the part of the **TextFile** API illustrated in Figure 3-3. The **@param** on line 82 is the tag that identifies each of a method's parameters so javadoc can display them in the Parameters section of the documentation it generates for the method.

Unit Testing with main

TextFile objects are not much use on their own. You can imagine that the **TextFile** class is just one of many classes you would need to model the behavior of a complete computer system. But it is important to be able to test the **TextFile** API without first having to build all those other classes. To do that, we need a **main** method somewhere

appendLine

```
public void appendLine(String text)
```

Append a new line of text to the end of the file.

Parameters:
        text - the text to be appended.

Figure 3-3: The javadoc fragment for **appendLine**

that creates and exercises **TextFile** objects. We can follow our past practice and write class **TestTextFile** (like **Temperatures**) with just **main** in it. Or we can declare a **main** method right in **TextFile.java** and thus avoid writing a special testing class. Then we can test **TextFile** by itself, separate from any larger program of which it might be a part. This kind of testing, where we test just a single class on its own, is called *unit testing*. Always unit test classes you write so that you can know that they behave correctly. Then you will know that the errors which inevitably appear when your class is used in a larger program are due to the interactions of the classes and not to any particular class (provided, of course, that the other programmers on the project have unit tested the classes they are responsible for!).

The **main** method in the **TextFile** class creates a single **TextFile** object, then exercises the public methods by sending that object messages. The tests are hard coded and self-documenting. Here is the output from the unit test:

```
%> java TextFile

TextFile myTextFile contains 13 characters.
Created by bill, Sat Dec 29 14:02:37 EST 2001
Hello, world.

append new line "How are you today?"
Hello, world.
How are you today?
TextFile myTextFile contains 32 characters.
Modified Sat Dec 29 14:02:38 EST 2001
```

Here is the code for **main**. It is easy to see which lines of code are responsible for which lines of output.

```
158    public static void main( String[] args )
159    {
160       Terminal terminal = new Terminal();
161       TextFile myTextFile
162          = new TextFile( "bill", "Hello, world." );
163       terminal.println( "TextFile myTextFile contains " +
164                          myTextFile.getSize() +
165                          " characters.");
166       terminal.println( "Created by " +
167                          myTextFile.getOwner() + ", " +
168                          myTextFile.getCreateDate() );
169       terminal.println( myTextFile.getContents() );
170       terminal.println();
171       terminal.println(
```

```
172                    "append new line \"How are you today?\"" );
173        myTextFile.appendLine( "How are you today?" );
174        terminal.println( myTextFile.getContents() );
175        terminal.println( "TextFile myTextFile contains " +
176                          myTextFile.getSize() +
177                          " characters." );
178        terminal.println( "Modified " +
179                          myTextFile.getModDate() );
180   }
```

Class Methods and Class Variables

All the methods in the **TextFile** class *except* **main** are associated with **TextFile** instances. These methods are called ***instance methods***: You send a **TextFile** instance a message to invoke an instance method. The **main** method is clearly different. It runs when the **java** command says "start with **main** in the **TextFile** class." Methods like this one that are not triggered by messages passed to objects are called ***class methods***. Class methods are declared with the keyword **static**.

There is no keyword specifying that a method is an instance method – that is the default. If a method is not declared **static**, then it's an instance method. That is appropriate because most methods in well-designed object-oriented programs are instance methods. But there are a few places where class (that is, **static**) methods are called for. The **main** method for starting program execution is one. Here is the complete header for the declaration of **main**. It's the same in all the programs we have seen so far (**Bank.java**, **Change.java**, **Temperatures.java**, and **TextFile.java**):

```
public static void main( String[] args )
```

The keyword **void** tells us that **main** does not return a value. The formal parameter list tells us that **main** expects a single parameter of type **String[]**. In the next chapter we will learn the meaning of the square braces. It's safe to ignore them for now (as long as you type them).

Class methods are also used to package some arithmetic calculations. Suppose we wish to compute the square root of 2.0 in a Java program. The object-oriented model suggests that we should do that by sending a message to 2.0 asking it to find its square root. But we can't do that because 2.0 is a primitive type, not an object.[7] To compute

---

[7] In the object-oriented language Smalltalk, there are no primitive types. Everything is an object, and you do in fact send messages to numbers.

square roots in Java, we use the class method **sqrt**, declared this way in the **Math** class in the Java library:

```
public static double sqrt( double d )
```

Because it's a class method, we invoke it by sending the **sqrt** message to the **Math** class itself, not to an instance of any class. Thus the expression

```
Math.sqrt( 2.0 )
```

returns the value 1.4142135623730951.[8]

Java also supports the notion of a ***class variable***, which is a variable associated with a class rather than with an instance of a class. For example, the library class **Double** declares the public class variable **MAX_VALUE**. You examine it by asking the **Double** class for its **MAX_VALUE** field: **Double.MAX_VALUE**.[9] The expression

```
terminal.println(Double.MAX_VALUE)
```

prints the largest positive value of type **double** that Java allows, expressed in scientific notation:

```
1.7976931348623157E308
```

That's about 1.8×10^{308}, which is big enough for most purposes![10] You can find out more about static fields and methods by studying class **StaticDemo.java** (Example 3-1).

Shapes

We will continue our study of the structure of Java programs with an example that models shapes displayed on a computer screen. We begin small, with just two simple shapes: a horizontal line and a rectangular box. We'll build more shapes in the exercises.

Shapes are painted onto an imaginary screen using characters. For example, a horizontal line of length 5 and character z would be painted as

```
zzzzz
```

A box of width 6 and height 4 with character # would be painted as

```
######
######
######
######
```
[11]

---

[8] Because the square root of 2 cannot be expressed as an exact double, this is of course an approximation.

[9] You can see at work here the conventions we established in Chapter 2. We know **Double** is a class because it starts with an uppercase letter. We know **MAX_VALUE** is a constant because it is all uppercase. The two words that make up that identifier are separated by an underscore.

[10] See Exercise 3-27 for a chance to deal with *really* large numbers.

[11] This 6×4 box looks square because characters are higher than they are wide.

The character used for drawing any particular shape instance (for example, # above) is called its *paint character*.

We model our shapes using objects. An **HLine** object, modeling a horizontal line, will have two private fields, one for its length and one for its paint character. Its API will have a public method for painting itself on a **Screen**. A **Box** object, modeling a rectangular box, will have private fields for its width and its height instead of a single field for its length.

A **Screen** is a two-dimensional grid onto which shapes may paint themselves. When programming graphical output devices like computer screens and television sets, we address locations on the screen using a coordinate system in which the origin (0,0) is at the top left corner, the x-axis extends to the right, and the y-axis extends downward, as in Figure 3-4, which shows a **Screen** of width 7 and height 3 with an x at position (3,1). The numerical labels and the horizontal and vertical borders of + characters aren't part of the **Screen**; they are there to make it easier to read the figure. Note that the first screen location in the upper left corner is (0,0), not (1,1). It may take you a while to get used to that convention.

Each particular **Screen** object is an instance of the **Screen** class. We will not study the implementation in **Screen.java** now. All we need to know in order to use a **Screen** is its API. The complete **Screen** javadoc API may be found on the *Java Outside In* CD-ROM and online on the *Java Outside In* Web page. To see how **Screen**, **HLine**, and **Box** objects work together, consider the **main** method in class **DemoShapes** (Listing 3-2).

Listing 3-2: DemoShapes.java

```
18      public static void main( String[] args )
19      {
20          Terminal t = new Terminal();
21          Screen s = new Screen( 36, 12 );
22
23          HLine h1 = new HLine( 10, 'R' );
24          Box   b1 = new Box( 5, 6, 'G' );
25          Box   b2 = new Box( 5, 6, 'B' );
26
```

```
        0   1   2   3   4   5   6

    +   +   +   +   +   +   +   +   +

0   +                               +

1   +               x               +

2   +                               +

    +   +   +   +   +   +   +   +   +
```

Figure 3-4: A graphical coordinate system

```
27            h1.paintOn( s ); // at position (0,0)
28            b1.paintOn( s, 2, 2 );
29            b2.paintOn( s, 4, 5 );
30
31            t.println("A Screen with an HLine and two Boxes:");
32            s.draw( t );
33       }
```

main creates a **Terminal t**, a **Screen s**, an **HLine h1**, and two **Boxes b1** and **b2**. It then paints **h1** to the **Screen** with its leftmost character at the default position (0,0), **b1** with its upper left corner at (2,2), and **b2** at (4,5). Now the **Screen** contains the three shapes, but nothing shows on the **Terminal** yet. Line 31 prints a message telling what will happen next. Then line 32 asks the **Screen** to draw itself on **Terminal t**. The output produced looks like this:

```
A Screen with an HLine and two Boxes:
++++++++++++++++++++++++++++++++++++++
+RRRRRRRRRR                          +
+                                    +
+   GGGGG                            +
+   GGGGG                            +
+   GGGGG                            +
+   GGBBBBB                          +
+   GGBBBBB                          +
+   GGBBBBB                          +
+     BBBBB                          +
+     BBBBB                          +
+     BBBBB                          +
+                                    +
++++++++++++++++++++++++++++++++++++++
```

The **Screen** itself provides the + characters that form the border. Our program does not explicitly ask for them.

The HLine Class

Listing 3-3 is the declaration for class **HLine**. An **HLine** has private fields for its length and its paint character (declared on lines 15 and 16). It has one constructor (line 25), which expects the length and paint character as arguments. It has two methods for painting itself on a **Screen**: The first (declared on line 39) requires us to specify a position; the second (line 52) always draws the **HLine** at (0,0). Finally it has methods for getting and setting its length (lines 69 and 80) and a **main** method with a self-documenting unit test (line 84).

The Box Class

Listing 3-4 is the declaration for class **Box**. Its definition is similar to that for **HLine**. A **Box** knows its width, height, and paint character. It has a constructor that expects the width, height, and paint character as arguments. It has two methods for painting itself on a **Screen**: The first requires us to specify a position; the second always draws the **Box** at (0,0). Finally it has methods for setting and getting its width and height and a **main** method with a self-documenting unit test.

Most of the features of these two classes are not new to us. We will focus on those parts that are.

The for Loop

Consider the first **paintOn** method in the **HLine** class. Its declaration header shows that it is **public**, returns no value, and expects a **Screen** object and two integers as arguments. Its job is to ask the **Screen** to put this **HLine**'s **paintChar** onto itself **length** times at the right places. It need not know how the **Screen** does that – it just sends the **Screen paintAt** messages, whose behavior is documented in the **Screen** class API.

```
39      public void paintOn( Screen s, int x, int y )
40      {
41          for ( int i = 0; i < length; i = i+1 ) {
42              s.paintAt( paintChar, x+i , y );
43          }
44      }
```

The new feature in this code is the **for** statement on line 41. Most flow control structures in Java are self-explanatory. When we first saw **while** loops and **if-else** statements in Chapter 1, we could see how they worked from the ordinary English meanings of the Java reserved words. We made that understanding explicit in our discussion of flow control at the end of Chapter 2. The **for** loop is a lot less intuitive – it needs more explanation, because it's not at all obvious what the Java code on line 41 means.

A **for** loop consists of

- the **for** statement itself, with syntax

  for (*start* ; *test* ; *step*)

- a body, usually surrounded by braces

The *test* statement is like the test in a **while** loop. In this example, the test statement is

i < length

That expression evaluates to **true** or **false**. If it's **true**, the loop body is executed. If it's **false**, then the **for** loop is over and control passes to the next statement after the body (line 44, the end of the method, in the example). This test statement compares the values of two variables, **length** (the length field of the **Hline**) and the variable **i** declared and initialized in the *start* statement

```
int i = 0
```

So the first time the test is evaluated, the JVM compares **0** with **length**. If **length > 0** (probably it is – who would make a line of length 0?), the body executes:

```
42      s.paintAt( paintChar, x+i , y );
```

asking the **Screen s** to paint a character on itself at position (x+0,y).

After the body executes, it's time for the *step*:

```
i = i+1
```

Now **i** has value $0 + 1 = 1$, and the test runs again. If the **length** is greater than 1, the body runs again, and the **Screen** again paints a character on itself, this time at position (x + 1, y). The pattern is clear: The body in line 42 runs **length** times, with the ***loop variable* i** taking on successive integer values:

$$i = 0, i = 1, i = 2, \ldots, i = \text{length} - 1$$

causing the paint character to be painted at successive grid locations on the **Screen**:

$$(x + 0, y), (x + 1, y), (x + 2, y), \ldots, (x + \text{length} - 1, y).$$

Then the step increases **i** from **length-1** to **length**, the test **i < length** fails, and the loop is done.

The **paintOn** method declared on line 52 of **Box.java** uses a **for** loop too.

```
52      public void paintOn( Screen s, int x, int y )
53      {
54          HLine hline = new HLine( width, paintChar );
55          for ( int i = 0; i < height; i++ ) {
56              hline.paintOn( s, x, y+i );
57          }
58      }
```

It paints a (**width** × **height**) box by painting **height** horizontal lines, each of which is **width** characters long. To do that, it declares a local variable of type **HLine** on line 54 and initializes it with a newly created **HLine** whose length is the **width** of the **Box**. Then it asks that **HLine** to paint itself **height** times, using the **for** statement on line 55 to execute the body (line 56)

```
hline.paintOn( s, x, y+i );
```

with the loop variable **i** taking on successive integer values

$$i = 0, i = 1, i = 2, \ldots, i = \text{height} - 1$$

causing **hline** to be drawn at successive grid locations on the screen:

$$(x, y + 0), (x, y + 1), (x, y + 2), \ldots, (x, y + \text{height} - 1).$$

There is one new Java idiom to learn here. The step statement in the **for** loop is the expression **i++**. That is an abbreviation for the statement **i = i + 1**. Either version will do. The shorter one is a little easier to read (once you know what it means). The longer version, though correct, isn't stylish. It marks the programmer who wrote it as a novice.

We could have painted the **Box** one character at a time using the **Screen**'s **paintAt** method directly instead of painting it as a sequence of **HLine**s. That would have required nested **for** loops in the method body:

```
for ( int i = 0; i < height; i++ ) {
    for ( int j = 0; j < width; j++ ) {
        s.paintAt( paintChar, x+i, y+j );
    }
}
```

But the solution we've chosen in **Box** delegates work to a class we've already defined. That's often good software practice and so worth practicing even in this simple example.

Here are the first things to remember about **for** loops:

- Use a **for** loop when you know in advance how many times you want to execute the body. Use a **while** loop if the decision about how long to continue looping is made in the body itself.
- Declare the index variable in the start statement. If the index should increase by 1 each time through the loop (that's often the case), increment it in the step with the **++** idiom.
- Ordinary people and mathematicians count to three this way: "1, 2, 3." Computer programmers count "0, 1, 2." You are learning to be a programmer, so always start your index variable at 0.

• Remember to create a block for the body with curly braces (**{}**), prettyprinted as in the examples above. A common programming error is to write

```
1    for (int i = 0; i < 3; i++ )
2        terminal.println("iteration " + i);
3        terminal.println("something interesting");
```

expecting to see

```
iteration 0
something interesting
iteration 1
something interesting
iteration 2
something interesting
```

when what actually appears is

```
iteration 0
iteration 1
iteration 2
something interesting
```

That happens because the prettyprinting in the code suggests that lines 2 and 3 are both part of the **for** loop body. In fact only line 2 will execute three times. The correct formatting for this code is

```
1    for (int i = 0; i < 3; i++ )
2        terminal.println("iteration " + i);
3    terminal.println("something interesting");
```

and the correct formatting for what the programmer *meant* to write is

```
1    for (int i = 0; i < 3; i++ ) {
2        terminal.println("iteration " + i);
3        terminal.println("something interesting");
4    }
```

To avoid this error, we recommend using the braces even when the body contains just one line of code.

   The **for** loop is actually a much more flexible tool for flow control than these simple examples and guidelines indicate. Indeed, anything that can be expressed using a **for** loop can be expressed using a **while** loop, and vice-versa. In general, the idiom

```
for ( <start>; <test>; <step> ) {
    <do something>
}
```

is the same as the idiom

```
<start>;
while ( <test> ) {
    <do something>
    <step>;
}
```

You can look at some examples of this now in the program **ForDemo.java** (Example 3-2). Examples using the **break** and **continue** statements within a **for** statement may be found in **BreakAndContinueDemo.java** (Example 3-3).

Method Signatures

The **Box** class has *two* **paintOn** methods – the one we have just studied, declared on line 52, with three formal parameters, and this one:

```
66    public void paintOn( Screen s )
67    {
68        paintOn( s, 0, 0 ); // or this.paintOn(s,0,0);
69    }
```

This second **paintOn** method has just one formal parameter. We describe this distinction by saying that the methods have different *signatures*. A method's signature consists of its name together with the number and types of its parameters (in order).[12] In the **Box** class, the first method has the signature **paintOn(Screen, int, int)** while the second has signature **paintOn(Screen)**. A class may have several methods with the same name, as long as they have the same return type and different signatures.

When a **Box** object receives a message that invokes the second **paintOn** method, it delegates the task of drawing itself at the default screen location (0,0) by sending itself (**this Box**) a message whose signature matches that of the other **paintOn** method. The comment in the program makes that clear by indicating that the statement **this.paintOn(s, 0, 0)** is equivalent to the one that's there. The compiler will accept either form. Our convention says that we omit the **this** when the method name is in scope (that is, when the method is defined in the same class). But you may use it from time to time in your programs in order to clarify your own thinking about what is happening.

---

[12] It's easy to confuse the signature and the method header. The header is everything before the curly braces that surround the method body, including the method's return type. The signature consists only of the method name and the typed formal parameter list.

Constructors also have signatures, and a class may declare several constructors as long as their signatures differ. For example, we might declare a second constructor for **TextFile** that creates an empty **TextFile** owned by the user executing the program:

```
public TextFile()
{
    this( System.getProperty( "user.name" ), "" );
}
```

Now, *this* is a mouthful. Our constructor's body uses **this** in a new, special way to invoke the other **TextFile** constructor[13] (with signature **TextFile(String, String)**), supplying the current username for its owner and the empty **String** **""** for its contents. Our knowledge of Java conventions allows us to read the code fragment

```
System.getProperty( "user.name" )
```

without having to consult a reference. **System** begins with an uppercase letter, so it must be a class, probably in the Java library.[14] Here, we are sending the **System** class a **getProperty** message, so **getProperty** must be a **public static** method in that class. It accepts a **String** (in this case **"user.name"**) as an argument and returns a **String** to be passed to the **TextFile** constructor. So our detective work leads us to suspect that somewhere in file **System.java** we should find the method whose declaration has the header

```
public static String getProperty( String propertyName )
```

Names and Scope Rules

In Java we distinguish between a ***simple name***, which is a name that can be written as a single identifier, and a ***qualified name***, which is a name followed by the . token followed by an identifier. In the line

```
s.paintAt( paintChar, x+i, y );
```

paintChar is a simple name and **s.paintAt** is a qualified name.

The ***scope*** of a declaration is that region of the program where the entity (the variable or method) being declared can be referred to by a simple name. Let's review the scopes of declarations that we have seen in our examples.

- The scope of an instance variable declaration is the entire body of the class declaration.

---

[13] It might have been better if Java's designers (mortals like us) had prescribed the use of the class name, e.g. **TextFile**, here.

[14] If you did Exercise 2-10, you have already seen the **System** class, when you used **System.out** for output.

- The scope of a constructor or method declaration is the entire body of the class declaration.
- The scope of a formal parameter to a method (or constructor) is the entire body of the method (or constructor).
- The scope of a local variable declaration is the rest of the block in which it is declared.

A **block** is any sequence of zero or more statements between two enclosing curly brackets (**{** and **}**). The body of a method (or constructor) is a block. But we can create a block anywhere we want to treat a sequence of statements as a single statement. That use is most common when we want to execute more than one statement in a loop or after a conditional expression. For example, consider this fragment of code from the **processTransactionsForAccount** method in **Bank.java**:

```
120        else if ( command.equals( "deposit" ) ) {
121            int amount = atm.readInt( "amount: " );
122            account.deposit( amount );
123        }
```

Without the braces on lines 120 and 123, only line 121 would execute when the command was "deposit". Clearly that's not the programmer's intent. Declaring the local variable **amount** in this block means it exists only here, so it can't be confused with any variable of the same name anywhere else in the program.

- The scope of a local variable declared in the start part of a **for** statement,

```
for ( start ; test; step ) {
    // body
}
```

is all of start (after the declaration), test, step, and the body of the loop.

Good programming practice demands that one declare variables as locally as possible, so that they are in scope only where they are actually used.

Uses of this

The **this** keyword refers to the object at hand. We've seen three uses of **this**:

- To get at an instance variable hidden by a method's (or a constructor's) formal parameter, as in the constructor

```
37    public Box( int width, int height, char paintChar )
38    {
39        this.width    = width;
40        this.height   = height;
```

```
41              this.paintChar = paintChar;
42      }
```

- To invoke one constructor from another, as in

```
public Box( int width, int height )
{
    this( width, height, '+' );
}
```

which would construct a **Box** with default **paintChar '+'**. Java requires that when one constructor invokes another with **this,** that invocation must be the first statement in the constructor's body.

- Optionally, when we want to make particularly clear the fact that a variable is a field in the object we are working on, or a message is being sent to that object by another of its methods, as in

```
paintOn( s, 0, 0 ); // or this.paintOn(s,0,0)
```

What Happens When a New Object Is Constructed?

In all but the simplest of our examples, our programs have been object oriented, as promised. Now we will look systematically at material we have been hinting at all along: How are objects created?

When we wish to create a new instance of a class, we invoke one of its constructors using the Java keyword **new**. For example, to create a 4×5 **Box** object with **paintChar 'R'** we would write

```
new Box( 4, 5, 'R' );
```

Think of the **new** operator as sending an order to a **Box** factory. The arguments to the constructor tell the factory what kind of **Box** we want. In fact it is the Java Virtual Machine (JVM) that acts as the factory. When it evaluates that expression, here is what happens (more or less):

1. Storage space (computer memory) is allocated for the new object.
2. The argument list is evaluated, giving (4, 5, 'R') in our example. These values are assigned to the constructor's formal parameters.
3. The constructor's body is executed; **this** refers to the object allocated in Step 1.
4. The object is returned as the value of the instance creation expression **new**.
5. Execution is transferred back to the place in the program that invoked **new**.

After Step 3 above has completed, the computer's memory contains a completed object. Figure 3-5 shows how we represent that object symbolically, using the conventions we introduced earlier for box-and-arrow pictures. In this case the object is an instance of the **Box** class. It's important to understand that Figure 3-5 is the **Box** as we visualize it in the computer, just as Figure 3-1 represents our visualization of a **TextFile** object. It's not the way the **Box** object would be drawn on a **Screen**!

References, Boxes, and Arrows

We create objects in order to send them messages to get work done. So we need a way to refer to those objects using variables in our program. We will study that process in pictures by looking at part of the unit test in **Box.java**:

```
137        Screen screen = new Screen( 20, 6 );
138
139        Box box1 = new Box( 4, 5, 'R' );
140        Box box2 = new Box( 3, 4, 'G' );
141
142        box1.paintOn( screen );
143        box2.paintOn( screen, 2, 2 );
144
145        // test reference model for objects
146        box2 = box1;
147        int oldWidth = box2.getWidth();
148        box1.setWidth(oldWidth+3);
149        box2.paintOn( screen, 4, 5 );
150
151        screen.draw( terminal );
```

Line 139 declares variable **box1** of type **Box**, creates a **new Box**, and makes **box1** refer to that **Box**. Line 140 does the same for variable **box2**. Figure 3-6 represents the results symbolically. The variables **box1** and **box2** contain references (arrows pointing to) the two newly created **Box** objects. Those variables are not themselves fields in any object – they are local variables in the **main** method.

Lines 142 and 143 ask the two **Box**es to paint themselves on the **Screen** referred to by variable **screen**. We won't look at those lines further now.

Figure 3-5: A **Box** object in computer memory

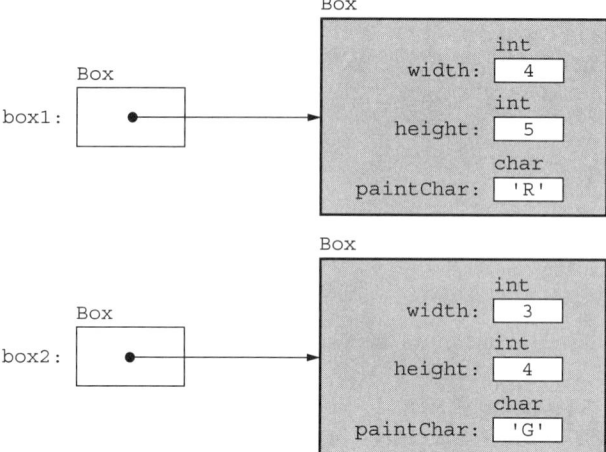

Figure 3-6: Two **Box** objects referred to by two variables

Line 146 changes the value of variable **box2**. That variable now refers to the same **Box** referred to by variable **box1**. Figure 3-7 represents the new situation. It's important to understand that line 146 does not make a copy of **Box box1**. Moreover, our program now has no way to refer again to the **Box** that variable **box2** used to refer to.

Figure 3-7 helps us understand how the next two lines of code work. Line 147 sends a message to **box2** to get its width, which is 4. Then line 148 sets the **width** of **box1** to be 4 + 3, or 7. Those operations all deal with the only **Box** that's available. Figure 3-8 shows the computer's memory after line 158 has executed.

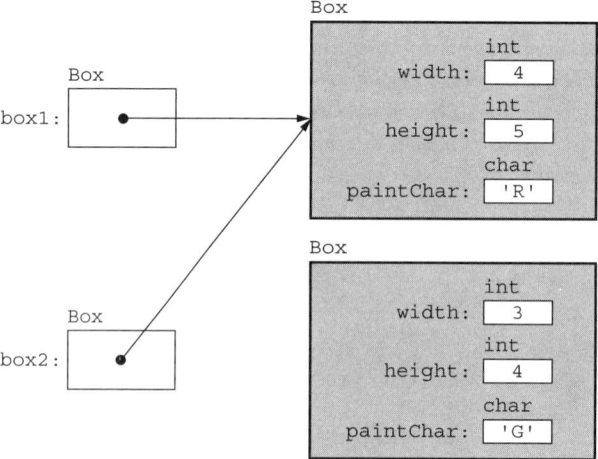

Figure 3-7: One **Box** referred to by two variables

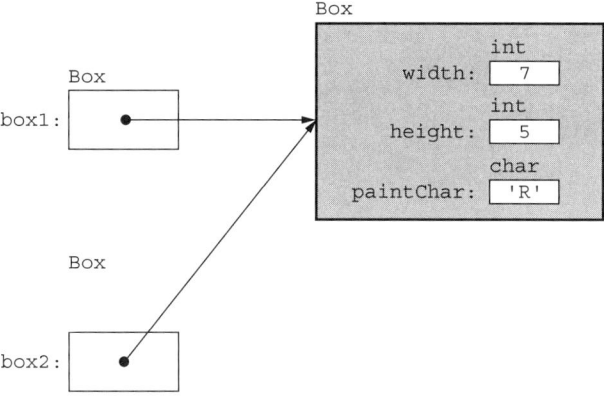

Figure 3-8: One **Box** referred to by two variables

What Happens When an Object Receives a Message?

A method is invoked when an object is sent a message. Figure 3-9 shows our convention for picturing the execution of the message expressions **box2.getWidth** and **box2.setWidth** on lines 147 and 148. Even though it uses a box to represent an object (in this case a **Box** object), the arrow pointing to that box has a different meaning than the arrow in Figure 3-8. It is not a reference to this object in memory; instead, it symbolizes a message being sent to the object. We use a dashed arrow for that purpose and label the arrow with the message and the actual arguments the corresponding method

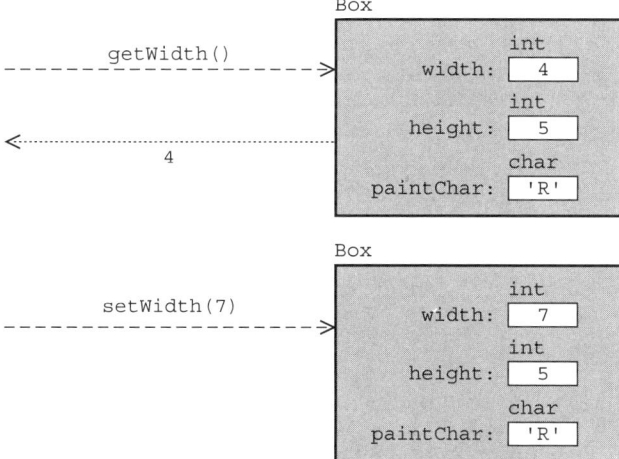

Figure 3-9: Sending messages to a **Box**

will use. When the method returns a value, we indicate that with a dotted arrow leaving the box representing the object and label the arrow with the value being returned.

When the Java Virtual Machine (JVM) evaluates a message expression like

```
box2.getWidth();
```

or

```
box1.setWidth(oldWidth+3);
```

here is what happens (more or less):

1. The object expression (**box1** or **box2**) is evaluated to produce a reference to an object (the single **Box** here).
2. The argument list is evaluated. In the first example, there are no arguments (Java requires that we indicate we know that by using the empty parentheses). In the second case, the expression **oldWidth+3** is evaluated to give the value $4 + 3 = 7$.
3. The method with a matching signature is found (**getWidth** and **setWidth** in these examples). The values of the actual arguments are assigned to the method's formal parameters: 7 is assigned to parameter **width** declared in the **setWidth** header

```
100      public void setWidth( int width )
```

4. The method's body is executed; **this** refers to the object computed in Step 1.
5. If a return value is specified in the declaration, that value becomes the value of the message expression.

Summary

In this chapter we dealt in detail with the form and function of objects by studying two new applications – a class that models text files and a set of classes modeling shapes drawn on a **Screen**. We learned how to declare fields and methods and provide controlled access using setters and getters. That study of encapsulation led to a discussion of javadoc for documenting APIs. We explained several important Java keywords: **static**, **new**, and **this**. We introduced the **for** loop. Finally, we used box-and-arrow pictures to explain how variables hold references to objects.

In the next chapter we will study collections: objects that model groups of objects.

Exercises

3-1   Create a text file for your journal for this chapter. Use your journal for questions that call for written answers and to record any observations about your work.

3-2   Consider the following rewritten version of **TextFile**'s constructor.

```
public TextFile( String owner, String contents )
{
    this.owner    = owner;
    this.contents = contents;
    createDate = new Date(); // date and time now
    modDate = new Date();
}
```

- How does this change the nature of a new **TextFile** object?
- Redraw Figure 3-1 so that it reflects this change.
- Which version is better, this or the original? Why?

3-3   If you execute the unit test for **TextFile** with the command

```
%> java TextFile
```

you will probably find that the sample **TextFile**'s final modification date is the same as its creation date even though the contents have been changed. That is because the program runs so fast that the creation and modification times are less than one second apart.[15] In order to test for a changed modification date more reliably, write method

public long getModDateInMilliseconds( )

and invoke it from **main**. Consult the online javadoc API for class **Date** to see how your method should delegate its work.

3-4   The **TextFile** API does not have a public method to set the modification date to the current date and time without actually changing the **contents**. Sometimes that functionality is useful.[16] Here is javadoc and the declaration header for such a method:

```
/**
 * Change the modification date of this TextFile to the
 * current date and time.
 */
```

public void setModDate( )

- Add that method in **TextFile.java**. Think about a sensible place to put it in the file.

---

[15] We were lucky when we ran that unit test for this text – we saw creation date **Sat Dec 29 14:02:37 EST 2001** and modification date **Sat Dec 29 14:02:38 EST 2001**.
[16] touch is the command in the Unix operating system for changing the modification date of a file. If you have access to a Unix system, test touch there.

- Modify **main** so that it provides a test of your **setModDate** method.
- Change the existing code, replacing each expression that sets the modification date directly by a delegation to the **setModDate** method. Do that with **this** even though the **this** is optional.
- Should the **TextFile** API offer another public **setModDate** method with this functionality?

```
/**
 * Change the modification date of this TextFile.
 *
 * @param date the new modification date.
 */

public void setModDate( Date date )
```

3-5   If you did the previous exercise, you may have noticed that many of the methods in the **Date** class are marked as ***deprecated*** in the API. (If you didn't, look now.) Those methods still work in this version of Java, but they are not guaranteed to work in future releases of Java. So it's best not to use them in new programs. The documentation tells you that the **Calendar** class is the right place to do this work. So change the type of the **createDate** and **modDate** fields in **TextFile** from **Date** to **Calendar** and replace the line

```
41    createDate = new Date(); // date and time now
```

with

```
41    createDate = Calendar.getInstance();
```

Then use the **Calendar** API to figure out how to change **getCreateDate** and **getModDate** so that their behavior is unchanged (the first thing to try is **toString** – perhaps it works).

Write a note in your journal explaining how encapsulating data in private fields and accessing it with public methods made this upgrade possible.

3-6   Provide **TextFile** objects with the alternate constructor (discussed in the text) that accepts no arguments:

```
public TextFile()
{
    this( System.getProperty( "user.name" ), "" );
}
```

Add a test for this constructor to **main**.

3-7   The code in the constructor in the previous exercise is compact and perhaps hard to read. We could consider rewriting it this way, for clarity:

```
public TextFile()
{
```

```
        String userName = System.getProperty ( "user.name" );
        String emptyContents = "";
        this( userName, emptyContents );
}
```

Try that version in your code. The compiler will complain. This is a common error, quite annoying, and difficult to puzzle out when you encounter it for the first time. Explain the error message you see and learn the lesson it teaches.

3-8   Try the command

```
%> java Terminal
```

to see what the unit test in the **Terminal** class does.

3-9   Compile the shapes classes **Screen**, **HLine**, **Box**, and **InteractiveShapes** (Listing 3-6, an interactive version of **DemoShapes**). Run **InteractiveShapes**, creating and painting shapes of zero size, negative size, and shapes with sizes or positions that might cause things to be drawn outside the boundaries of the **Screen**. Discuss the results of your experiments in your journal.

3-10   Find all the declarations in **HLine.java**. For each, indicate the kind of thing being declared (class, field, variable, parameter, or method), its type, and its scope. For example, line 52

```
52    public void paintOn( Screen s )
53    {
54        paintOn( s, 0, 0 );
55    }
```

declares the **paintOn** method returning nothing (**void**) with scope the entire body of **HLine** and the parameter **s** of type **Screen**, with scope the body of this **paintOn** method.

3-11   Find all the places in **HLine.java** in which a message is sent to an object. For each, give the type of the object to which the message is sent, its class, and the declaration header for the method that will respond to the message.

3-12   Identify the various uses of **this** in **HLine.java**.

- Find places where the code would be wrong to if you left **this** out.
- Find places where **this** could be safely removed.
- Find places where a **this** that's absent but understood could be safely added.

3-13   The **for** loop in **Hline**'s **paintOn** could be written this way:

```
for ( int col = x; col < x + length; col++ ) {
    s.paintAt( paintChar, col , y );
}
```

Why did the programmer choose the identifier **col** for the index variable in the loop? Discuss this design. In what ways is it better than the one that's in the code? In what ways it is worse?

3-14   Add a setter method for the **paintChar** field in class **HLine** class, honoring the setter naming convention we have established. Modify the unit test in **HLine.java** so that *its output remains exactly the same* but *uses just one* **HLine** *object* instead of the three that are there now. Remember to write properly formatted javadoc for your new method.

3-15   Answer the previous exercise for the **Box** class.

3-16   Write a class declaration for **VLine**, whose instances model vertical lines. A vertical line of length 3 and paint character * would be drawn as

```
*
*
*
```

A **VLine's** position on a screen is the position of its topmost character.

VLine and **HLine** have the same API, so you might want to save typing by beginning with a copy of **HLine.java**. Then change what needs changing. If you do that, be sure to change variable and field names and comments when appropriate. If you wrote a **setPaintChar** method for **HLine** in a previous exercise, keep it for **VLine**.

Give your **VLine** class a **main** method with a self-documenting noninteractive unit test.

Modify the **DemoShapes**, **InteractiveShapes**, and **UnitTests** classes so that they exercise your **VLine** class.

3-17   Write a class declaration for **Frame** to model framed rectangles. A **Frame** of width 5, height 4, and paint character **f** would be painted as

```
fffff
f   f
f   f
fffff
```

Frames and **Box**es have the same API, so you might want to save typing by beginning with a copy of **Box.java**. Then change what needs changing. If you do that, be sure to change variable and field names and comments when appropriate.

Give your **Frame** class a **main** method with a self-documenting noninteractive unit test.

Modify the **DemoShapes**, **InteractiveShapes**, and **UnitTests** classes so that they exercise your **Frame** class.

Warning: **Frame**s are hollow. Figures behind a **Frame** will show through, so you cannot paint a **Frame** by painting a blank **Box** inside a filled **Box**! Be sure your unit test shows that you have implemented hollow **Frame**s.

3-18   Write a class declaration for **SquareBox** to model a box whose four sides are of equal length. Like **Box**, a **SquareBox** has both a width and a height – that is, there are setters and getters for each. But changing one (with a setter) automatically changes the other. How many fields will a **SquareBox** need to manage its size?

Modify the **DemoShapes**, **InteractiveShapes**, and **UnitTests** classes so that they exercise your **SquareBox** class.

3-19   Write a class declaration for **Triangle** to model triangles. A **Triangle** with height 4 and paint character * paints itself as

```
   *
  * * *
 * * * * *
* * * * * * *
```

The **Triangle** constructor should accept a height and a paint character as arguments. The width of a **Triangle** can be computed from its height. For example, the width of the **Triangle** above with height 4 is 7; in general, the width of a triangle is $2 \times$ height $- 1$. The position of a **Triangle** on a **Screen** is the position of the smallest rectangle enclosing it.

The **Triangle** API is very much like the **Box** API: two **paintOn** methods and setters and getters for the **height** and the **width**. The constructor should be told the height and the paint character.

Implementing **setHeight** and **setWidth** will be tricky, because the height and the width are not independent, and the width must always be an odd number (why?). Describe in your journal the difficulties you encounter. Decide what to do if **setWidth** is passed an even number, and discuss your decision in your journal.

Write a **main** method in **Triangle.java**, providing a self-documenting unit test.

Modify the **DemoShapes**, **InteractiveShapes**, and **UnitTests** classes so that they exercise your **Triangle** class.

3-20   Old-fashioned line printers often printed a cover page showing the name of the file being printed in a banner. In that banner the letter E might have been written this way

```
EEEEEEEEEEE
EEEEEEEEEEE
EEE
EEE
EEE
EEEEEE
EEEEEE
EEE
EEE
EEE
EEEEEEEEEEE
EEEEEEEEEEE
```

Write a class declaration for **BannerE** to draw that shape on a **Screen**. Both the height and width should be 12, and the **paintChar** should be **E** so the **BannerE** class needs no fields and no constructor. It does need two **paintOn** methods and a unit test.

3-21   Answer the previous exercise for your favorite character. Your shape's height should be 12. You can make it as wide as seems right: **I** will need less space than **W**.

3-22   Write a class declaration for **TextLine** whose instances model a horizontal line of text to be painted on a **Screen**. A **TextLine** with contents "Hello, world." would be drawn as

Hello, world.

with the position of the H specified in the **paintOn** invocation.

Although **TextLine**s resemble **HLine**s, the APIs differ in several important ways. To help you, we have provided a *stub* implementation in **TextLine.java** (Listing 3-7). That file contains javadoc and declarations for all the public methods, but the method bodies are empty. Read and understand that API before you begin. Then plan your code before you type. A **TextLine** won't need a **paintChar** field, but it will need a field to hold the **String** that is supposed to be painted on the **Screen**. How will you declare that? How will it get its value in the constructor? Why can't **TextLine** have a **setLength** method?

The **for** loop in **paintOn** will need to get at the characters of the **String** to be painted one at a time. You will find the tools you need for that task in the **String** API: Look at the methods **length** and **charAt**.

Draw a box-and-arrow picture of the **TextLine** object for the **String** "Hello, world.".
Write a good unit test in **main**.

3-23   Add two **paintOn** methods to class **LinearEquation**, with the same signatures as those in **HLine**. When you ask the **LinearEquation** modeling the line $y = f(x) = mx + b$ to paint itself on a **Screen** at position (a, b), the character ***** should be painted at positions

$$(a, f(a)), (a + 1, f(a + 1)), \ldots$$

as long as those points are on the **Screen**. As usual, **paintOn(Screen s)** should delegate to **paintOn(s, 0, 0)**.

There are several potentially tricky parts to this exercise:

- You do not want the **for** loop that paints to the **Screen** to go on forever. Use the **Screen**'s **getWidth** method to figure out where to stop.
- The value of **paintOn**'s **y** parameter is ignored.
- The **LinearEquation**'s **compute** method returns a **double** value for the y coordinate, but the **Screen**'s **paintAt** wants to be told an **int**. Here is the Java that will do that conversion for you:

```
int y = (int)this.compute(x);
```

- The pixel resolution on the **Screen** is very coarse. Most **LinearEquation**s will paint themselves as very jagged lines because of the rounding from **double** to **int**. That may make it hard to see whether your code is doing the right thing. So test with lines with slopes like 0, 1, 2, and -1. (How will you test?)
- Why should you not be surprised when lines with a positive slope fall rather than rise as x increases?

3-24   Write **BoxAndArrow.java**, whose **main** method creates and draws a character representation of the **TextFile** object illustrated in Figure 3-1. You can save yourself lots of tedious work by painting your picture on a **Screen** using the various shapes discussed in the text and in previous exercises and then drawing the **Screen**.

3-25   Add a **main** method to the **BankAccount** class that contains a self-documenting test showing that the public API for that class behaves correctly. Explain why it would be harder to write a unit test for the **Bank** class.

3-26   Explore the Java library API to find the maximum and minimum values for the primitive numerical types **byte**, **short**, **int**, and **long**. You will see the answers in decimal (base 10) notation. They are more informative when written in binary (base 2) or algebraically as numbers close to powers of 2.

3-27   Although the range of values for each of the primitive numerical types is finite, Java provides the **BigInteger** class, whose instances can represent arbitrarily large integers.

Read about that class in the Java API and use it to write the application **Exponentiate**, which prompts for a base and an exponent and performs the computation. Here are two test runs:

```
%> java Exponentiate
base: 2
exponent: 10
2 raised to the power 10 = 1024
%> java Exponentiate
base: 3
exponent: 70
3 raised to the power 70 = 2503155504993241601315571986085849
```

Hint: When you find the signature for the **BigInteger** constructor in the API, you will discover that you want to get the base as a **String** by sending your **Terminal** a **readWord** message, not as an **int** with a **readInt** message.

Your program may misbehave if you give it bad input. You should document that behavior in your journal, but you need not make any effort to deal with it.

3-28   As an **EStore** exercise, write method **main** containing a hard-coded self-documenting unit test for the **ShoppingCart** class. Be sure to test all the methods. You will need **Item.class** (compiled from **Item.java**) because your test will have to create some **Item** objects to add to the **ShoppingCart** you create (with **new**) in **main**.

Chapter 4

Collections

When computers were first envisioned as serious tools, in the middle of the twentieth century,[1] it was thought that their main function would be to carry out repetitive numerical calculations for scientists (and the military). But present-day reality is quite different. Now most computers manipulate more general data most of the time. A bank's information system does a little arithmetic, adding and subtracting from balances to implement deposits and withdrawals. But most of the bank's software manages the bank accounts – locating the records for an account when the user inserts a card in an ATM, checking the PIN against the number stored in the bank's records, and making sure that two people with access to a bank account do not simultaneously withdraw all the money using two ATMs on opposite sides of town.

Each program that manages a collection of objects (bank accounts in a bank, shapes on a screen, files in a directory, parts in a warehouse) must provide a way to

- create a new, empty place to store the items
- put items into the collection
- retrieve items from the collection
- loop through (iterate through, cycle through) all the items in the collection

In this chapter we will start to study three kinds of Java objects whose purpose is to maintain a collection of data: array,[2] **ArrayList**, and **TreeMap**. These tools will allow us to build a more sophisticated **Bank**, to model a **Directory** containing **TextFile** objects, and to improve our shapes package.

Arrays

The most primitive way to maintain a collection of objects is in an ***array***: an object that stores its contents in order, so that they can be accessed using an integer index.

An Array of BankAccounts

In Version 1 of the banking system, we declared a separate field for each **BankAccount** in the **Bank** (recall **account1**, **account2**, and the **account3** you added in an exercise). The **Bank** class in the new release of the banking system (Listings 4-1,

---

[1] Or in the middle of the nineteenth if you count Babbage's Difference Engine.
[2] "Array" isn't capitalized in the text because there is no array class in Java, even though arrays are objects.

Bank.java, and 4-2, **BankAccount.java**) uses a single field to hold all the **BankAccount** objects in an array. The declaration

```
32     private BankAccount[] accountList;³
```

tells the Java compiler that **accountList** is a variable (a private field in this case) whose type is **BankAccount[]**. We read **BankAccount[]** out loud as "array of BankAccounts."[4]

Later, in the **Bank** constructor, we use the keyword **new** to create the array object the **accountList** field refers to. That resulting array can store references to three **BankAccount** objects because field **NUM_ACCOUNTS** was assigned the value 3 when it was declared on line 34.

```
60     accountList    = new BankAccount[NUM_ACCOUNTS];
```

We might have declared the array and created it all at once on line 32:

```
32     private BankAccount[] accountList
              = new BankAccount[NUM_ACCOUNTS];
```

but decided instead to leave that task to the constructor. There, after creating the array, we fill it by creating three new **BankAccount** objects:

```
66     accountList[0] = new BankAccount( 0, this);
67     accountList[1] = new BankAccount(100, this);
68     accountList[2] = new BankAccount(200, this);
```

These lines show how to use square brackets to refer to particular entries in the **accountList** array. Note that indexing starts at 0, not at 1: The three accounts are numbered 0, 1, and 2, not 1, 2, and 3. That should not surprise you if you remember that computer scientists always begin counting at 0 rather than at 1.

Figure 4-1 illustrates what we have constructed, showing our convention for a box-and-arrow picture of an array. We have omitted the internal structure of the **BankAccount** objects in that figure; we will return to it later.

The **accountList** field in the **Bank** is a collection of **BankAccount** objects that allows us to find an account when we know its number. The **Bank**'s **whichAccount** method prompts the user for that number (line 188), finds the entry in the array

---

[3] If you consult the program listing you will find an extra comment on this line, and others. Those comments are referred to in several of the exercises.

[4] The Java compiler accepts the alternative array declaration syntax

```
BankAccount accountList[];
```

for historical reasons – Java syntax mimics the syntax of the C programming language in many ways. We will not use this alternative construction. The new way is better because it follows the convention that puts the type of the variable – in this case **BankAccount[]**, for "array of BankAccounts" – first, followed by the name of the variable.

Bank

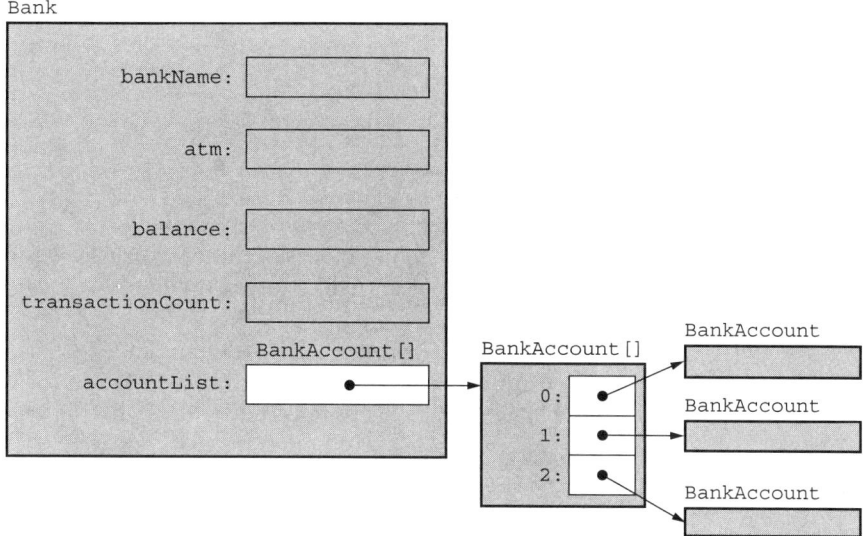

Figure 4-1: Object structure of a **Bank** and its **BankAccounts**

(if it's there), and returns it (line 194); otherwise, it prints a message and returns
null:

```
184 private BankAccount whichAccount()
185 {
188     int accountNumber = atm.readInt("account number: ");
189
193     if (accountNumber >= 0 && accountNumber<NUM_ACCOUNTS){
194         return accountList[accountNumber];
195     }
196     else {
197         atm.println("not a valid account");
198         return null;
199     }
200 }⁵
```

Line 194 shows again how we use the array name and square brackets to refer to an
element stored in the array at a particular place. Before we get to that line, line 193

---

⁵ Pay no attention to the missing lines in this listing. The comments there will help you later with the
exercises.

checks to see that the user entered a legal account number – in our example, that's 0, 1, or 2. It uses the test

```
accountNumber >= 0
```

to eliminate negative account numbers (allowing 0) and the test

```
accountNumber < NUM_ACCOUNTS
```

to check that the account number is less than the number of objects in the **accountList** array. It's always wise to use that field rather than a hard-coded number (which would be 3 here) so your program will still work when the array happens to have a different size.

The two tests are combined with the token **&&**, signifying "and."

The **Bank** uses its **accountList** field in one more place: When the **Bank** shuts down, it reports the status of each of its accounts. That's done with our friend the **for** loop:

```
211  for (int i = 0; i < NUM_ACCOUNTS; i++ ) {
212      atm.println(i + "\t" +accountList[i].getBalance()+
213          "\t" + accountList[i].getTransactionCount());
214  }
```

which sets **i** to be 0, 1, and 2 in turn to look at each account, printing the account number **i** and then the value returned when the **BankAccount accountList[i]** is sent a **getBalance** message and a **getTransactionCount** message (the **"\t"** is a tab character, to separate those numbers).

The missing lines in these fragments of code from **Bank.java** hint at features of this release that we haven't looked at yet. We will do that at the end of this chapter. Now we want to focus on learning how to use arrays.

An Array of Prime Integers

Arrays can store primitive types as well as references to objects. This code declares a variable for an array of integers and then creates such an array with five places (in positions 0, 1, 2, 3, and 4).

```
int[] primes = new int[5];
```

The **int[]** on the left in this expression tells the Java compiler the type of the variable **primes**. The **new int[5]** on the right invokes the array constructor.

After the array has been constructed, we can fill it with the first five prime numbers:

```
primes[0] = 2;
primes[1] = 3;
primes[2] = 5;
```

```
primes[3] = 7;
primes[4] = 11;
```

The first entry in the array is the 2 at position 0. It's the first prime number.[6]

Java allows you to initialize the values in an array all at once when you declare it by listing those values in order separated by commas in a block surrounded by curly braces:

```
int[] primes = {2, 3, 5, 7, 11};
```

Figure 4-2 illustrates the array we have constructed.

Arrays are objects. Objects do work when they receive messages. The syntax for sending messages to arrays is special: It uses the square brackets rather than a method name. The expression

```
primes[0] = 2;
```

is really sending the **primes** array a message asking it to store the **int** 2 in its first place. The expression

```
int thirdPrime = primes[2];
```

is really sending the **primes** array a message asking it to get the **int** stored in its third place (the place with index 2); that value (which happens to be 5) becomes the value of the variable **thirdPrime**.

An attempt to execute

```
primes[5] = 13;
```

or

```
int r = primes[-1];
```

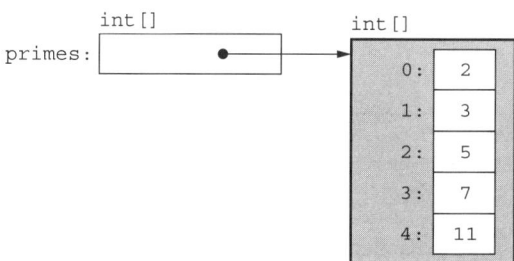

Figure 4-2: A variable referring to an array of five integers

---

[6] Mathematicians have good reasons for their convention that 1 is not prime, so 2 is the first prime.

will generate an **ArrayIndexOutOfBoundsException**. One of the exercises at the end of this chapter has you make these kinds of errors intentionally to see what happens.

We can always find out how many elements there are in an array by examining its **length** field:

```
int primeCount = primes.length;
```

assigns the value 5 to the variable **primeCount**.

If we create an array of **int**s with **new**, and do not specify what is to fill it, Java fills it with zeros:

```
int[] mystery = new int[3];
```

creates an array of three zeros (by default), as illustrated in Figure 4-3.

Arrays themselves can be assigned, so long as the type rules are followed. Because both **primes** and **mystery** refer to integer arrays, we can say,

```
mystery = primes;
```

After this assignment, both **primes** and **mystery** refer to the same array. Figure 4-4 shows that. The array of zeros that used to be the value of the variable **mystery** is no longer accessible to our program.

The statement

```
mystery[4] = 13;
```

would change the fifth (not the fourth!) element of the **mystery** array – and hence the **primes** array as well – to 13.[7]

The **for** loop is the standard idiom for looking at each element stored in an array in turn. We saw that idiom in the **report** method in class **Bank**. Here are two more examples: loops to print the **primes** array, first in order and then in reverse order:

```
for (int i = 0; i < primes.length; i++) {
    System.out.println( primes[i] );
}
```

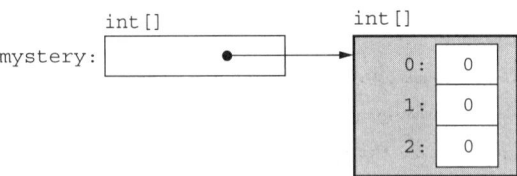

Figure 4-3: A variable referring to an array of three integers

---

[7] The Java is still correct, but now the mathematics isn't, because our array of primes skips 11.

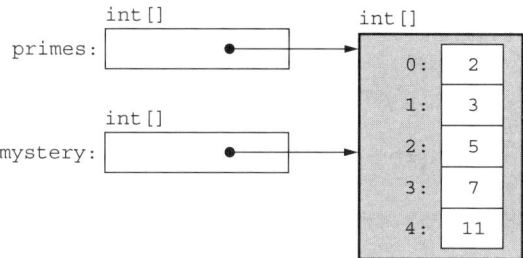

Figure 4-4: Two variables that refer to the same array

```
for (int i = primes.length-1; i >= 0; i--) {
    System.out.println( primes[i] );
}
```

The expression **i--** decreases the value of **i** by 1 just as **i++** increases it by 1.

In each of these examples we use the **length** field of the **primes** array to manage the number of iterations. That guarantees that our code will work properly even if in some later version of the program the **primes** array is created with a **length** other than 5.

Arguments to main

The declaration header for the **main** method where Java programs start is

```
public static void main( String[] args )
```

We now know how to read what's between the parentheses. The formal parameter **args** is an array of **String** objects. Thus **main** expects an array of **String**s as its single parameter. Those **String**s are the *command-line arguments* passed to the program: the words following the class name on the command line. Class **CommandLineArgsDemo** (Example 4-1, displayed below) shows how to access command-line arguments. If **main** in **CommandLineArgsDemo** is invoked this way

```
%> java CommandLineArgsDemo Hi there,  neighbor
```

then the actual argument passed to **main** will be an array of length 3 containing the **String**s **"Hi"**, **"there,"** and **"neighbor"** in positions 0, 1, and 2. Java has broken the rest of the command line (after the name of the class with **main**) into tokens, using white space (blanks or tabs) as separators, and put those tokens into an array. The program then prints those **String**s one to a line, surrounded by vertical bars to show that the blanks have been deleted:

```
Echo command line arguments,
surrounded by |...|
|Hi|
|there,|
|neighbor|
```

The code is a straightforward application of what we have learned about arrays:

```java
public class CommandLineArgsDemo
{
    public static void main( String[] args )
    {
        System.out.println("Echo command line arguments, ");
        System.out.println("surrounded by |...| ");
        for (int i = 0; i < args.length; i++) {
            System.out.println('|' + args[i] + '|');
        }
    }
}
```

The Screen Class: Two-Dimensional Arrays

The **Screen** on which we drew our shapes in Chapter 3 is a two-dimensional grid of characters. We implement this grid with a two-dimensional array. In Java we do that by building an array of arrays. In class **Screen** (Listing 3-8), the grid is represented by the private field **pixels** declared on line 20:

```
20    private char[][] pixels;
```

The type of this field is **char[][]**. That is, it is an array of objects of type **char[]**: an array of arrays of **char**s. Variable **pixels** is initialized on line 33 in the **Screen**'s constructor when the size of the **Screen** is known:

```
29    public Screen( int width, int height )
30    {
31        this.width  = width;
32        this.height = height;
33        pixels = new char[width][height];
```

```
34        clear();
35    }
```

Figure 4-5 shows the box-and-arrow representation of a 2×3 **Screen**.

A **Screen** clears itself by assigning the blank character to every location. Nested **for** loops do the job, illustrating a common idiom for looping over a two-dimensional array:

```
41    public void clear()
42    {
43        for (int x = 0; x < width; x++) {
44            for ( int y = 0; y < height; y++ ) {
45                pixels[x][y] = BLANK;
46            }
47        }
48    }
```

Line 45 shows how painting a character at position (x,y) on the grid means assigning that character to the variable **pixels[x][y]** .

Figure 4-5 makes clear the fact that a two-dimensional array is simply an array of (one-dimensional) arrays. Indeed, each of those one-dimensional arrays is an object in its own right, so we can say:

```
char[] firstRow = pixels[0];
```

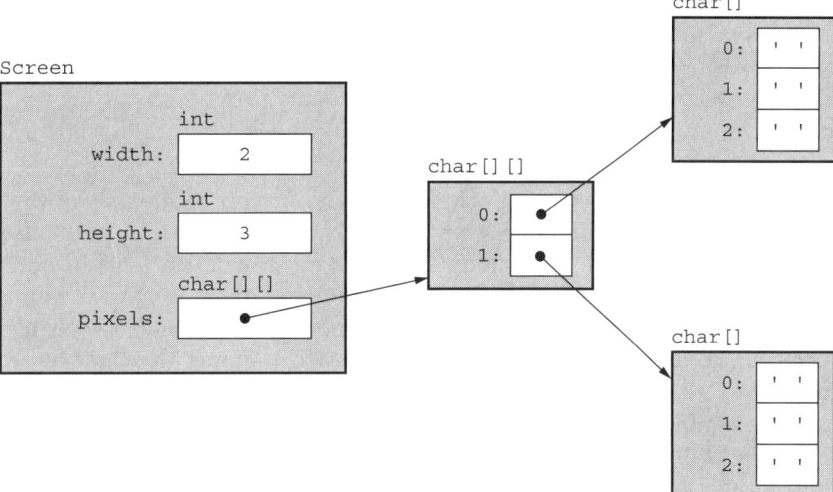

Figure 4-5: Object structure of a 2×3 **Screen**

Array Summary

Use an array when you need a collection of objects that are all of the same type and when you know in advance how many objects there will be.

- To declare an array to store objects of a given **Type**:

  Type[] myArray;

- To create an array to store **N** objects, once the array has been declared:

  myArray = new Type[N];

- To discover the length of an array:

  myArray.length

- To put something at position **i** (when **0 <= i < myArray.length**):

  myArray[i] = something;

- To get something from position **i** (when **0 <= i < myArray.length**):

  something = myArray[i];

- To loop through an array:
  ```
  for( int i = 0; i < myArray.length; i++) {
      // do something with myArray[i]
  }
  ```

Program **ArrayDemo.java** (Example 4-2) illustrates all these array features and others. Study it to learn more about how arrays behave. Borrow code from it to paste into your own programs when you are using arrays.

ArrayList

We use an array when we know in advance how many elements we want to store in an indexed list. But sometimes we do not know when we create the list how many elements there will be. For example, a **Bank** must maintain a list of **BankAccount**s that allows for the possibility of new customers' opening new accounts. Then the **ArrayList** class in the Java library comes to the rescue. We can think of an **ArrayList** as like an array but capable of expanding to whatever size it needs to be.

For example, suppose we want to read lines the user types at the keyboard and, when she is done, print them out *in reverse order*. Because we cannot print any line until all the lines have been typed, we must *remember* the lines as they are typed and print them afterward. But we can't use an array to store the lines, because we do not know when we start the program how many lines will be typed. Class **Reverse** (Listing 4-7) uses an **ArrayList** to do the job:

```
6      import java.util.ArrayList;


22     public static void main( String[] args )
23     {
24         Terminal  t    = new Terminal();
25         ArrayList list = new ArrayList();
26         String line;
27
28         while ((line = t.readLine()) != null ) {
29             list.add(line);
30         }
31
32         for (int i = list.size()-1; i >= 0; i--) {
33             line = (String)list.get(i);
34             t.println( line );
35         }
36     }
37 }
```

Line 6 is new to us.[8] It uses the Java keyword **import** to tell the compiler to recognize **ArrayList** as a class from the **java.util** package in the Java library.

On line 25 we declare variable **list** of type **ArrayList** and create a new **ArrayList**, just as we would an object of any other class. Our new **ArrayList** is empty, ready to have elements added to it.

To add an object at the end of an **ArrayList**, we send the **ArrayList** an **add** message. Our **Reverse** program does that on line 29. The object that's added is the **String line** returned by **Terminal t**'s **readLine** method on line 28. When there are no more lines of input,[9] method **readLine** returns **null** and the test on line 28 ends the **while** loop. That loop should not be a **for** loop because we do not know when it starts how long it will continue.[10]

But once input has ended, we have all the lines the user wants us to reverse. They are stored in our **ArrayList**. Then we print them out with a **for** loop. We find out how many elements our **ArrayList** contains by sending it a **size** message, and we

---

[8] If you noticed the import of the **Date** class in **TextFile.java**, then it's not new to you.

[9] When typing, enter Ctrl+Z to end input (on Windows), Ctrl+D to end input (on Unix).

[10] Because anything **while** can do, **for** can do too, you could write this as a **for** loop (but we don't recommend that):

```
for (String line; line = t.readLine()) != null ; list.add(line))
```

use the returned value to initialize the loop index **i** on line 32, remembering that an **ArrayList**, like an array, starts at position 0 and ends at the position whose index is one less than its size. The body of the **for** loop sends the **ArrayList** a **get** message to retrieve the object at position **i** – there is no shortcut like the square bracket syntax honored by arrays. Line 33 has one feature we have not seen before: the class name **String** in parentheses. That construction is a ***cast***. It tells the Java compiler what kind of object was returned by the **ArrayList get** method – in this case, a **String**, because that's what we put in. We will learn more about casts later.

ArrayList Summary

Use an **ArrayList** when you need a collection of objects and the size of the collection is not known in advance.

- To use an **ArrayList** in your class definition, you must import it before the class declaration in the file:

  ```
  import java.util.ArrayList;
  ```

- To declare a variable of type **ArrayList**:

  ```
  ArrayList myList;
  ```

- To create an empty **ArrayList** once an **ArrayList** variable has been declared:

  ```
  myList = new ArrayList();
  ```

- To discover the length of an **ArrayList**:

  ```
  myList.size()
  ```
  [11]

- To put something at the end of the list:

  ```
  myList.add(something);
  ```

- To get something from position **i** (**0 <= i < myList.size()**), send a get message and cast the returned value to the proper type:

  ```
  Type something = (Type) myList.get(i);
  ```

- To loop through an ArrayList:

  ```
  for( int i = 0; i < myList.size(); i++) {
      // do something with (Type)myList.get(i)
  }
  ```

---

[11] It's unfortunate that you learn the size of an array by looking at its *length field* but you learn the size of an **ArrayList** by sending it a *size message*. You are sure to try **myArray.size()** and **myArrayList.length** from time to time, and grumble when the compiler complains.

- An **ArrayList** may contain only objects, unlike an array, which may contain primitive types.
- An **ArrayList** may contain the same object at different locations.
- An **ArrayList** may contain many different kinds of objects – unlike an array, which must be declared to contain objects of just one type. Because the contents of an **ArrayList** are heterogeneous, when you get an object from an **ArrayList** you must cast it to its proper type.

The **ArrayList** class supports lots of additional functionality, including methods to add an element in the middle of the list, either replacing the element there or moving all the later elements down to make room. All of these are documented in the API that comes with the Java library. You can find that API at **http://java.sun.com/j2se/1.4/docs/api/java/util/ArrayList.html**. Browse it now. Program **ArrayListDemo.java** (Example 4-3) illustrates many **ArrayList** features. Study it to learn more about how **ArrayList**s behave. Figure 4-6 shows a box-and-arrow picture of the **ArrayList** in that program.

Borrow code from **ArrayListDemo.java** to paste into your own programs when you must work with an **ArrayList**. In the exercises we will use one to improve the **Bank** so you can open as many new **BankAccount**s as you like while the **Bank** simulation is running, without having to edit the source code.

TreeMaps

Telephone books and library catalogs are everyday instances of *maps*: collections that allow you to look up a *value* (like a telephone number) associated with a *key* (a name).

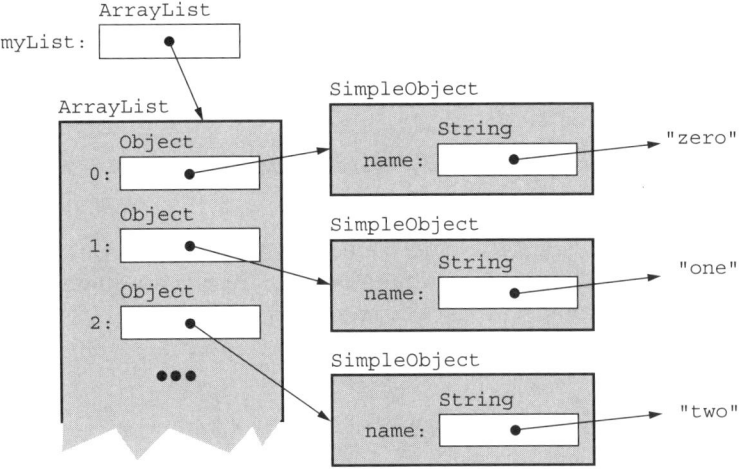

Figure 4-6: Boxes and arrows for **ArrayList**

So we say that a map *stores key–value pairs* or *maps keys to values.* A telephone book is a collection in which the keys are names and the values are telephone numbers. The Social Security Administration maintains a (large!) database in which the keys are Social Security numbers and the values are records containing information about a person's employment history. A library catalog is a more complicated kind of map because the record for each book can be found using either the book's title or the author's name as a key. You can even think of the World Wide Web as a map, where the keys are URLs like **www.cs.umb.edu/joi** and the values are the Web pages that correspond to those URLs.

Class **TreeMap** in the Java API implements map functionality.[12] We will learn how to use a **TreeMap** by designing class **Dictionary**,[13] whose instances allow us to look up the definitions of words. **Dictionary.java** is Listing 4-8.

First we tell the compiler how to find several classes from the **java.util** package:

```
6 import java.util.*;
```

Then we declare a private field for our **TreeMap**:

```
18     private TreeMap entries;
```

and create an empty **TreeMap** in the **Dictionary** constructor:

```
24     public Dictionary()
25     {
26         entries = new TreeMap();
27     }
```

A **Dictionary** entry associates a word (which is a **String**) with a definition (which is an object of type **Definition**). To add an entry to the **Dictionary**, we send it an **addEntry** message, passing as arguments the information it needs:

```
36     public void addEntry(String word, Definition definition)
37     {
38         entries.put( word, definition );
39     }
```

The one-line body of **addEntry** delegates the work to the **put** method in the **TreeMap** class. After line 38 executes, the **TreeMap entries** knows that a particular **Definition** is associated with the **String word**.

---

[12] You will find out in Chapter 10 why this class is not just **Map**. You will find out in a later course in computer science why it's a **TreeMap**.

[13] The Java library contains a **Dictionary** class, but it's obsolete. New Java doesn't use it, so we have no qualms reusing the name here.

To look up a word, we send the **Dictionary** a **getEntry** message, telling it the word we are interested in:

```
48    public Definition getEntry( String word )
49    {
50        return (Definition)entries.get(word);
51    }
```

The body of **getEntry** delegates the lookup to the **get** method in class **TreeMap**. That method returns the object associated with the key. **TreeMap**s, like **ArrayList**s, store objects anonymously, so we must cast the value returned by **get** to type **Definition** before we can return it from **getEntry**.

These code fragments illustrate the essentials involved in using a **TreeMap**: putting items in and getting them out. Making these fragments work in a complete program requires a little more work. You will find the declaration for the **Definition** class in Listing 4-9. Class **Lookup** (Listing 4-10) has a **main** method that builds a **Dictionary** and then allows you to look up the **Definition**s of words. Here is a fragment of an interaction with **Lookup**:

```
%> java Lookup
look up words, "quit" to quit
word> square
a rectangle having equal sides
word> quit
```

and here is the code from **Lookup.java** that implements that interaction (without line numbers, because we are omitting lots of lines). You will note that **Lookup.java** uses several static fields and methods in addition to **main**, to make the code easier to read.

```
private static Terminal t = new Terminal();
private static Dictionary dictionary = new Dictionary();

private static void fillDictionary()
{
    dictionary.addEntry( "quadrilateral",
        new Definition("a polygonal shape with four sides"));
}

private static void printDefinition(String word)
{
    Definition definition = dictionary.getEntry(word);
    t.println(definition.toString());
}
```

```
public static void main( String[] args )
{
    while (true) {
        word = t.readWord("word> ");
        if (word.equals("quit")) {
            break;
        }
        printDefinition(word);
    }
}
```

We do not need to know more about **Definition** objects than we can guess from this code fragment. The **Definition** API has

- a public constructor that accepts a single **String** – in this case, the definition of a quadrilateral
- a public **toString** method that acts as a getter for that **String**

You can read all of **Definition.java** in Listing 4-9.

Figure 4-7 shows the convention we have adopted for box-and-arrow pictures of **TreeMap**s. It shows a **Dictionary** object containing two word-**Definition** pairs.

What if the Entry Isn't There?

If we try to look up a word that's not in the **Dictionary**, the **TreeMap**'s **get** method invoked on line 50 in the **Dictionary**'s **getEntry** method returns the special object literal **null**. That special value is then returned to whoever called **getEntry**. Here is

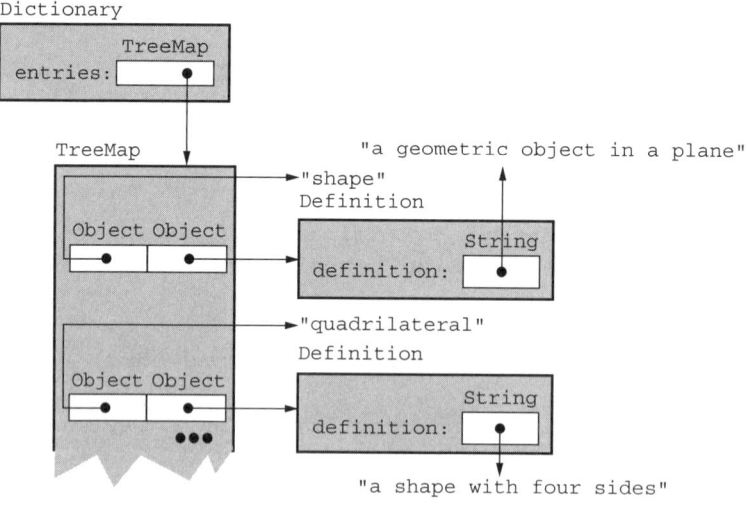

Figure 4-7: A **Dictionary** with two entries

the complete text of the method in **Lookup.java** that prints the definition requested by the user:

```java
private static void printDefinition(String word)
{
    Definition definition = dictionary.getEntry(word);
    if (definition == null) {
        t.println("sorry, no definition found for " + word);
    }
    else {
        t.println(definition.toString());
    }
}
```

Duplicate Entries?

In a simple **TreeMap**, putting a second item with the same key as another causes the first value to be overwritten. But there is no restriction on how many keys map to the same value: Several words may have the same **Definition**. Several people may have the same telephone number.

Because each key corresponds to a unique value, we need to think about how to deal with the fact that a person may have more than one telephone number and a word may have more than one definition. One strategy is to have the value corresponding to a given key be an **ArrayList** rather than a simple object. You will program that strategy in one of the exercises.

Looping Over a TreeMap: Iterators

Sometimes we want to know about the **TreeMap** as a whole, rather than about any single item stored there. Our **Dictionary** application allows that: We can see all the words and their definitions by passing **Lookup** the command-line argument "all":

```
%>  java Lookup all
The whole dictionary (4 entries):
-------------------
quadrilateral:
a polygonal shape with four sides
rectangle:
a right-angled quadrilateral
shape:
a geometric object in a plane
square:
a rectangle having equal sides
-------------------
```

This code in **Dictionary.java** (invoked by **Lookup**) produces that output:

```
59    public int getSize()
60    {
61        return entries.size();
62    }


70    public String toString()
71    {
72        String str = "";
73        String word;
74        Definition definition;
75        Set allWords = entries.keySet();
76        Iterator wordIterator = allWords.iterator();
77        while ( wordIterator.hasNext() ) {
78            word = (String)wordIterator.next();
79            definition = this.getEntry( word );
80            str += word + ":\n" + definition.toString() + "\n";
81        }
82        return str;
83    }
```

The **getSize** method is straightforward. The **Dictionary** has no size field – this getter delegates the job to the **size** method in the **TreeMap** class.

The **toString** method is tricky. It constructs a multiline **String** with all the words in the **Dictionary** and their definitions. To do that, we need a way to loop over all the key-value pairs in the **TreeMap**. Without a proper tool, that would be hard to do, because they are not indexed 0,1,2 . . . as are the entries in an array or an **ArrayList**. Fortunately, Java provides class **Iterator**, whose API has just the methods we want for a loop: a way to find out whether there are any more elements to look at and a way to get the next element. Getting an **Iterator** for the keys in a **TreeMap** is a two-step process. First we ask the **TreeMap** for the **Set** of its keys by sending a **keySet** message:

```
75    Set allWords = entries.keySet();
```

As its type implies, **allWords** is assigned the **Set** of all the keys used in the **TreeMap**. Like **TreeMap**, **Set** is a class in the Java library. To iterate (loop) over all of the keys in this **Set**, we use an **Iterator**, which we get by sending the **Set** an **iterator** message:

```
76    Iterator wordIterator = allWords.iterator();
```

Then we send **wordsIterator** (not the **TreeMap entries**, not the **Set allWords**!) messages to look at the words:

```
77    while ( wordIterator.hasNext() ) {
78        word = (String)wordIterator.next();
79        definition = this.getEntry( word );
80        str += word + ":\n" + definition.toString() + "\n";
81    }
82    return str;
```

This **while** loop is a common idiom for iteration. Method **hasNext** in the loop test (on line 77) returns **true** until **next** (on line 78) has run through all the keys. Note the cast to **(String)** for the object returned by **next**. The objects in an **Iterator**, like those in a **TreeMap**, have an anonymous type. We must cast them after retrieving them in order to send them messages they can understand.

Because we want to see both the words and the accompanying definitions, we look up the value each time we get the next key. Then we append two lines to the **String** we are building. We return that **String** when the iterator loop ends.

The words in the output appear in alphabetical order, even though they were not put into the **TreeMap** in that order earlier in **Lookup**. This is no coincidence: The order in which an **Iterator** sees the keys of a **TreeMap** is based on the natural ordering of the keys.

Although it's hard to imagine why one would want a list of definitions separate from the list of words to which they apply, sometimes we do want to look just at the values in a **TreeMap** without bothering with the keys. To do that, we ask the **TreeMap** for an **Iterator** over the **Set** of values:

```
Iterator defIterator = entries.values().iterator();
while (defIterator.hasNext()) {
    Definition def = (Definition)defIterator.next();
    // do something with def
}
```

The values are ordered by their keys, even though the keys are not present.

TreeMap Summary

Use a **TreeMap** when you need a collection of objects indexed by a key rather than by their position in the collection.

• Import the **java.util** package before the class declaration in the file:

```
import java.util.*;
```

You should import all of **java.util**, not just **java.util.TreeMap**, because you will probably want to iterate over your **TreeMap**.

- To declare a `TreeMap`:

  TreeMap myMap;

- To create an empty `TreeMap` once a **TreeMap** variable has been declared:

  myMap = new TreeMap();

- To discover the number of key–value pairs in a **TreeMap**:

  myMap.size()

- To add a key–value pair to the **TreeMap**:

  myMap.put(key, value);

  Any kind of object may be the value of an entry in a **TreeMap**. Keys must be objects too. In this text we will always use **String** keys.[14]

- To look up the value corresponding to a key send a **get** message and cast the returned value to the proper type:

  Type something = (Type)myMap.get(key);

- To loop through a **TreeMap**, use an **Iterator** on the **Set** of keys (remember to cast the key and value before you use them):

  ```
  Iterator iter = myMap.keySet().iterator();
  while ( iter.hasNext() ) {
      String key = (String)iter.next();
      Type value = (Type)myMap.get(key);
      // do something with key and value
  }
  ```

- A **TreeMap** may contain the same value associated with different keys, but each key is associated with just one value.

- A **TreeMap** may contain many different kinds of objects, like an **ArrayList**, but unlike an array, which must be declared to contain objects of just one type. Because the contents of a **TreeMap** are heterogeneous, when you get a key or a value from a **TreeMap** you must cast it to its proper type.

The **TreeMap** class supports lots of additional functionality, documented in the API that comes with the Java library.

Whenever your program needs a way to store objects so that they can be retrieved by name, a **TreeMap** with **String** keys is a good candidate. In the previous chapter we introduced **TextFile** objects to model files in a computer system. In the exercises

---

[14] The real requirement is that in a **TreeMap**, key objects can be ordered, as can **String**s. There are other kinds of maps – for example, **HashMap**, which don't require that the keys be orderable; the order in which an **Iterator** loops over the elements of a **HashMap** is therefore unpredictable. But that's more general than what you need to think about this early in your career as a programmer.

at the end of this chapter you will build a **Directory** containing **TextFile**s keyed by their names and will improve the **Bank** so you can open as many new **BankAccount**s as you like while the **Bank** simulation is running, without having to edit the source code. You may borrow code from **TreeMapDemo.java** (Example 4-4) to paste into your own programs when you do these exercises.

What's in a Name?

The names for the ways to find out how many elements are stored in a collection present an interesting puzzle. In **TextFile.java** we saw that we could send a **length** message to a **String** to get the number of characters in a **String**. For arrays, we look directly at the public instance field **length** rather than send a **length** message. For **TreeMap** and **ArrayList**, we send a **size** message to find the number of elements stored. There is no common pattern, and none of these follows our convention for naming getters, which would dictate **getLength** or **getSize**.

Some of these names are historical. For example, **length** was used for the length of a string long before Java, and long before the convention of using getters and setters was established. For arrays, the direct access to the **length** instance field might have been a design decision driven by a wish for runtime efficiency: Although arrays are like objects, they are implemented specially by Java to make them faster. But even given that special treatment, there is no technical barrier to making a **length** method as efficient as a public instance field. There are always retrospective ways to see how things could have been done better. But programming languages are never perfect. They are designed by mortals like us; they have histories and they evolve as do human languages.

Banks Revisited

The **Bank** we worked with in Chapter 1 had just two accounts – three, if you did the exercise. The version we studied at the beginning of this chapter has three accounts stored in a fixed-length array. We now have tools with which we can build a **Bank** that allows accounts to be added while the application is running rather than by editing the source code: A **Bank** object could keep accounts in an **ArrayList** instead of in an array. Or it could keep accounts in a **TreeMap** instead of in an array, if we wanted accounts to have names rather than numbers.

We leave these improvements as exercises. Whether or not you choose to do them, you should study the new versions of **Bank** (Listing 4-1) and **BankAccount** (Listing 4-2). They reflect an important redesign.

In addition to its **balance** field, a **BankAccount** object maintains a **transactionCount** field for keeping track of the number of transactions performed by the account. The **Bank** maintains its own **balance** and **transactionCount** fields for keeping track of the total balance on hand and the total number of transactions performed by the various accounts. Every time a **BankAccount** object performs a transaction, it must update not only its own fields but also one or more of the fields in the issuing **Bank**. In order to do this, each **BankAccount** object must know the **Bank** that created it. To implement that functionality, we construct a **BankAccount** this way in a **Bank** object:

```
68    accountList[2] = new BankAccount(200, this);
```

The second argument in the **BankAccount** constructor is the **Bank** that is creating the account – **this** in the code fragment above. The **BankAccount** deals with that information by declaring field

```
20    private Bank issuingBank;
```

which it initializes in its constructor:

```
31    public BankAccount(int initialBalance, Bank issuingBank)
32    {
33        this.issuingBank = issuingBank;
34        deposit( initialBalance );
35    }
```

Figure 4-8 shows the box-and-arrow picture of a **Bank** with three **BankAccount**s. It's an elaboration of Figure 4-1.

To see how we use this design, consider the **BankAccount** method **countTransaction**, which is invoked for each transaction performed:

```
125    public void countTransaction()
126    {
127        transactionCount++;
128        this.getIssuingBank().countTransaction();
129    }
```

Method **countTransaction** first increments this **BankAccount**'s **transactionCount** field (using the autoincrement operator **++**), then sends a message to the issuing **Bank** so that it can increment *its* **transactionCount** field.

Summary

We have begun to study three of the many ways Java programs can store collections of objects. An array is useful for storing a fixed number of objects (or primitive values) of a particular type, indexed by an integer. An **ArrayList** stores objects in an array that may grow over time. A **TreeMap** stores arbitrary objects keyed by **String**s. We discussed several examples in the text. In the exercises, you will use collections to improve the **Bank** application and to implement a **Directory** class whose instances

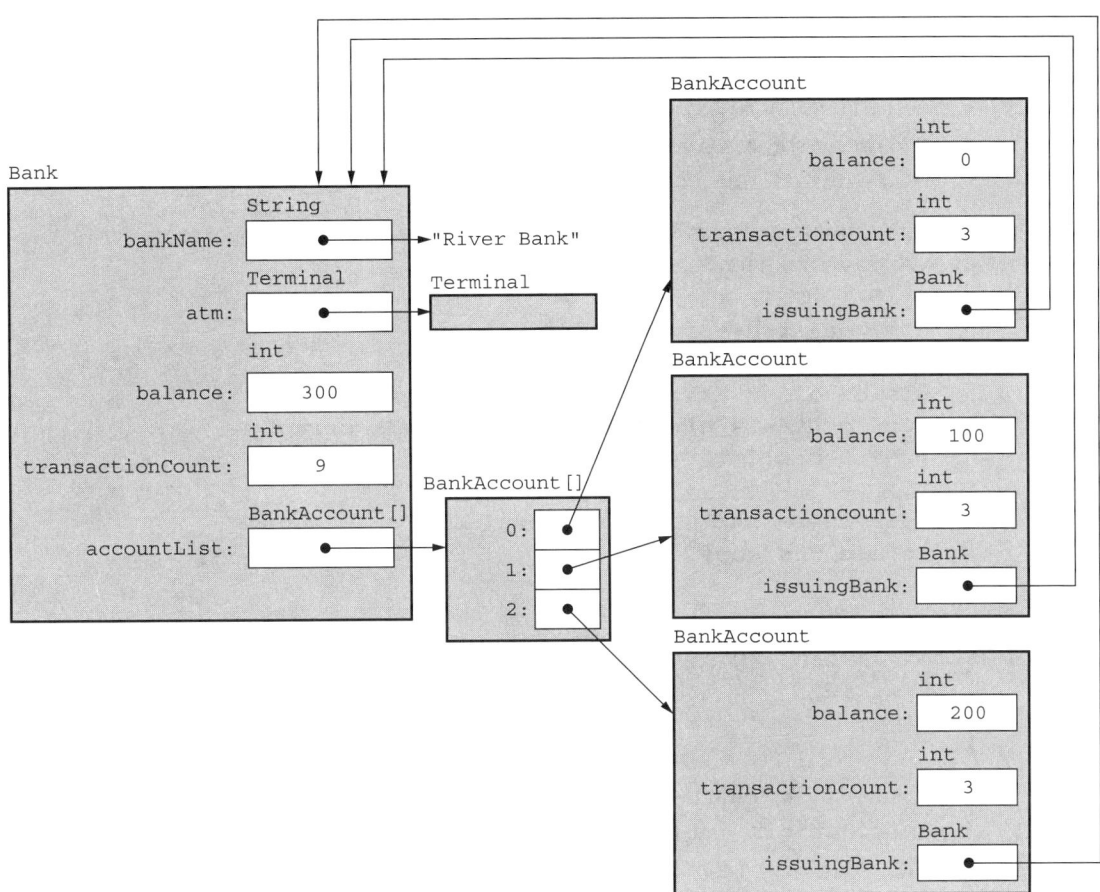

Figure 4-8: A **Bank** object and its fields

manage a collection of **TextFile**s. We will use all three kinds of collections frequently throughout the remainder of this text.

In the next chapter, we will learn about inheritance – Java's strategy for managing classes that have a lot in common.

Exercises

4-1   Create a text file for your journal for this chapter. Use your journal for questions that call for written answers and to record any observations about your work.

4-2   Write class **BadArrays** with a **main** method that intentionally makes several array usage errors. Declare and instantiate **int[] myArray = new int[3]** and discuss the following experiments. Which cause compile time errors? Which cause runtime errors?

- Set the length of **myArray** with the statement **myArray.length = 4;**
- Try to access **myArray[-1]**, **myArray[100]** and **myArray[2.5]**.
- Try to store a **double** in **myArray**.

4-3   Java programmers often discover that they need to make a copy of an array. Write class **CopyArray** implementing the static method

```
/**
 * Copy an array of integers.
 *
 * Create a new array as long as necessary,
 * copy contents of input array to that array
 * and return it.
 *
 * @param src the array to copy.
 * return the copy.
 */

public static int[] copyIntArray( int[] src )
{

}
```

- Explain why it would be wrong to implement **copyIntArray** this way:
  ```
  public static int[] copyIntArray( int[] src )
  {
      int[] newArray = src;
      return newArray;
  }
  ```
  (A box-and-arrow picture might help.)
- Write a **main** method to test **copyIntArray**. Be sure your test can detect the faulty implementation above.
- **copyIntArray** is not nearly as general as we'd like. It deals only with arrays of integers. Why can't we just write **copyArray** and use it to copy any kind of array?
- You probably used a **for** loop to copy the contents of **src** to a new array. Arrays are so common that Java provides an efficient way to copy them without using a loop.[15] Look in the Java API for the static method **arraycopy** in the **System** class

---

[15] That is, without using an explicit loop written in Java. The underlying implementation may loop somehow.

and use it instead of your **for** loop to implement **copyIntArray**. (Leave the **for** loop in the code, commented so that the Java compiler does not see it.)

4-4   Rewrite the initialization of the **accountList** array in the **Bank** constructor using the **{...}** syntax:

```
accountList = { new BankAccount( 0, this), ...};
```

4-5   When a shape like an **HLine** paints itself on a **Screen**, the **Screen** boundary crops the shape if it won't fit. One of the exercises in Chapter 3 asked you to observe this fact. Read **Screen.java** and explain how its **paintAt** method crops shapes.

4-6   Modify **Screen.java** (Listing 3-8) so that drawing a **Screen** surrounds the grid with a double frame like this:

```
@@@@@@@@@@@@@@@@@@@@@
@@@@@@@@@@@@@@@@@@@@@
@@                @@
@@                @@
@@                @@
@@                @@
@@                @@
@@@@@@@@@@@@@@@@@@@@@
@@@@@@@@@@@@@@@@@@@@@
```

4-7   To sort a sequence of integers, write **main** in class **SelectionSort** to prompt for an integer *n* and then read *n* more integers. After those integers have been entered, the program prints them in increasing order. Use the **Terminal** method **readInt** to collect input. Here is a sample program run:

```
%> java SelectionSort
Integers to sort? 3
> 4
> 100
> -4
-4
4
100
```

Here is the *selection sort* algorithm:

- find the index of the smallest integer in the array and swap the integer there with the first integer in the array (the one in position 0)
- find the index of the smallest integer in the rest of the array (starting at position 1) and swap the integer there with the one currently in position 1

- and so on . . .

The real code will use nested **for** loops. The inner one to find the minimum in the rest of the array is one you wrote in an exercise in Chapter 2. The only other trick you will need is the one for swapping the values of two integer variables **a** and **b**:

```
int tmp = a
a = b;
b = tmp;
```

4-8   Sorting (reprise). *Bubble sort* and *insertion sort* are simple sorting algorithms that use nested loops like the selection sort in the previous exercise. Look up those algorithms and code them in Java.

4-9   Sorting (reprise). In the previous exercises you probably did all the work in **main**. Rewrite your solution, reading the integers into an array in **main** as before but then invoking

```
public static void sort( int[] nums )
```

to do the actual sorting. This works because the **nums** parameter passed to the **sort** method is a *reference* to an array. When **sort** rearranges the contents of this array, the original array is modified.

This design makes your sorting algorithm generally available; other Java programs can use it by invoking the class method **Sort.sort**.

4-10   Finding primes. Write class **Eratosthenes**. The API has just two public methods, a constructor accepting an **int** argument:

```
public Eratosthenes( int n )
```

and a method returning an array of **boolean** values:

```
public boolean[] isPrime()
```

The array returned by **isPrime** should have value **true** at position **i** just when **i** is prime. So sample code like

```
boolean[] isPrime = (new Eratosthenes(10)).isPrime();
for (int i = 2; i < isPrime.length; i++) {
    System.out.println(i + "\t" + isPrime[i]);
}
```

Should produce

```
2    true
3    true
4    false
5    true
```

```
6    false
7    true
8    false
9    false
```

If you think about what you've just read, you should realize that this is the unit test for **Eratosthenes**.

You may use any algorithm you choose to fill the array that **isPrime** returns. The most elegant is the *sieve of Eratosthenes*. That ancient algorithm is on the Web in lots of places. Any good search engine should find it (as long as you spell "sieve" and "Eratosthenes" correctly). You might hit on a Java version. If you do, feel free to use it as long as you credit it.

4-11   Sums of squares. Write class **SumsOfSquares**. The API has just two public methods, a constructor accepting an **int** argument:

```
public SumsOfSquares( int n )
```

and a method returning an array of integer values:

```
public int[] getCount()
```

In the array returned by **getCount**, the value at position i should be the number of ways to write i as a sum of two squares. So sample code like

```
SumsOfSquares sos = new SumsOfSquares(10);
int[] count = sos.getCount();
for (int i = 0; i < count.length; i++) {
    System.out.println(i + "\t" + count[i]);
}
```

should produce

```
0    1    // 0 = 0 + 0
1    2    // 1 = 1 + 0 = 0 + 1
2    1    // 2 = 1 + 1
3    0    // no way
4    2    // 4 = 4 + 0 = 0 + 4
5    2    // 5 = 4 + 1 = 1 + 4
6    0    // no way
7    0    // no way
8    1    // 8 = 4 + 4
9    2    // 9 = 9 + 0 = 0 + 9
```

(Of course, the comments are not part of the output.)

If you think about what you've just read, you should realize that this is the unit test for **SumsOfSquares**.

If number theory intrigues you, find the smallest integer that's a sum of squares four ways. What are the four ways? Which numbers will be the sum of squares exactly one way? Compare the output from **SumsOfSquares** and **Eratosthenes** and try to guess which *primes* can be written as the sum of two squares.

4-12   Design (do not implement) a more sophisticated **Definition** class for the dictionary application. What fields, getters, and setters would a real **Definition** need? Will it be possible to make that information available to a user of your **Dictionary** without changing the **Dictionary** class or the interactive loop in **Lookup**? (Of course, you will have to change the part of **Lookup** that fills the **Dictionary**.)

4-13   Rewrite the **Definition** declaration so that it allows for multiple meanings for a word. For example, the **toString** method for the **Definition** of "square" might return the multiline **String**

```
1. a rectangle having equal sides
2. not cool
3. a peg that won't fit in a round hole
```

Implement this functionality by providing a **Definition** object with a private **ArrayList** of **String**s instead of the single **String** field it has now. To test your code, write method

```
public void addMeaning( String definition )
```

that **fillDictionary** in class **Lookup** can invoke.

Note that the list of meanings is numbered $1, 2, 3, \ldots$, not $0, 1, 2, \ldots$, because we should not assume that the users of our **Dictionary** are computer programmers. You should still *store* these meanings starting at position 0 in the **ArrayList**. Just report those positions in this user-friendly way.

4-14   Rewrite the **for** loop in class **Reverse** so that it uses an **Iterator** for the **ArrayList** rather than an explicit index.

4-15   Rewrite **Reverse** so that it writes each line backward (reversing the order of the characters) as well as reversing the order of the lines. Use the **toCharArray** method in the **String** class.

4-16   We have learned to loop through the contents of a **TreeMap** by getting an **Iterator** for the set of keys and then looking up the value for each key we get from the **Iterator**. That idiom is the best for reinforcing the idea of a **TreeMap**, but there is a more efficient way. The **entrySet** method in the **TreeMap** API returns the set of key–value pairs: objects of type **Map.Entry**. If you ask that set for an **Iterator**, you can loop through the pairs and retrieve both the key and the value from each pair you see. Rewrite **toString** in class **Dictionary** using this idiom.

4-17 Write a class declaration for **Directory**. A **Directory** should store **TextFile**s, keyed by their names. You can start with the skeletal version of **Directory.java** we have provided (Listing 4-12). That file contains commented declaration headers for all constructors and methods but only empty bodies. It has most of a unit test too. Methods like these with empty bodies are often referred to as *stubs*. **Directory.java** will compile and run, but it won't do what it is supposed to do. It is your job to supply bodies so that the unit test in **main** will run properly. The practice of starting with stubs and slowly filling in the bodies is called *stub programming*. It is often a good approach to program development.

Here is what the output from **main** should look like when you are done (with current dates, of course):

```
%> java Directory
bill  17  Sun Jan 06 19:40:13 EST 2002 diary
eb    12  Sun Jan 06 19:40:13 EST 2002 greeting
```

We have designed the **Directory** class so that a **Directory** contains only **TextFile**s. A directory on your computer system can contain other directories as well. We'll provide for that when we discuss inheritance in the next chapter.

4-18 Draw a box-and-arrow picture of the **Directory** object containing the two **TextFile**s built in the **main** method in class **Directory**. Show the references to all the fields of all the objects referred to, and their fields, and so on.

4-19 Both **Bank.java** and **BankAccount.java** have been drastically redesigned. Write (in your programmer's journal) about the important changes compared with the version in Chapter 1. Comment particularly on how each individual **BankAccount** does some bookkeeping[16] not only for itself but also for the **Bank** that it is in. If you want to run this banking system, copy these two files to your work area, compile them, and run the application with the command **java Bank**. You will note that some things don't work yet.

4-20 Experiment with the command line arguments the **Bank** program accepts. Change the name of the **Bank**. See what the **-e** flag does. Then read and explain the argument parsing code in **Bank.java**.

4-21 Big banks are impersonal. Their accounts have numbers. Complete **Bank.java**, using an **ArrayList** to store numbered bank accounts. The file **bigbank.out** (Listing 4-4) is the result of running this **Bank** using **bigbank.in** (Listing 4-3) for input. Complete **Bank.java** so that it implements this functionality.

---

[16] This is one of our favorite words because it has three double letters in a row. Do you know another such? (We don't.)

You will have to declare your **ArrayList** in the right place and complete the stubs in the methods **openNewAccount**, **whichAccount**, **report**, and **getNumberOfAccounts**. We've marked all the places you need to change with the comment string **///**. When your big **Bank** code is complete you can test it using the contents of **bigbank.in** as input without having to retype all that stuff by using *input output redirection* (in Unix and in Windows). Try

```
%> java Bank -e < bigbank.in
```

(The **-e** flag tells **main** to instantiate a **Terminal** that echoes its input to its output. See what happens if you leave it out.) Then try

```
%> java Bank -e < bigbank.in > mybank.out
```

That captures the output from your program in the file **mybank.out**. Then you can compare that file with **bigbank.out** to see if your program is working correctly. (Your computer system may even have a command that compares files for you.)

4-22   Little banks are friendly. Their accounts have names. The file **littlebank.out** (Listing 4-6) is the result of running this **Bank** using **littlebank.in** (Listing 4-5) for input. Complete **Bank.java** using a **TreeMap** to store named bank accounts. Follow the instructions and the hints from the preceding exercise.

4-23   The methods **incrementBalance** and **countTransaction** are public in class **Bank**. That means anyone can send a **Bank** a message asking it to change its balance. Shouldn't those methods be private, to prevent bank fraud? Try changing the declarations and explain what goes wrong.

4-24   Add an "audit" option to the banker commands. When the banker asks for an audit, the **Bank** should loop through its accounts, summing the balances and the transaction counts, and then check the results against what its own fields say those values should be.
This exercise needs two solutions, one for a big **Bank** and one for a little **Bank**.

4-25   Add code to the **Bank** application that allows the manager to close an account. When an account is closed, you can assume that its balance has been handed over to its owner. Make sure the **Bank**'s bookkeeping is correct.
This exercise needs two solutions, one for a big **Bank** and one for a little **Bank**.

4-26   Modify Figure 4.8 so that it illustrates your big or little **Bank**.

4-27   You will have noticed that your big **Bank** and little **Bank** are *almost* identical. All the code is the same except for the pieces dealing with how the collection of accounts is managed. Try to think of a way you might write a single **Bank.java** that could work either as a big or a little **Bank** with very few editing changes (or even none). But don't try to rewrite anything this way. Write about your ideas in your journal and wait to see how Java solves the problem – that's the meat of the next chapter.

4-28   Add functionality to the **BankAccount** class that allows a **BankAccount** to maintain a transaction history – a list of the transactions it has performed. Add an option in the **Bank** that allows a customer to see her account's history. Start by designing class **Transaction** so you can keep **Transaction** instances on your list.

EStore exercises

The following exercises refer to release 4 of the **EStore** application: classes **EStore**, **ShoppingCart**, **Item**, and **Catalog** (Listings 4-13, 4-14, 4-15, and 4-16).

4-29   This release of the **EStore** application differs in several ways from the one we saw in the exercises in Chapter 1. Discuss the differences in the user interface. You will find some places where functionality is promised but does not yet exist. Comment on those too.

4-30   Implement the missing method **show** in **Catalog.java**.

4-31   Implement the promise that the **ShoppingCart** can maintain a list of the **Item**s it contains rather than just a total count and a total cost. We've marked the places in **ShoppingCart.java** that need work with comments flagged by **///**.

4-32   Write the **showContents** method in the **ShoppingCart** class so that when the **ShoppingCart** contains more than one **Item** of a particular kind, that **Item** appears just once in the output, with its quantity. (This is tricky.)

4-33   Add a "return" option in the **EStore customerVisit** method so that a customer can change her mind and remove an **Item** from her **ShoppingCart** before checkout. Prompt for the name of the **Item** to be returned. Be sure to tell the customer that returns are possible.

4-34   Think about how you would allow the manager to change the cost of an **Item** in the **Catalog**, then implement your design. Would a change of cost affect an **Item** that happened to be in a customer's **ShoppingCart** at that moment?

4-35   Arrange for the **EStore** to keep track of all the **Item**s sold. Allow the manager to see the number of **Item**s or the total cost of the **Item**s or the list of **Item**s. *Hint:* Create a **ShoppingCart** field for the **EStore** and put an **Item** into it each time a customer buys an **Item**.

4-36   Draw a box-and-arrow picture of an **EStore** with two **Item**s in its **Catalog**.

4-37   Draw a box-and-arrow picture of a **ShoppingCart** containing two **Item**s of one kind and a third **Item** of a different kind.

Chapter 5

Inheritance: Putting Things in Their Proper Place

Object-oriented programming provides two special features that make programs easier to read and write. One is message passing, which encourages the encapsulation of implementation details in the private fields and methods of objects, giving the outside world access only through the methods in the public API. The second is *inheritance*, which allows us to define classes for objects that are alike in some ways and different in others. We study inheritance in this chapter.

We have already seen similarities among kinds of objects. Each shape has a **paintChar** field, a way to specify its size, and a **paintOn** method for painting itself onto a **Screen**. In the exercises in Chapter 4, we saw that big and little banks share lots of functionality and hence lots of code. So do the text files and directories we modeled there. In each of those examples, we wrote the code for one class by starting with the code for a related class and changing just a few lines.

For several reasons, we want to describe these common properties in one place rather than copying code from one class declaration to another. First, having the descriptions in one place saves work. Second, having the descriptions in one place makes it easier to make changes when changes are needed. Third, having a common place to describe common properties encourages us to think about what properties are common and thus encourages a cleaner design for our objects.

Object-oriented programming languages like Java provide a way to do just what we want to do. We've already seen how to describe objects in terms of the classes to which they belong. Now we go one step further and describe classes partly in terms of other classes. We put common properties in a single *superclass*. Other classes are then defined as *subclasses* of this superclass from which they *inherit* the common properties. This is a powerful tool for organizing classes and programs.

In this chapter we use inheritance to improve the design of some of our applications. First we will reorganize the source code for the shapes classes. Then we'll address the problem of modeling a file system in which directories can contain other directories as well as text files. Next we'll address the problem of providing bank customers with both checking accounts and savings accounts, leaving much of the implementation as an exercise in using inheritance. Finally, we will see how to change some of the default behavior Java provides for all objects. Along the way we will learn a little more Java too.

Shapes Revisited

In Exercise 3-16 we wrote class **VLine**, modeling vertical lines just as **HLine** models horizontal ones. We did that by starting **VLine.java** with a copy of **HLine.java** and then changing a small fraction of the code. That's not good software engineering practice. Should someone find a bug in one of the common methods, we would have to fix both **HLine** and **VLine** in the same way. At best that's annoying. At worst we might forget to make one of the changes. We solve that problem by identifying what **HLine** and **VLine** have in common and then learning how Java allows us to put the common code in just one place.

What's Common to HLine and VLine?

HLine and **VLine** have the same fields: **paintChar** and **length**. The setters and getters for those fields are the same in both classes. So is the **paintOn(Screen)** method, which delegates to **paintOn(Screen, int, int)**.

What's Specific to HLine and VLine?

The primary difference between these classes is in their **paintOn(Screen, int, int)** methods. One paints characters horizontally, the other vertically. The unit tests in **main** differ too, of course.

How do we organize this distinction in Java?

Subclasses, Superclasses, and Inheritance

We declare a new class, **Line**, to manage the properties common to **HLine** and **VLine**. We keep only the features specific to **HLine** and **VLine** in the declarations of those classes. Finally, we declare **HLine** and **VLine** to be *subclasses* of the (superclass) **Line**. That relationship gives **HLine** and **VLine** access to the common material in **Line**. Figure 5-1 illustrates this relationship, using a diagram like a family tree, where superclasses appear above subclasses. Where appropriate, we use boxes to contain the fields and methods that are defined at any particular level (for any particular class) in the inheritance *hierarchy*.

The figure shows that both **HLine** and **VLine** are subclasses of **Line**. Conversely, **Line** is a superclass of both **HLine** and **VLine**. The Java keyword *extends* specifies the subclass relationship: We say that **HLine extends Line** and **VLine extends Line**.

A subclass inherits all of the properties of its superclass. That means that instances of **HLine** and **VLine** inherit the instance variables and methods defined in **Line**, just as if they had declared them themselves.

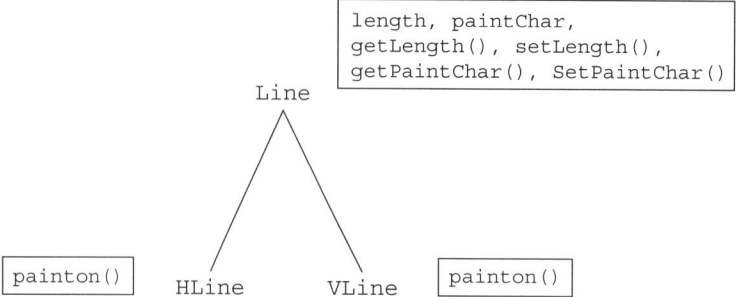

Figure 5-1: Line and its subclasses: HLine and VLine

The Java Program: Abstract Methods and Classes

Listings 5-1, 5-2, and 5-3 contain the Java source for classes **Line**, **Hline**, and **VLine**. We begin our reading with the superclass **Line**, declared this way:

```
16 public abstract class Line
17 {
18    protected int length; // length in (character) pixels.
19    protected char paintChar; // character used for painting.
```

The **Line** class declares the two fields we expect. But this short fragment contains two unexpected tokens: **abstract** and **protected**. The keyword **abstract** tells the Java compiler that we will never create a **Line** object that is just a plain **Line**. It's clear why we would not want to. Any particular **Line** must be either an **HLine** or a **VLine**.

The modifier **abstract** appears once more in **Line.java**:

```
86    public abstract void paintOn( Screen s, int x, int y );
```

This is a strange method declaration. It has no body. The header is followed by a semicolon instead of a block delimited by braces. Of course the body for **paintOn** can't possibly be in the **Line** class, because it's different for **HLine** and **VLine**. We must look there for the two separate implementations. **HLine.java** starts with the header

```
11    public class HLine extends Line
12    {
```

indicating that **HLine** inherits from **Line**. Later in **HLine.java** we find the method body we expect for **paintOn**:

```
33    public void paintOn( Screen screen, int x, int y )
34    {
```

```
35              for ( int i = 0; i < length; i++ )
36                  screen.paintAt( paintChar, x+i, y );
37          }
```

The variables **length** and **paintChar** referred to on lines 35 and 36 are the fields we declared in **Line.java**. They are visible (in scope) in **HLine** because they are **protected** in **Line**, which means they can be seen in any class that inherits from **Line**.[1] If they were **private**, they would not be available here in **HLine**. If they were **public**, anyone could see them – which would not be good object design.

The **length** and **paintChar** fields are set in the usual way in the **Line** constructor:

```
28      protected Line( int length, char paintChar )
29      {
30          this.length   = length;
31          this.paintChar = paintChar;
32      }
```

That constructor is **protected** too – visible to the child classes but not to the public.[2] To see how it's invoked we look at the corresponding constructor in **HLine**:

```
20      public HLine( int length, char paintChar )
21      {
22          super( length, paintChar );
23      }
```

The Java keyword **super** on line 22 means "my parent". It's analogous to **this**, which means "me". Here, **super** is used to invoke the parent's constructor with signature **(int, char)**. That's the one in **Line.java** we just looked at. Thus **HLine** delegates the initialization of its fields to its parent **Line**.

To see how inheritance works in practice, we look at part of the unit test in **HLine**:

```
64      Line hline = new HLine( 10, 'x' );
65      hline.paintOn( screen );
66
67      hline.setLength(5);
68      hline.paintOn( screen, 0, 1 );
```

Line 64 declares variable **hline** of type **Line** and then initializes it with a new **HLine** instance. We can declare a variable of type **Line** even though **Line** is an abstract class and so cannot be instantiated. The value for that variable can be any kind of **Line** – that is, an instance of any class that extends **Line** – in this case, **HLine**.

---

[1] The true meaning of the keyword **protected** is a little more complicated, but this approximation will do for now.

[2] In this case the **protected** designation is redundant. The class is **abstract**, so no one could use this constructor even if it were declared **public**.

On line 68 we send **hline** a **paintOn** message. The JVM does its usual job. It looks in class **HLine** for a **paintOn** method with signature **(Screen, int, int)**, finds it, and executes the code there.

On line 67 we send **hline** a **setLength** message. The JVM looks in class **HLine** for a **setLength** method. This time the search fails – no such method exists. But all is not lost. When it fails to find the method in class **HLine**, it looks in the parent class, **Line**, where we put **setLength**. So the code there executes, and the length is changed to 5.

Line 65 is even more interesting. We send **hline** a **paintOn** message with signature **(Screen)**. There is no such method in **HLine**, so the JVM looks in the parent class **Line**, where it finds

```
94      public void paintOn( Screen s )
95      {
96          paintOn( s, 0, 0 );
97      }
```

The code on line 96 shows this **Line** delegating to its fully parameterized **paintOn** method with signature **(Screen, int, int)** by sending *itself* a message. We could have written that line this way:

```
96          this.paintOn( s, 0, 0 );
```

Because the object at hand is really an **HLine**, that's where the JVM looks for the **paintOn** method. It finds it there and executes it.

We have barely begun to exploit the power of inheritance, even in this simple example. Suppose we want to add class **Box** and class **Frame** to our application. All the shapes – **HLine**, **VLine**, **Box**, and **Frame** – have a **paintChar** with a setter and a getter and a **paintOn** with signature **(Screen)**. That suggests that we create an abstract class **Shape** to hold that information. Then we can have **Line** extend **Shape** and delete common code from **Line.java**. To incorporate **Box** and **Frame**, which have a lot in common, we make them subclasses of an abstract class **Rectangle**, which in turn extends **Shape**.

Figure 5-2 illustrates the inheritance hierarchy we have just postulated. In the exercises you will implement this design.

Figure 5-3 is a box-and-arrow picture for a typical **HLine**, in the context of this new **Shape** hierarchy. Notice that we distinguish among fields defined in (and so inherited from) different classes in the hierarchy: **paintChar** is defined in **Shape**, and **length** is defined in **Line**.

A Hierarchical File System

Your computer's operating system probably organizes its file system as a *hierarchy* in which directories contain both files and other directories. (Both Unix and Windows do this.)

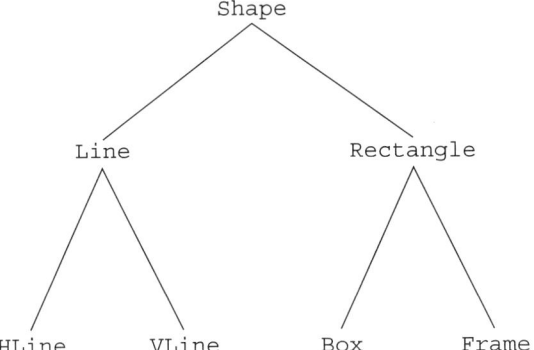

Figure 5-2: The class hierarchy for Shape

HLine

Shape

paintChar: char   'X'

Line

length: int   3

Figure 5-3: An HLine object

If your operating system has a graphical user interface, it probably displays the directory hierarchy in outline form, as in Figure 5-4.

Such pictures are often called "trees". The single item at the top is called the "root". Real trees grow upward, but computer scientists usually draw trees with the root at the top. Following this tree metaphor further, the items at the bottom levels (**insult**, **journal**, and **billhome** in Figure 5-4) are called "leaves".

Figure 5-4: Outline view of a file hierarchy

A second metaphor for hierarchical structures uses the parent–child vocabulary we introduced to study inheritance. In this file system example, we say, "**ebhome** and **billhome** are children of **root**" and "**ebhome** is the parent of **cs110**".

The metaphors are often mixed: The root has no parent, and leaves have no children.

Modeling a Hierarchical File System

To create a Java application that models a hierarchical file system, we modify the **TextFile** class from Chapter 3 and the **Directory** class from Exercise 4-17 so that **Directory** instances, which were originally designed to contain just **TextFile** objects, can contain other **Directory** objects as well. In order to use inheritance, we examine the **Directory** and **TextFile** classes to see what they have in common.

What's Common to Directories and Text Files?

Both have an owner, a creation date, a modification date, and the getters and setters to access these fields. Both have a parent: the **Directory** in which they live. Both have a size property, accessed by the public method **getSize**, but "size" has different meanings in each case. The size of a **TextFile** is the number of characters in its **String** contents. The size of a **Directory** is the number of objects (of type **TextFile** or **Directory**) it contains.

What's Specific to Text Files?

The **TextFile** API provides methods to set, append to, and get the **String** contents. These methods make no sense for a **Directory**.

What's Specific to Directories?

The **Directory** API provides methods to manage its contents: a collection of **TextFile** and **Directory** objects stored by name, so that those objects can be added, retrieved by name, and listed. These methods make no sense for a **TextFile**.

This analysis suggests that we declare a new class, **JFile**, to manage the properties common to **TextFile** and **Directory**. We describe the properties specific to **Directory** and **TextFile** in the declarations of those classes. Finally, we declare **Directory** and **TextFile** to be subclasses of **JFile**. Figure 5-5 illustrates this relationship.

It is important to distinguish between the file system illustrated in Figure 5-4 and the class inheritance structure illustrated in Figure 5-5. Each represents a hierarchy. Pictures like these are common in computer science because such treelike structures model many useful ideas. Figure 5-4 shows how the actual files in the file system are related. Figure 5-5 depicts the inheritance relationships among the *classes* we are using

Figure 5-5: The inheritance hierarchy for JFiles

in our model. Although they both happen to be hierarchical, the two figures have little relationship to each other.

The Java Program

Listings 5-5, 5-6, and 5-7 contain the Java source for classes **JFile**, **Directory**, and **TextFile**. Before we read the code we look at the unit test, which is the **main** method in **JFile**. That method tests the three classes by building the file system illustrated in Figure 5-4. It generates this output:

```
%> java JFile
Some hardwired, self documenting JFile system tests
create and then explore JFile hierarchy
    root                   (owner sysadmin)
        billhome           (owner bill)
        ebhome             (owner eb)
            cs110          (owner eb)
                journal    (owner eb)
            insult         (owner bill)
list contents of the root directory:

2 files:
bill    0        Thu Jan 24 23:12:44 EST 2002    billhome/
eb      2        Thu Jan 24 23:12:44 EST 2002    ebhome/

list contents of ebhome:
ebhome
```

```
2 files:
eb        1          Thu Jan 24 23:12:44 EST 2002     cs110/
bill      41         Thu Jan 24 23:12:44 EST 2002     insult

retrieve billhome, list its contents (empty)):
billhome
0 files:

retrieve insult, contents two line insult:
Your mother wore sneakers,
in the shower.

retrieve file "foo" from ebhome, try to display it:
no such file

list contents of cs110 (one file):
cs110
1 file:
eb        25         Thu Jan 24 23:12:44 EST 2002     journal
path to root:      /
path to ebhome:    /ebhome
path to cs110:     /ebhome/cs110
```

When we look at the implementation, we see that **JFile**, like **Line**, is an **abstract** class:

```
25  public abstract class JFile
26  {
...
31  public static final String separator = File.separator;
32
33  private String     name;
34  private String     owner;
35  private Date       createDate;
36  private Date       modDate;
37  private Directory  parent;
```

This declaration contains what we expect for the fields common to a **Directory** and **TextFile** – the familiar private instance variables **owner**, **createDate**, and **modDate** and the new **name** and **parent** fields, of type **String** and **Directory**. When we create a **JFile** (either a **Directory** or a **TextFile**) it must be put in some **Directory** with its name as key. The **name** field stores that name. The **parent** field stores the **Directory** this **JFile** is in, just as the **issuingBank** field in a **BankAccount** keeps track of the **Bank** that a **BankAccount** is in. **JFile** also declares public getters and setters appropriate for the fields it maintains.

TextFile and **Directory** each inherit from **JFile**, and each declares one more field of its own:

```
12   public class TextFile extends JFile
13   {
14       private String contents;   // The text itself
```

```
17   public class Directory extends JFile
18   {
19       private TreeMap jfiles; // table for JFiles
```

JFile declares (but does not implement) the method

```
95       public abstract int getSize();
```

which is abstract because the answer depends on the kind of **JFile** to which a **getSize** message is sent. A **TextFile** responds by returning the number of characters in its contents:

```
51   public int getSize()
52   {
53       return contents.length();
54   }
```

while a **Directory** returns the number of **JFile** objects it contains:

```
41   public int getSize()
42   {
43       return jfiles.size();
44   }
```

The **JFile** class declares another abstract method:

```
104      public abstract String getSuffix();
```

In **Directory** the **getSuffix** body returns the **String** **"/"**.[3] In **TextFile** it returns the empty **String** **" "**.

---

[3] **getSuffix** in the **Directory** class will return **"\"** when this program runs in a Windows environment and **"/"** when it runs in Unix; the code in **JFile.java** can determine the right value for the current environment.

We could have implemented **getSize** and **getSuffix** in each subclass and never mentioned them in **JFile**. We choose to declare them **abstract** there for three reasons.

- First, we tell the Java compiler that we wish to be able to send a **getSize** or **getSuffix** message to any **JFile**, without having to know at the time whether that **JFile** is a **Directory** or a **TextFile**.
- Second, we reaffirm our intention never to create a **JFile** object: Any class with an abstract method is necessarily an abstract class. The **abstract** keyword in the **JFile** class declaration header is required.
- Third, we ask the Java compiler to remind us to implement **getSize** and **getSuffix** in each subclass. It will complain if we forget.

Polymorphism

The first of these reasons is the most important. It illustrates ***polymorphism***, the feature in object-oriented programming that allows us to write a program that sends an object a message when we may not know precisely what kind of object it is. Different kinds of objects can then respond appropriately to the same message.[4] To see polymorphism at work, consider these lines of output from the unit test listing the contents of **Directory ebhome**:

```
ebhome
2 files:
eb        1       Thu Jan 24 23:12:44 EST 2002      cs110\
bill      41      Thu Jan 24 23:12:44 EST 2002      insult
```

In this listing we can tell that **cs110** is a **Directory** because a \ has been appended to its name. **Directory cs110** contains one file. **insult** is a **TextFile** (no suffix appended to its name) containing 41 characters.

Here is the code in **JFile.java** that generates these lines:

```
256     private static void list( Directory dir )
257     {
258         terminal.println( dir.getName() );
259         terminal.println( dir.getSize() +
260                             (dir.getSize() == 1
261                             ? " file:" : " files:") );
262
263         String[] fileNames = dir.getFileNames();
264         for ( int i = 0; i < fileNames.length; i++ ) {
```

---

[4] The word "polymorphism" comes from the Greek *poly* (many) and *morph* (shape). Objects of many (different) shapes can respond to the same message.

```
265              String fileName = fileNames[i];
266              JFile jfile = dir.retrieveJFile( fileName );
267              terminal.println( jfile.toString() );
268          }
269      }
```

The **getFileNames** message sent to **Directory dir** on line 263 returns an array containing the **String** names of the **JFile**s in the **Directory**. The following **for** loop steps through those names one at a time. For each name we send a message to retrieve the corresponding **JFile** from the **Directory** (line 266) and then send that **JFile** a **toString** message to get a **String** describing the file:

```
192      public String toString()
193      {
194          return getOwner() + "\t" +
195              getSize() + "\t" +
196              getModDate() + "\t" +
197              getName() + getSuffix();
198      }
```

The **String** returned begins with the owner of the **JFile**, followed by a tab (**"\t"**) and the size of this **JFile**, which we discover by sending a **getSize** message. The corresponding method responds with the right answer (either a character count or a count of files) even though we do not know at the moment what kind of **JFile** we are talking to. That is the essence of polymorphic behavior. The **String** ends with this **JFile** object's name, followed by the proper suffix, obtained using polymorphism with a **getSuffix** message.

Finally, the **list** method offers a chance to learn an elegant Java idiom, the *conditional expression*, which has the general form

test ? consequent : alternate

To compute its value, we evaluate the *test* part; if *test* is true, then the value is that of *consequent*; otherwise, the value is that of *alternate*. So the expression

(dir.getSize() == 1 ? " file:" : " files:")

on lines 260 and 261 evaluates to the **String " file:"** if the size of **dir** is 1, and to **" files:"** otherwise. That produces the correct English plurals "0 files", "1 file", "2 files", "3 files", and so on. We could have written the program without the conditional expression this way:

```
String whatever;
if (dir.getSize() == 1) {
    whatever = " file:";
}
else {
```

```
            whatever = " files:";
     }
     terminal.println( dir.getSize() + whatever );
```

But the conditional expression is much more elegant. It replaces seven lines of code that don't really help the reader understand what's happening, and it adds style to our program. Moreover, you must be able to read it even if you choose not to write it, because you will encounter it in other programmers' code.

Constructing a JFile

To create a new **TextFile**, we invoke the constructor, telling it the name of the file, its creator, the **Directory** the file is in, and the file's initial contents:

```
25    public TextFile(String name, String creator,
26                      Directory parent, String initialContents)
27    {
28        super( name, creator, parent );
29        setContents( initialContents );
30    }
```

Line 29 sets the contents of this **TextFile** to the fourth argument passed to the constructor, just as in Chapter 3. Line 28 uses **super** to invoke the **JFile** constructor, which deals with the name, creator, and parent:

```
49 protected JFile( String name, String creator,
                      Directory parent )
50 {
51    this.name   = name;
52    this.owner  = creator;
53    this.parent = parent;
54    if (parent != null) {
55        parent.addJFile( name, this );
56    }
57    createDate = modDate = new Date(); // set dates to now
58 }
```

Lines 52 and 57 are familiar. Line 51 shows how a **JFile** knows its name, and line 53 shows how it knows its parent – the **Directory** it is in. Line 55 asks the parent to add this newly constructed **JFile** to the list of files it contains.

But how does the world begin? If every **JFile** must belong to some **Directory**, you can't create the first **JFile** because you don't have a **Directory** to put it in. We solve this problem with a convention that says that if a **JFile** has **null** for a parent, it is the root of the file system hierarchy. Line 54 in the **JFile** constructor tests for that condition.

Line 218 in the **JFile** unit test creates a root **Directory** with no name, owner **"sysadmin"** and parent **null**:

```
218 Directory root = new Directory( "", "sysadmin", null );
```

Figure 5-6 shows (part of) the box-and-arrow diagram for the objects in our Java program that represent the file system constructed in that unit test, pictured in Figure 5-4.

The Bank Simulation, Again

We wish to improve our model of the banking system to allow several kinds of bank accounts: regular accounts, checking accounts, and fee accounts. Inheritance is the natural tool to use.

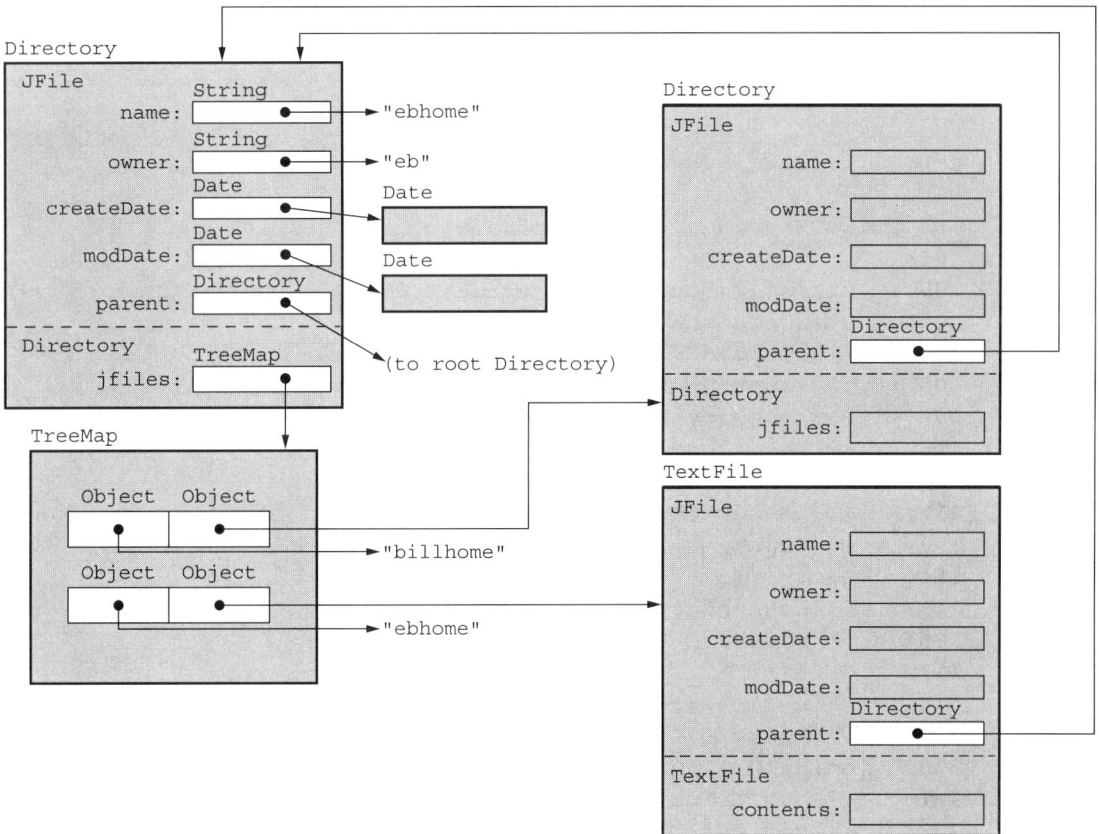

Figure 5-6: Object structure for ebhome tree

We'll begin with a **Bank** class that's a solution to Exercise 4-21, a little bank where accounts have names and an abstract **BankAccount** class (Listings 5-8 and 5-9). We've come a long way (in a short while) from Chapter 1's banking simulation. The banker now can open new accounts. Each **BankAccount** keeps track of the number of transactions it has performed as well as its balance, and informs the **Bank** it is in whenever either of these quantities changes. In this new release of the bank simulation the banker command to open a new account is followed by a query asking which type of account to open:

```
%> java Bank
Welcome to Faithless Trust
Open some accounts and work with them.
Banker commands: exit, open, customer, report, help.

banker command: open
Account name: groucho
Checking/Fee/Regular? (c/f/r): c
Initial deposit: 1000
opened new account groucho with $1000
```

The response "c", "f" or "r" causes a checking, fee, or regular account to be created, using the **Bank**'s **openNewAccount** method:

```
103 private void openNewAccount()
104 {
105    String accountName = atm.readWord( "Account name: " );
106    char accountType =
107      atm.readChar( "Checking/Fee/Regular? (c/f/r): " );
108    int startup = atm.readInt( "Initial deposit: " );
109    BankAccount newAccount;
110    switch( accountType ) {
111    case 'c':
112      newAccount = new CheckingAccount( startup, this );
113      break;
114    case 'f':
115      newAccount = new FeeAccount( startup, this );
116      break;
117    case 'r':
118      newAccount = new RegularAccount( startup, this );
119      break;
120    default:
121      atm.println("invalid account type: " + accountType);
122      return;
```

```
123       }
124       accountList.put( accountName, newAccount );
125       atm.println( "opened new account " + accountName
126                          + " with $" + startup );
127 }
```

The *switch statement* on lines 110–23 examines the value of the **char** variable **accountType** and chooses from among the cases provided to decide what to do next. The **break** statements on lines 113, 116, and 119 cause control to break out of the **switch** statement and resume on line 124 once a new account has been created. That account is put into the **TreeMap accountList** keyed by its name. Then lines 125–6 print a confirmation. If the user did not specify one of the legal options, the **default** case on line 120 executes, printing a message and returning from the method without creating a new account. There's no need for a break here.

Java allows you to write a **switch** based on the value of any variable with a primitive type. Switch syntax is straightforward: The keywords **case** and **default** are self-explanatory. The **break** statements at the end of each case are important. Without them, control would simply fall through to the next case. (Forgetting the **break** statements in a **switch** is a common programming error.) For more information about **switch**, read **SwitchDemo.java** (Example 5-1).

RegularAccount: Getting Back to Where We Were

Now that **BankAccount** is an abstract class, we can no longer create the plain old ordinary vanilla accounts we are used to working with. That's unfortunate. In general, a new release of a software package should add features not previously available and fix bugs, but not prevent the user from doing whatever she was able to do before. To restore the old-fashioned bank accounts, we create class **RegularAccount** (Listing 5-10), extending the abstract **BankAccount** class and putting nothing in it except a constructor that delegates to the parent:

```
12  public class RegularAccount extends BankAccount
13  {

24      public RegularAccount( int initialBalance,
                                Bank issuingBank )
25      {
26          super( initialBalance, issuingBank );
27      }
```

Now a **RegularAccount** inherits all the functionality provided by **BankAccount**.

CheckingAccount: Adding New Behavior

A checking account can do everything a regular bank account can do, and more: It can honor checks. We model that by writing class **CheckingAccount**, extending class **BankAccount** in order to add one new method. **CheckingAccount.java** is Listing 5-11:

```
14   public class CheckingAccount extends BankAccount
15   {
16       private static int checkFee = 2;

27       public CheckingAccount( int initialBalance,
                                  Bank issuingBank )
28       {
29           super( initialBalance, issuingBank );
30       }

41       public int honorCheck( int amount )
42       {
43           incrementBalance( - checkFee );
44           return withdraw( amount );
45       }
```

CheckingAccount inherits all the behavior declared for **BankAccount**. In addition, it provides an (exorbitant) **checkFee**, a constructor, and method **honorCheck** for honoring checks. As usual, the constructor delegates to the parent class constructor using **super**.

In method **honorCheck**, this **CheckingAccount** sends a message to itself to subtract the check fee using the inherited **incrementBalance** method. Then it delegates the actual withdrawal to the inherited **withdraw** method.

Code in **Bank.java** invokes **honorCheck** when a customer wants to cash a check:

```
151  else if ( transaction.startsWith( "c" ) ) {
152      int amount = atm.readInt( "  amount of check: " );
153      atm.println("  cashed check for " +
154          ((CheckingAccount)acct).honorCheck( amount ));
```

The cast to **CheckingAccount** on line 154 is necessary before you can send the account an **honorCheck** message. That's because **acct** is of type **BankAccount**, and **BankAccount** does not have an **honorCheck** method.

FeeAccount: Changing Old Behavior

The **Bank** offers a fee account as well as regular and checking accounts. A fee account charges itself $1 for each transaction it performs. We model fee accounts as instances of class **FeeAccount**, which extends **BankAccount**.

```
13   public class FeeAccount extends BankAccount
14   {
15        private static int transactionFee = 1;
```

Now we must arrange to charge the transaction fee whenever the user makes a deposit or a withdrawal or asks for the account balance. We might implement that by changing the corresponding inherited transaction methods: **deposit**, **withdraw**, and **getBalance**. Then, when the JVM looks for one of those methods, it will find the **FeeAccount** method before it looks for the corresponding method in **BankAccount**. Writing a method in the child class with the same signature as a (non-abstract) parent's method is called *overriding*.

But when we plan to make the same change in three places, our software instincts should sound a warning. It's easier and safer and better programming practice to make a change in just one place if possible. In this case, that place is the **countTransaction** method, which is invoked by each of the three methods we thought we might have to override. So we declare a **countTransaction** method here, confident that when the JVM sends a **FeeAccount** a **countTransaction** message, it is this code that will execute, overriding the **countTransaction** in the superclass.

```
34   public void countTransaction()
35   {
36       incrementBalance( - transactionFee );
37       super.countTransaction();
38   }
```

On line 36 this **FeeAccount** sends itself an **incrementBalance** message to subtract the transaction fee. The inherited **incrementBalance** method does the job. Then we want to count the transaction in the normal way any account would. We can't just send ourselves another **countTransaction** message.[5] We need to undo the override (temporarily) in order to do whatever the superclass **countTransaction** method does. **super** comes to the rescue on line 37. Recall that **super** is "myself, thought of as an instance of my superclass," so

```
super.countTransaction();
```

sends a message to this **FeeAccount** thought of as just a **BankAccount**. So it's the **BankAccount** **countTransaction** method that runs.

Nothing more need be done. In particular, the **Bank** does not need to remember that this is a **FeeAccount** in order to subtract the transaction fee when appropriate.

---

[5] Explore this in Exercise 5-16.

Every time a **FeeAccount** performs a transaction for itself, the overriding **countTransaction** is invoked, and the fee is charged – another instance of polymorphism at work.

Simulated Time

If you play with this release of the bank application, you may notice a new banker command: "newmonth." It's the banker's job to issue this command on the first day of each month. When that happens, the **Bank** should send a **newMonth** message to each of its accounts, asking it to take whatever action is appropriate. The **BankAccount** class declares the abstract method **newMonth**, so each concrete subclass must implement it. We have done that in each case, with a stub that does nothing. Nothing is the right behavior for regular accounts and checking accounts, but a **FeeAccount** should charge itself a monthly fee. Savings accounts (when we write them) credit themselves with interest. These improvements are addressed in the exercises.

Object: The Mother of All Classes

Inheritance is present in Java programs even when it is not introduced explicitly. The Java library comes with class **Object**. Any class that does not seem to extend anything actually extends **Object**. **Object** is the root of the class hierarchy – it's the only class with no superclass. Figure 5-7 shows the full picture of the class hierarchy for the redesigned shapes package, including the place of **Object**. Note that **Screen** is there as a direct descendant of **Object** – in the class hierarchy it has nothing to do with the descendants of **Shape** even though it is used by all of them.

Class **Object** implements several useful methods that all other classes inherit by default but are free to override when appropriate. We have in fact taken advantage of that feature several times.

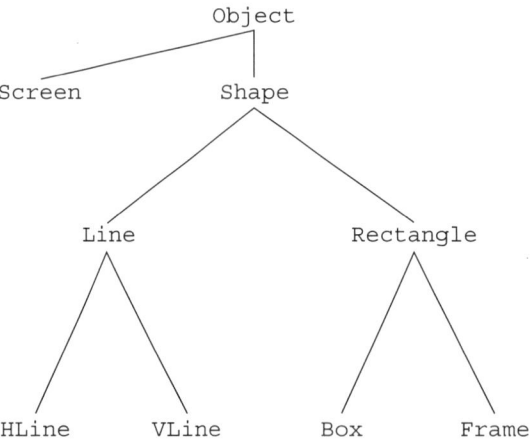

Figure 5-7: The class hierarchy for Shape and Screen (in the context of Object)

Equality

We know two ways to test whether two values are the same. One uses the operator **==**. If **a** and **b** are of type **int**, then   **a == b** is **true** just when **a** and **b** are the same integer, in the usual sense of the word. If **a** and **b** are reference types, then their values are of type **Object** (or some subclass of **Object**). In that case **a == b** is true just when they refer to the same location, so that in a box-and-arrow picture, the arrows from **a** and **b** point to the same place. The variables in Figures 3.7 and 4.4 refer to just one box and to just one array. Their values are **==** . But when deciding what to do in response to user input in the bank application, we used the test

```
if ( command.equals( "deposit" ) )
```

instead of the more natural

```
if ( command == "deposit" )
```

Now that we understand inheritance, we can think about why.

Class **Object** provides method

```
public boolean equals(Object obj)
```

that returns **true** just when this **Object** (the one receiving the **equals** message) is the same as the **Object** parameter **obj** – in other words, just when **this == obj**.

But there are times when that's not what "the same as" should mean. Two strings should be the same when they consist of the same characters in the same order, whether or not they happen to be the same **Object**. Fortunately, the **String** class overrides the **equals** method in class **Object**, providing exactly that interpretation. Program

```
public class TestStringEquals {
    public static void main( String[] args )
    {
        Terminal t = new Terminal();
        t.println("args[0] == args[1]: " +
                (args[0] == args[1]));
        t.println("args[0].equals(args[1]): " +
                args[0].equals(args[1]));
    }
}
```

produces this output:

```
%> java TestStringEquals hello hello
args[0] == args[1]: false
args[0].equals(args[1]): true
```

The variables **args[0]** and **args[1]** refer to two different **String** objects that happen to represent what we think of as the "same" **String**.

The collection classes override **equals** too: Two **ArrayList** instances are equal if they contain equal **Object** instances in the same order, even if they are not the same object. Two **TreeMap** instances are equal if they contain equal objects with equal keys. To see examples, look at class **EqualsDemo** (Example 5.3).

String Representation

Class **Object** provides method

public String toString()

that returns a representation of this object as a **String**. If class **SomeThing** does not override **toString**, then the code

System.out.println((new SomeThing()).toString());

produces output like

SomeThing@2103df64

That uninformative string is the class name followed by an '@' sign and then a hexadecimal integer. A friendly class will override **toString** in **Object** in order to provide more useful information. **JFile** is friendly in that way – earlier in this chapter, we read its **toString** method.

Java will send a **toString** message at appropriate times even if you don't ask for it. Line 277 in **JFile.java**

277   terminal.println(jfile.toString());

could be rewritten this way:

277   terminal.println(jfile);

The **ArrayList** and **TreeMap** classes also override the default **toString** from class **Object** to provide a useful view of the contents of those collections.[6] **OuerridingDemo** (Example 5.2).

Now that we know that everything extends **Object**, we can understand the labels in the **TreeMap** box in Figure 5-6. The **TreeMap** thinks its keys and values are **Object**s when in fact they are **String**s and **JFile**s (respectively).

Summary

Inheritance is a powerful tool with which we can structure our programs. With it we can

---

[6] When Zengyuan Zou first heard about **toString** in a lecture, he suggested that we ask for one for **ArrayList** as an exercise. That's before he knew that the authors of Java provided one.

- collect common functionality in one place, saving programming time and making future modifications possible
- write abstract classes, which allow us to take advantage of polymorphism, both for building structures (like our **Directory**) from heterogeneous (**JFile**) components, and for abstraction, so that we can send a message to an object without worrying about the object's type so long as the proper method has been defined

We learned to use **super** and how to override methods in a parent class. In particular, we saw how useful it could be to override the **equals** and **toString** methods in class **Object**. That's an exception to the general rule that it's not good design practice to extend concrete classes. When you do, it's difficult to modify the extended class without affecting the extension. All common functionality should go into abstract classes.[7]

But do not be carried away by the magic of inheritance. It's just a tool. When you design a program, focus on the objects you need to model and the messages they send one another. Then decide whether and where inheritance is appropriate.

In the next chapter we will assemble all the tools we have studied so far – message passing, collections, inheritance – to build Juno: an application that models a computer operating system.

Exercises

5-1   Create a text file for your programmer's journal for this chapter. Use your journal for questions that call for written answers and to record any observations about your work.

5-2   Change the declarations of **length** and **paintChar** in **Line.java** from **protected** to **private**. Explain the errors you get when you try to recompile **HLine**. Then rewrite **paintOn** in **HLine.java** so that it uses the public getters for those fields.

What are the advantages and disadvantages of each of these designs?

5-3   Comment out the implementation of **paintOn** in **HLine.java** and try to recompile. Explain the error message you see.

5-4   Delete the modifier **abstract** in the header of the declaration of class **Line** and try to recompile. Explain the error message you see.

5-5   Implement the shape class hierarchy discussed in the text and illustrated in Figure 5-2.

---

[7] A notable exception is the design of the Java Swing set of classes for representing graphical user interface components. The concrete classes in Swing – for example, the **JPanel** and **JFrame** classes we used in Chapter 1 to implement the traffic light application – were specifically designed to be extended.

5-6 Define a dotted HLine and a dotted VLine in classes **DottedHLine** and **DottedVLine**, each drawn as a sequence of alternating paint characters and periods (' . '). Of course, these classes should extend **Line**. Write good unit tests for your new classes.

5-7 This long exercise sketches a major upgrade of the shapes application. In the current version, each particular shape can paint itself on a **Screen**. Once it's done that, there is no way to erase it or move it around. A real graphics package is more flexible. A **Screen** maintains a list (perhaps an **ArrayList**) of the shapes on it. When asked to draw itself, it loops through the list, painting on itself each **Shape** it finds there in the position it wants to occupy.

Follow these steps:

a. Declare a field in the **Screen** class to hold an **ArrayList** of **ShapeOnScreen** objects. The **Screen** constructor should instantiate that list. Then write method

```
public void add( Shape s, int x, int y )
```

which behaves this way:

```
create a new ShapeOnScreen object holding the Shape s
        and its position (x,y)
add that object to the list
```

We have written class **ShapeOnScreen** (Listing 5-4).

b. Change the **draw** method in class **Screen**:

```
make the Screen blank
loop through the the list: for each ShapeOnScreen
    get the Shape it refers to
    send that Shape a message asking it
        to paint itself on this Screen
        at the correct position
output this Screen to the Terminal
```

c. Edit the **clear** method so that it removes everything on the list.
d. Write

```
public void cycle( )
```

which takes the **Shape** at the end of the list (the one that would be painted last) and moves it to the front of the list, so that it is painted first.

e. Write

```
public void bringToFront(int i)
```

which takes the **Shape** at position **i** on the list and puts it the first position. If index **i** is beyond the end of the list (or is negative), your program should silently do nothing at all – it should not crash.

f. Write

```
public void remove(int i)
```

which removes the **Shape** at position **i** from the list. If index **i** is beyond the end of the list (or is negative), your program should silently do nothing at all – it should not crash.

g. Design and write a method that allows you to move the **Shape** at position **i** in the list to a different location on the **Screen**.

5-8   Reverse the orders of lines 28 and 29 in **TextFile.java**. Explain the error message you see when you try to recompile.

```
28          super( name, creator, parent );
29          setContents( initialContents );
```

5-9   Remove the test for the **null** parent in the **JFile** constructor and comment on what happens when you run the unit test.

5-10   The unit test in **JFile** doesn't test **getParent**. To add such a test, introduce a **private static** variable **currentDirectory** of type **Directory**. In **main**, initialize it to the root of the file system.

Write method

```
private static void cd( String directoryName )
```

to change **currentDirectory** to its subdirectory with the given name. When **directoryName** is " . . ", **cd** should change **currentDirectory** to its parent.

Add self-documenting invocations of **cd** to **main**.

5-11   Could you use a **switch** instead of **if-else** logic in the **visit** method in class **Bank**? Try it and see what happens

5-12   What happens if you leave one or all of the **break** statements out of the **switch** statement in **openNewAccount**?

5-13   The **openNewAccount** method in class **Bank** does not detect an illegal entry in the **switch** until after the initial balance query. Fix that annoyance.

5-14   What would go wrong if **honorCheck** in class **CheckingAccount** sent a **withdraw(amt + checkFee)** message? Would it be OK to **withdraw(checkFee)** and then **withdraw(amount)**?

5-15   In the cash check clause in the customer transaction loop in class **Bank**, we cannot rely on polymorphism to get the right behavior. We really do need to be dealing with objects whose type is known. Try these experiments and report on what happens.

- Try to cash a check on an account that is not a checking account.
- Delete the cast to **(CheckingAccount)** in the source code.

5-16   Explain what happens if you replace **super.countTransaction( )** with **countTransaction( )** in the body of the **countTransaction** method in class **FeeAccount**.

5-17   (*) Finish the coding for the simulated time in the bank application. Class **Month** (Listing 5-13) needs work. Write the bodies for the **next** and **toString** methods. Do you have to change **report** in class **Bank** to see what **toString** returns? Complete **newMonth** in class **Bank** and **newMonth** in class **FeeAccount**.

5-18   (*) As currently implemented, the transaction fee for a **FeeAccount** is hard coded in the **FeeAccount** class. A better design puts a **transactionFee** field in the **Bank**, along with a getter and a setter. Then a **FeeAccount** queries its **Bank** for the transaction fee each time it must charge itself. Implement this feature, along with a new banker command, "transactionfee", that prompts for the new fee and sets it.

5-19   (*) Do for the check fee and the **CheckingAccount** class what the previous exercise does for the transaction fee.

5-20   (*) Savings accounts. On the first of each month, interest is added to the balance of each savings account. Suppose the annual interest rate is 5 percent. The stingy banks use a double value for the interest rate (for example, 0.05 for 5 percent) but keep all the pennies when they compute the interest. Thus the monthly interest at 5 percent on a balance of $120, which should be $(0.05/12) \times 120 = 0.5$, is in fact 0. The bank keeps the half dollar – what else would you expect?

Moreover, savings accounts are allowed only three free transactions in any month. After that, each transaction costs whatever a **FeeAccount** is charged for a transaction.

Edit **Bank.java** so that when a new account is opened the banker can choose the kind of account with the prompt

`Checking/Fee/Savings/Regular? (c/f/s/r):`

Write class **SavingsAccount** extending **BankAccount**. First write the **newMonth** method to take care of crediting interest when the month changes. Get the interest rate from the **Bank** with a **getInterestRate** message as in the previous exercise.

Finally, figure out a way for a **SavingsAccount** object to remember how many transactions it has executed in the current month, in order to deduct the fee when that number exceeds the maximum allowed.

Be sure to test as you go.

5-21   If you did the exercise in Chapter 4 in which bank accounts maintain a transaction history, then arrange to reset that history to empty when the month changes.

5-22   Should two **TextFile**s be equal if they have equal contents? The same contents and the same owner? The same contents, owner, and name? The same contents, owner, name, and parent (this last is a trick question – think carefully before answering it).

5-23   Design and implement an **equals** method for **Month** objects and test it in **main**.

5-24   In Exercise 4-25 you speculated on the fact that the **Bank.java** files for the big and little banks were nearly identical. Now that you know about inheritance you should say to yourself, "I know a better way: Build an abstract **Bank** class with two subclasses, **BigBank** and **LittleBank**." Your job now is to design those classes. You do not need to code them. You may if you like (it may be hard to resist the temptation), but that's optional. The point of this exercise is to think about the design.

5-25   (*) Implement the design you wrote in the previous exercise. In order to make sure that your big and little banks still work after you have made the changes, use a *regression test*. Write a file of input commands for a little bank, run the simulation with that input, and capture the output with *input-output redirection*

```
%> java Bank -e < littebank.in > littlebank.out
```

Then you can compare the output you get after you have written class **LittleBank**. (Your computer system may even have a command that compares files.)

Do the same for a big bank.

EStore exercises

The following exercises refer to the **EStore** application.

5-26   Write **toString** methods for class **Item**, class **Catalog**, and class **ShoppingCart**. Use those methods to simplify your program.

5-27   An **EStore** will probably stock several kinds of items. Make the **Item** class **abstract** and extend it for each kind of **Item** you think the store might offer its customers. Build some polymorphism into your design.

Chapter 6

Juno

In Chapter 5 we developed classes that model a hierarchical file system like those found on Unix and Windows. In this chapter, we begin building a command-line operating system around that file system. Users of our operating system will register for accounts. Registered users can log in and play in the file system by entering commands at a prompt. We call our application "Juno", for "Juno's Unix – not."[1] In succeeding chapters and exercises we will improve and extend Juno and learn more Java. By Chapter 10 we will be ready to give Juno a graphical user interface.

As we build Juno, we will want to keep track of which version we are studying. Doing so is a common problem in software engineering as applications are developed and marketed. A company might have one version of its product in production, several old versions still used by customers, a new one being tested, and one still newer under development. Each version has a release number so that users and programmers can know which release they are playing with. In a Windows application the About selection (perhaps under Help) will usually tell you the current version of the software. In both Unix and Windows, the command

```
%> java -version
```

produces information about the version of Java running on your computer. Juno, like Java, will tell you about itself if you ask. For example:

```
%> java Juno -version
```

Juno version 6

We number Juno releases according to the chapter in which they are discussed. This is Chapter 6, so the first release of Juno is version 6. Juno 6 is built from the following classes:

- Class **Juno**, describing what a **Juno** instance looks like, with code to initialize the system and **main** to start it running
- Class **User**, representing users having accounts on the system

---

[1] Creating an acronym this way follows a Unix tradition. The Free Software Foundation names its tools "gnu", which stands for "gnu's not unix". And Douglas Comer at Purdue University supports the xinu operating system. "xinu" is both "unix" backward and an acronym for "xinu is not unix". We wanted a name with a J in it, because our not Unix is written in Java. You do not need to be working in a Unix environment to appreciate Juno – it also resembles the command-prompt system available in Windows environments.

- The **JFile**, **Directory**, and **TextFile** classes from Chapter 5, used to construct Juno's hierarchical file system. The classes here differ from those in Chapter 5 in only one respect: a file's owner is a **User** object instead of a **String**
- Class **LoginInterpreter**, encapsulating how Juno manages user registration and login
- Class **Shell**, encapsulating how Juno manages a user's session once she has logged in
- An abstract class **ShellCommand** that captures the generic notion of an operating system command like "create a directory" or "list the contents of the current directory." Each actual command is represented by a (concrete) subclass of **ShellCommand**
- A **ShellCommandTable** object that supports an elegant dispatching mechanism that treats the command name the user enters as a key for which the corresponding value is a command object.

We start Juno by invoking **main** in class **Juno**:

```
%> java Juno
```

In the following sample session, a user named "bill" registers, creating his account on the Juno virtual machine. Next, user eb registers. Then bill logs in, creates a directory he names "empty", asks for help, creates a file named "memo", looks at that file, and then logs out. Then we shut down Juno:

```
Welcome to mars running Juno version 6
help, register, <username>, exit

Juno login: register bill Bill Campbell
Juno login: register eb Ethan Bolker
Juno login: bill
mars> mkdir empty
mars> help
shell commands
  help: display ShellCommands
  mkdir: create a subdirectory of the current directory
  newfile: create a new TextFile
  type: display contents of a TextFile
mars> newfile memo I am a one-line file
mars> type memo
I am a one-line file
mars> logout
goodbye
Juno login: exit
```

We will spend the rest of this chapter studying the Java that makes all this happen. Before you read on, compile and run Juno (see Exercise 6-2).

Class Juno

Main

Method **main** in **Juno** (Listing 6-1) parses the command-line arguments, looking for "-version", which we have seen above, "-e", which will cause Juno to echo any input it receives before it takes action on that input, and an optional host name to replace the default "mars"[2] in the sample session.

Exercise 6-3 asks you to explain how **main** works.

The Juno Environment

A **Juno** object's fields define the Juno system environment. Following our practice of information hiding, we declare them private and grant access to them using getters and setters.

```
29    private String     hostName;    // host machine name
30    private Map         users;       // lookup table for Users
31    private Terminal    console;     // for input and output
32
33    private Directory   slash;       // root of JFile system
34    private Directory   userHomes;   // for home directories
35
36    private ShellCommandTable commandTable; // shell commands
```

The Juno Constructor

The constructor initializes the Juno environment, creating a single **User**, named "root", who serves as system administrator, a root **Directory** ("slash") for the file system, and a subdirectory to hold new users' home directories. Finally, it constructs a **LoginInterpreter** and sends it a **CLILogin**[3] message.

```
45    public Juno( String hostName, boolean echoInput )
46    {
47        //  initialize the Juno environment ...
```

---

[2] "mars" is the default host name because that is the name of the computer hosting CS110 at UMass-Boston, the course for which we developed Juno.
[3] In Chapter 1 we noted that "CLI" is a standard computer science abbreviation for "command-line interface", In Chapter 10 we implement a GUI (graphical user interface) for Juno.

```
48
49      this.hostName = hostName;
50      console       = new Terminal( echoInput );
51      users         = new TreeMap();
52      commandTable  = new ShellCommandTable();
53
54      // the file system
55
56      slash      = new Directory( "", null, null );
57      User root = new User( "root", slash, "Rick Martin" );
58      users.put( "root", root );
59      slash.setOwner(root);
60      userHomes = new Directory( "users", root, slash );
61
62      // create, then start a command line login interpreter
63
64      LoginInterpreter interpreter
65          = new LoginInterpreter( this, console );
66      interpreter.CLILogin();
67  }
```

Token Parsing with StringTokenizer

The **LoginInterpreter** takes care of registering and logging in users by responding appropriately to whatever is typed at the Juno login prompt. The sample session above shows that a user interacting with Juno may type a multiword command like

```
register bill Bill Campbell
```

at the login prompt or

```
type memo
```

at the shell prompt after logging in. That is a feature we haven't seen yet. The bank simulation refuses to deal with the natural input

```
deposit 1000
```

It just reads the first word, "deposit", ignores the rest of the line, and prompts for the amount to be deposited.

In order to handle multiword lines, we need a tool to break a **String** into words. Fortunately, Java provides the **StringTokenizer** class, whose instances do just that. For example, the expression

```
StringTokenizer st = new StringTokenizer( "now is the time" );
```

declares the variable **st** of type **StringTokenizer** and initializes it with a **StringTokenizer** instance for the **String** "now is the time". A **StringTokenizer** behaves very much like an **Iterator**. Once we have created one, we can ask it to loop over the words in the **String** by sending it the messages **nextToken** and **hasMoreTokens**. Thus, to print out these four words one to a line, we would write

```
while ( st.hasMoreTokens() )  {
    System.out.println( st.nextToken() );
}
```

to produce output

```
now
is
the
time
```

This **StringTokenizer** defines a token to be a word: any substring that's as long as possible without containing any white space (blanks, tabs, and newlines). But a **StringTokenizer** can be asked to break a **String** into tokens using delimiters other than the default white space. Both the constructor and the **nextToken** methods accept an optional second **String** argument listing the delimiters. Thus

```
StringTokenizer st = new StringTokenizer("abc,d f.ghi", ",.");
```

will cut the **String** using the punctuation marks '.' and ',' as delimiters, producing tokens

```
abc
d f
ghi[4]
```

---

[4] The **StringTokenizer** API isn't quite powerful enough to be used easily by the javac compiler when it must split code like

```
new TextFile( filename, sh.getWhoami(), sh.getDot(), contents );
```

into the tokens

```
new
TextFile
(
filename
,
sh
.
getWhoami
(
)
,
```

Class LoginInterpreter

The Juno constructor sends its **LoginInterpreter** (Listing 6-2) a **CLILogin** message, invoking method **CLILogin**.

```
55   public void CLILogin()
56   {
57     welcome();
58     boolean moreWork = true;
59     while( moreWork ) {
60       moreWork = interpret(console.readLine("Juno login: "));
61     }
62   }
```

CLILogin sends a **welcome** message and then loops, each time prompting the user with the prompt

Juno login:

reading the line the user types at the terminal, and sending that line to **interpret**, until such time as **interpret** returns **false** for the value of **moreWork** . Then the **while** loop ends and Juno shuts down.

The heart of a **LoginInterpreter** is its **interpret** method:

```
69     private boolean interpret( String inputLine )
70     {
71         if (inputLine == null) return false;
72         StringTokenizer st =
73             new StringTokenizer( inputLine );
74         if (st.countTokens() == 0)  {
75             return true; // skip blank line
76         }
77         String visitor = st.nextToken();
78         if (visitor.equals( "exit" ))  {
```

```
sh
.
getDot
(
)
,
contents
)
;
```

(See Chapter 2 for a review of token parsing.)

```
79                  return false;
80          }
81          if (visitor.equals( "register" ))  {
82              register( st );
83          }
84          else if (visitor.equals( "help" ))  {
85              help();
86          }
87          else  {
88              User user = system.lookupUser(visitor);
89              new Shell( system, user, console );
90          }
91          return true;
92      }
```

The **String** argument passed to **interpret** is the line the user types in response to the Juno login prompt. Because that line may contain several words, **interpret** creates a **StringTokenizer** for the **inputLine String** (lines 72 and 73). A blank line will have no tokens on it. Because that is acceptable input, line 75 returns **true**. Line 77 then grabs the first word on the line and assigns it to the **String** variable **visitor**. We chose that name for the variable because most of the time we expect that token to be the name of a Juno user about to log in. But there are other things we must check for. We do that using straightforward "**if-else if-else if**" logic, checking for the legal command strings in each **if** clause. We have seen this design pattern before in the bank simulation. In this case, the four branches deal with the four cases:

- **exit** – return **false**, to end the login loop and shut down Juno
- **help** – remind the user of the possible login commands
- **register** – invoke method **register** to create a new **User**
- *username* – Juno interprets any other **String** as the login name for a registered **User**, looks up that name in its **User** map, and creates a new **Shell** for a Juno session.

When the request is to register a new user, the rest of the input line (after the word "register") contains the rest of the information Juno needs to create a **User**: a login name ("bill") and a real name ("Bill Campbell"). That is precisely what is left in the **StringTokenizer** for the **inputLine** because we have already examined the first token ("register"). So we pass the **register** method the **StringTokenizer** as an argument.

```
100 private void register( StringTokenizer st )
101 {
102     String userName = st.nextToken();
```

```
103     String realName = st.nextToken("").trim();
104     Directory home = new Directory( userName, null,
                                    system.getUserHomes() );
105
106     User user = system.createUser( userName, home,  realName );
107     home.setOwner( user );
108 }
```

Line 102 gets the next token ("bill") from the **StringTokenizer** and puts it in variable **userName**. It then invokes **nextToken** again on line 103, this time passing the empty **String ""** as a second argument. That means that the next token, which we assign to variable **realName**, should be computed using no delimiters at all. Thus **realName** will be the rest of the original input line ("Bill Campbell"). We send **String realName** a **trim** message to get rid of any leading or trailing white space. Then lines 104–7 create a new **User** and a home **Directory** for that **User**.

Class Shell: using a dispatch table

The most common and most interesting thing the **LoginInterpreter** does is to start a **Shell** for a registered **User**:

```
88              User user = system.lookupUser(visitor);
89              new Shell( system, user, console );
```

Class **Shell** (Listing 6-3) declares four fields for **Shell** attributes:

```
22  private Juno system;      // the operating system
23  private User user;        // the user logged in
24  private Terminal console; // the console for this shell
25  private Directory dot;    // the current working directory
```

The **Shell** constructor initializes those fields, sets the current directory **dot** to be the **User** home directory, and starts the **Shell** command-line interpreter in method **CLIShell**:

```
35  public Shell( Juno system, User user, Terminal console )
36  {
37      this.system  = system;
38      this.user    = user;
39      this.console = console;
40      dot   = user.getHome(); // default current directory
41      CLIShell(); // start the command line interpreter
42  }
```

The **CLIShell** method (lines 47–54) is almost a clone of **CLILogin**. We won't show it here. It loops until the user logs out, getting a line of input from the console and passing it on to the **interpret** method:

```
60    private boolean interpret( String inputLine )
61    {
62        StringTokenizer st = stripComments(inputLine);
63        if (st.countTokens() == 0) {
64            return true; // skip blank line
65        }
66        String commandName = st.nextToken();
67        if (commandName.equals( "logout" )) {
68            return false; // user is done
69        }
70        ShellCommand commandObject =
71            system.getCommandTable().lookup( commandName );
72        if (commandObject == null ) {
73            console.errPrintln( "Unknown command: " +
                                      commandName );
74        }
75        else {
76            commandObject.doIt( st, this );
77        }
78        return true;
79    }
```

Like any good programming language, Juno allows the user to insert comments. The comment character is the pound sign, '**#**'. Method **stripComments** treats it the way the Java compiler treats the string "**//**" – it throws it and everything following it away. Then it creates and returns a **StringTokenizer** for what's left. Line 63 asks the **StringTokenizer** how many tokens it has. If there are none, the line is blank (empty, or all white space). There is nothing to interpret, so the **interpret** method returns **true** to indicate that it is ready for more input.

If there is work to do, then the first word on the line tells us what that work is: Line 67 gets that word and puts it in variable **commandName**.

If the **commandName** is "logout", **interpret** returns **false** to **CLIshell** (line 68), and control returns to the Juno login loop to wait for another user to register or log in.

Usually, there will be real Juno work to do. The next lines do that work, in a new and interesting way. We might expect a sequence of **if...else if...else if** clauses testing the value of the **commandName String** by sending it **equals** messages. That logic was fine for the bank and for the **interpret** method in class **LoginInterpreter**, where there were only a few commands and those commands rarely changed. But **if...else** would be poor design here. There will be very many Juno shell commands, and we will be adding new ones often. We do not want to have to modify the **interpret** method each time. So we store all the commands in a table, using the command name as a key. Lines 70 and 71 send the Juno system a message asking for its command table, then send that table a message asking it for the **ShellCommand** object associated with the **commandName** key. If there is such an object (if the returned **ShellCommand** isn't **null**), we execute the command by sending that **ShellCommand** object a **doIt** message.

This may seem like magic: The **interpret** method executes the user's command *without knowing what it does*. That wasn't the case at all in the **LoginInterpreter**. But of course it's not magic; it's good design that takes advantage of polymorphism. **ShellCommand** is an **abstract** class, with an abstract **doIt** method that's invoked on line 76, where it is passed both the **StringTokenizer** containing any unscanned input line arguments and this **Shell**. What happens then depends on the particular command.

Class NewfileCommand

Let's look at one example, the Juno command that creates a new **TextFile**. This line from the sample session

```
mars> newfile memo I am a one-line file
```

shows that the syntax for that command is the command name "newfile", then the name the file is to have, then its initial contents. The **doIt** method in class **NewfileCommand** (Listing 6-8) does the work:

```
36    public void doIt( StringTokenizer args, Shell sh )
37    {
38        String filename = args.nextToken();
39        String contents = args.nextToken("").trim();
40        new TextFile( filename, sh.getUser(),
                        sh.getDot(), contents);
41    }
```

The **StringTokenizer** argument **args** contains the original input from the user, with the command name token ("newfile" in this case) already used up. The next token on that line is the file name, "memo" in this case. That's assigned to variable **filename** on line 38. Line 39 treats the rest of the input as a single token using the technique[5] we used previously in the **LoginInterpreter register** method.

The only other method in class **NewfileCommand** is the constructor:

```
24   public NewfileCommand()
25   {
26       super( "create a new TextFile", "filename contents" );
27   }
```

That constructor invokes the parent class constructor, passing it two strings. The first is a short description of what the command does. The second gives the syntax of its arguments. To see what happens to those strings, we must look at the parent class.

Class ShellCommand

The **abstract ShellCommand** class (Listing 6-4) declares the abstract method

```
54   public abstract void doIt(StringTokenizer args, Shell sh);
```

and private fields and getters for the two attributes that all **ShellCommand** objects share – strings that can be used to provide help for the user:

```
19       private String helpString; // documents the command
20       private String argString;  // any args to the command
```

These are set in the constructor in the usual way.

When you design an application, it's important to think ahead about how to offer online help to the end user. The structure we have chosen requires the programmer implementing a **ShellCommand** to provide that help. His concrete **ShellCommand** class won't compile without it, so he can't avoid facing the question from the start.[6]

---

[5] The first time you see an idiom like this it's a *trick*. Thereafter it's a *technique*.

[6] Programmers have been known to cheat. In this case, that might mean writing a concrete **ShellCommand** constructor with the body

```
super ("help string goes here", "arg string goes here")
```

When the customer sees those strings in the final release, she will not be happy, though she may not be surprised.

The Concrete ShellCommand Classes

Juno version 6 provides four shell commands:

- **newfile** constructs a new **TextFile** in the current directory. We studied its implementation previously.
- **type** displays the contents of a **TextFile**.
- **mkdir** creates a new **Directory** in the current **Directory**.
- **help** displays help for all of the shell commands known to Juno. Its implementation uses the help strings and argument strings provided by each concrete **ShellCommand**.

That's a very thin set of commands. Many you would want to see are missing. The most important is **list**, to list the contents of a directory. Without it you can't know that **mkdir** works properly. In the exercises we ask you to write many new Juno commands. Because Juno uses a polymorphic dispatch table, that is a straightforward job:

1. Declare a subclass of **ShellCommand**, implementing **doIt** with the correct semantics and a constructor with useful help information.. Follow the naming convention that implements command named "foo" in class **FooCommand**. If you start with a copy of the source code for a similar existing command, you can save lots of typing. Just be sure to update the comments – preferably before you begin editing the Java.
2. Add your new command to the dispatch table by editing method **fillTable** in class **ShellCommandTable**.

Class ShellCommandTable

A **ShellCommandTable** object (Listing 6-9) manages the lookup table of **ShellCommand** objects by maintaining a private **TreeMap** field for those objects, keyed by command names. The public interface is just a thin wrapper delegating work to **TreeMap** methods in order to create a user-friendly API to the table, hiding its implementation as a **TreeMap**. Here is that API and some of the private methods that support that API, with some description of the implementation.

- **public ShellCommand lookup(String key)** retrieves a **ShellCommand** object, given the name of the command. The implementation delegates the **lookup** by sending a **get** message to a **TreeMap**, then casts the anonymous returned object to a **ShellCommand**. If there is no **ShellCommand** in the map to match the key, **lookup** returns **null**. Method **interpret** in class **Shell** is a client for this service. So is the loop in method **doIt** in class **HelpCommand**.
- **private void install(String commandName, ShellCommand command)** stores the shell command, keyed by its command name, in the table. The

implementation delegates the installation by sending a **put** message to the **TreeMap**.

- **public ShellCommandTable()** invokes the (private) **fillTable** method, which in turn invokes **install** once for each command.

- **public String[] getCommandNames()** returns an array of the command names – the keys for the **TreeMap**. Building this array warrants some discussion. The obvious construction is one we learned in Chapter 4: Get the **keySet** from the **TreeMap**, declare and instantiate an array of the proper size, and iterate over the **keySet**, putting each **String** it contains into the array. That will do. But it's clumsy. A neat advanced Java idiom does it all on one line:

```
56    return (String[]) table.keySet().toArray( new String[0] );
```

In Chapter 4 we saw that

```
table.keySet()
```

returns a **Set** of objects (in this case **String** objects) representing the command names. Sending the message

```
toArray( new String[0] )
```

to this **Set** returns an array of **String**s. The cast **(String[])** is necessary to keep the compiler happy. This is a pretty sophisticated use of interfaces and collections that you need not be able to write at this point. But you should be able to read it, because it's the right way to return the array of command names to a client.

The JFile system

The classes **JFile**, **Directory**, and **TextFile** come from Chapter 5, with minor changes discussed earlier. The current versions can be found in Listings 6-10, 6-11, and 6-12.

Class User

Each instance of class **User** (Listing 6-13) models a registered Juno user. It maintains the user's login name and home directory in the file system. Someday it will hold the user's password too. The public interface consists mainly of getters, giving access to the private instance fields. It also provides a **toString** method, overriding the default in class **Object**. We define the **String** representation of a **User** object to be the Juno login name. You can experiment with this construction in one of the exercises.

Exercises

6-1   Create a text file for your journal for this chapter. Use your journal for questions that call for written answers and to record any observations about your work.

6-2   Compile the **Juno** classes. Play with Juno. Register some new users, log them on, and create some files in their home directories. Write about your experience. What new commands would you like to see implemented right away? Consider creating a file (say, **juno.in**) of Juno commands and using input redirection to run Juno:

```
%> java Juno -e < juno.in
```

A word of warning: It's easy to crash Juno. That's because the program does not try to detect faulty input. In that way it resembles the bank application, which allows customers to withdraw more money than they have in their accounts. In the next chapter we will fix these problems.

6-3   Read method **main** in class **Juno** and write pseudocode explaining what is happening there. In particular,

- Look up **System.exit** in the Java API
- Why don't we need an **else** after the first **if**? Why do we need one after the second **if**?
- The last line of **main** creates a new **Juno** instance but does not assign it to any variable. How can the program work if it can never refer to that object again?

6-4   **Juno** contains straightforward getters and setters for various fields. But the methods **lookupUser** and **createUser** dealing with the **Map** of **User** objects do lots of real work. Those methods really belong in class **UserTable**, to wrap a **TreeMap** the way **ShellCommandTable** wraps a **TreeMap** of **ShellCommand** objects. Design and write **UserTable** and install it in **Juno**.

6-5   Class **InetAddress** in the **java.net** package has a static method that returns the name of the computer on which it is running. Modify **Juno** so that name replaces "mars" as the default.

6-6   *Dealing with potential circular references.* A **Directory** has an owner – an instance of class **User**, passed as an argument to the **Directory** constructor. A **User** has a home **Directory**, passed as an argument to the **User** constructor. So you need to create each of these objects before you create the other. Study the **Juno** code to see how this problem is solved. Describe the solution in words (pseudocode). Then modify **Juno** so that the root **User** is the owner of the root of the file system.

6-7   Describe what happens, and why, if you try to register a Juno user but fail to supply enough information on the register command line. What if you try to register a user who already exists? Don't try to fix these problems – that's a job for the next chapter.

6-8   To make Juno easier for a Unix user, modify **fillTable** in class **ShellCommandTable** so that "type" and "cat" each do the same thing at the Juno prompt. Will you use one **TypeCommand** instance or two? Does it matter? Draw a box-and-arrow picture of the **ShellCommandTable** object illustrating each possibility.

6-9   Implement the Juno command **alias**. After issuing the command

```
mars> alias newname existingname
```

at the Juno shell prompt, you should be able to type "newname" at the Juno prompt instead of "existingname". Thus

```
mars> alias cat type
```

would solve the previous problem.

6-10   (*) Implement the Juno command **list** in class **ListCommand**. **list** takes no arguments and lists the files in the current directory. The format for your **Directory** listing should be the one used by the static **list** method in the **JFile** unit test in Chapter 5. **ls** is the Unix command that lists a directory. In some operating systems the command **dir** does the same job. Add lines to **fillTable** making **dir** and **ls** aliases for **list**.

6-11   (*) Implement the Juno command **pwd** in class **PwdCommand**. **pwd** stands for "print working directory." That command should print the full path name to the current directory.

Then modify Juno so that the shell prompt is

```
mars:[full path to current directory]>
```

6-12   (*) Implement the Juno command **cd** in class **CdCommand**. **cd** stands for "change directory." If at the Juno shell prompt the user types

```
mars> cd foo
```

- if there is a **Directory** named "foo" in the current **Directory**, go there (make that the current **Directory**).
- if "foo" is the **String** ".." go to the parent **Directory** of the current **Directory**.
- If **cd** is entered with no argument, then go to the user's home **Directory**.

Do not worry about any errors that might occur when you try to go to a **Directory** that isn't there.

The best way to test whether your **cd** command works is to have written **pwd** or **list**.

6-13   Implement the Juno command **copy** in class **CopyCommand**. After issuing the command

    mars> copy source target

the current directory should contain **TextFile** target with the same contents as **TextFile** source. Do not worry about errors that might occur if you copy from a source that isn't there, or to a target that is, or from a **Directory**.

6-14   Implement output redirection in Juno, for the **type** command. The Juno command

    mars> type source > target

should have the same effect as

    mars> copy source target

Think about how you might implement output redirection for arbitrary commands:

    mars> anycommand followed by its arguments > target

should put the output from **anycommand** in **JFile** target instead of printing it at the console.

6-15   (*) Implement the Juno command **remove** in class **RemoveCommand**. This command removes text files and directories. To write it, you will have to write method **removeJFile** in class **Directory**.

6-16   The **remove** command in the previous exercise will trash anything you tell it to – even a **Directory** with things in it. Write command **removeall** in class **RemoveallCommand** that removes a **TextFile** in the ordinary way, but when it is asked to remove a **Directory** it calls itself (recursively) to remove everything in that **Directory**, and then removes the **Directory**.

To do this you will have to check whether a **JFile** is a **TextFile** or a **Directory**. This is not a place where you can rely on polymorphism. Use the Java keyword **instanceof** this way:

    if (something instanceof Directory) ...

6-17   Implement the Juno command **rename** in class **RenameCommand**. After issuing the command

    mars> rename source target

the current directory should contain **TextFile** target but not **TextFile** source. Can you implement **rename** by invoking **copy** followed by **remove** in the **doIt** method in class **RenameCommand**?

6-18   The comment character in Juno is hardwired to **'#'**. Implement the Juno command **cc** in class **CcCommand**. After issuing the command

```
mars> cc $
```

the comment character should become **'$'**.
You will need to look in the **String** class API to find out how to get the char **'$'** from the **String** "$" you get from the **StringTokenizer**.

Explain what happens if you set the comment character to be 'e' and then try to get help in Juno.

6-19   Implement the Juno command **finger** in class **FingerCommand.**. After issuing the command

```
mars> finger someone
```

Juno should display the login name and the real name of the **User** with login name "someone". If **finger** is entered with no argument, it should display the login name and real name of the current **User**. You might want to rewrite **toString** in class **User** to make your job easier.

6-20   Implement the Juno command **touch** in class **TouchCommand**. The command

```
mars> touch afile
```

should set the modification date of the **JFile** afile to now if the file exists, and create a new empty **TextFile** with that name if it doesn't.

6-21   Modify the Juno help command in two ways:

    a. Make use of the **ShellCommand argString** field to provide more information for each command.

    b. If the user enters a command name after typing "help", provide help for just that command.

6-22   (*) Modify the banking application so that all banker commands and all user commands can be read from a single line instead of prompting the user for more input. For example, to deposit $50 a user should type

```
deposit 50
```

To make this work you will need a way to convert the **String** "50" that's the second token on the line to the **int** 50 that the **deposit** method wants. Look at class **Integer** in the Java API. The static **parseInt** method there will help.

EStore exercises

6-23 Modify the **EStore** application so that all commands can be read from a single line instead of prompting the user for more input.

6-24 Design class **Customer** to represent shoppers at the **EStore**. Each customer should register when she first visits. Then the **EStore** creates a **Customer** object and saves it. A returning customer need not register again. You can decide what information the store should remember about its customers. The minimum is the customer's name. Consider tracking how many times someone has visited, how much he or she has spent, and how many items were purchased. You could even keep track of what those items were. The store might want to welcome its best customers with a friendly message, or advertise discounts on items it knows a customer is interested in.

For design hints look at how **Juno** handles **User** instances.

If you are so inclined, implement your design.

Chapter 7

When Bad Things Happen to Good Programs

In most places in most of the programs we have studied, we casually assumed that all went well. No one tried to withdraw more money from a bank account than it contained or to cash checks on a savings account. Juno users did not try to list the contents of a text file or to type a directory. But the real software world is less reliable. Good programs must be written *defensively*, so that they can detect errors and act appropriately before damage is done. And good languages like Java provide tools that make it easy for programmers to do the right thing when users do the wrong thing.

Clearly no bank would allow a customer to withdraw more money from a bank account than it contains.[1] We've deliberately waited to deal with that error it until we developed the proper programming tools. Now we're ready. Here is the essence of the code for method **withdraw** in class **BankAccount** before we do any error checking:

```
public void withdraw( int amount )
{
    incrementBalance( -amount );
}
```

It's easy enough to test whether the balance is sufficient to cover the amount being withdrawn:

```
public void withdraw ( int amount )
{
    if ( amount <= balance ) {
        incrementBalance( -amount );
    }
    else {
        // an error; do something
    }
}
```

When a running program encounters an error like this, it should

- Tell someone that something went wrong.
- Continue working in some reasonable way.

---

[1] Some banks offer overdraft protection – for a fee, of course.

For this attempt to withdraw more than is in the account, the solution seems simple:

```
public void withdraw( int amount )
{
    if ( amount <= balance ) {
        incrementBalance( -amount );
    }
    else {
        // Report the error and do nothing more
        System.out.println( "Insufficient funds" );
    }
}
```

This works well in our toy **Bank**. But it may fail in a real one. The error-handling code prints a message to **System.out**, but the rest of the banking system uses a **Terminal** object for its input and output. Imagine using instances of our **BankAccount** class in a bank where there is a real ATM that acts as the **Terminal**. Then it is not at all clear where the "Insufficient funds" string will be printed – perhaps somewhere at the bank's headquarters, where it will do the user at the ATM no good. Nor is it clear where it should be printed: When we write the **BankAccount** class, we have no idea what kind of screen or display the ATM will have.[2] The **BankAccount** objects do not know (and should not know) what **Terminal** the **Bank** is using. Or perhaps the **withdraw** message is being sent not by a person at an ATM but by another program that is paying the customer's monthly bills by electronic funds transfer (EFT).[3]

We will soon study error-handling solutions that do not involve printing at all. But if for some reason you *must* print, consider printing to *standard error* instead of to *standard output*:

```
public void withdraw( int amount )
{
    if ( amount <= balance ) {
        incrementBalance( -amount );
    }
    else {
        // Report the error and do nothing more
      System.err.println( "Insufficient funds" );
    }
}
```

We handle normal output by sending a **println** message to **System.out**. Java provides an alternative place to which to send error messages: **System.err**.

---

[2] Or even what language the user speaks.
[3] The world is full of abbreviations. This is one common in the banking industry. There, "ATM" means "automatic teller machine," but in computer networks "ATM" means "asynchronous transfer mode."

When you are running the JVM from a command prompt, both **System.out** and **System.err** print to the screen. But sometimes they go to different places – for example, if you redirect i/o. We have provided **errPrintln** methods in our **Terminal** class to wrap that functionality. Develop the habit of reporting to standard error when appropriate.

But printing, even to standard error, is usually a bad idea. The urge to print follows from the often mistaken assumption that when our program finds an error we should have it tell the user – the person who is running the program. We must arrange to tell *someone*, but we often don't know who the user is, because we have detected the error somewhere in a method providing a service to some client elsewhere. The best thing to do is to design programs so that when something goes wrong in a method, the method can inform *its client* (the object that sent the message).

Java provides an elegant way to do that: We can have our method *throw an* **Exception**. Before we take up that important idea, we will explore several other ways a method can use to return error information to its client. Sometimes they provide better solutions than throwing an **Exception**. And if you are writing code in a language that does not provide exceptions, you will have to use one of them.

The word "return" in the previous paragraph is a clue to one such way. The declaration of our **withdraw** method shows that it returns nothing. We could rewrite it this way:

```
public boolean withdraw( int amount )
{
    if ( amount > balance ) {
        return false; // signal trouble
    }
    incrementBalance( -amount );
    return true; // all went well
}
```

Then we rewrite the calling code to take advantage of the new information:

```
if ( ! account.withdraw( amount ) ) {
    // ... An overdraft - take appropriate action
}
```

What have we accomplished? What should happen when **withdraw** discovers that the account balance won't cover the withdrawal? We haven't answered that. All we have done is move the responsibility for dealing with it from the **withdraw** method to its client. But that is in fact a significant part of the solution to the problem. The client (the **Bank**) is likely to have a much better idea of what to do than the **BankAccount** object itself. If the client is a human teller (typing at her terminal), then she can talk to the customer standing in front of her. If the client is code in an ATM, then the ATM will know how to report that the money can't be delivered as requested. If the client is a method making EFT withdrawals, it may not know what to do – but it can pass along to *its* client the fact that there isn't enough money in the account.

We can generalize this idea of *returning* information rather than *reporting* it. Our new **withdraw** method returns either **true** or **false**: It can tell its client that a withdrawal was impossible, but not why. Suppose there is enough money in the account, but the owner of the account has not paid his taxes and the Internal Revenue Service has seized the account. Then the code for **withdraw** must test twice:

```
public boolean withdraw( int amount )
{
    if ( amount > balance ) {
        return false; // signal trouble
    }
    if ( irsHasSeizedThisAccount ) {
        return false; // signal another kind of trouble
    }
    incrementBalance( -amount );
    return true;      // all went well
}
```

When the client tests the value returned by **withdraw**

```
if ( ! account.withdraw( amount ) ) {
    // ... some problem, but what problem?
}
```

it knows only that *something* has gone wrong with the withdrawal, but not *what* has gone wrong. We could let the client know by redesigning **withdraw** so that it returns a **String**:

```
public String withdraw( int amount )
{
    if ( amount > balance ) {
        return "insufficient funds";
    }
    if ( irsHasSeizedThisAccount ) {
        return "has been seized";
    }
    incrementBalance( - amount );
    return null; // all went well
}
```

with the convention that a **null** return means success. Then the client could deal with the information this way:

```
String errorMessage;
if ( ( errorMessage = account.withdraw( amount )) != null ) {
    // look at errorMessage and decide what to do
}
```

Another design has **withdraw** return an integer. In fact, **withdraw** in version 5 of the **BankAccount** class already does just that: It returns the amount withdrawn. Because that amount can't be negative (an error condition we plan to test for elsewhere), we can use negative return values to signal particular errors:

```java
public int withdraw( int amount )
{
    if ( amount > balance ) {
        return -1;
    }
    if ( irsHasSeizedThisAccount ) {
        return -2;
    }
    incrementBalance( -amount );
    return amount;        // all went well
}
```

Then the client could deal with the information with a **switch** on the value returned by **withdraw**:

```java
int returnValue = account.withdraw( amount );
switch (returnValue) {
    case -1:
        System.err.println("insufficient funds");
        break;
    case -2:
        System.err.println("account has been seized");
        break;
    default:
        // do whatever you would do with a normal return
}
```

If you do use integer return values to signal particular error conditions, it's better to use *symbolic constants* instead of magic numbers like −1 and −2. In class **BankAccount**, declare

```java
public final static int INSUFFICIENT_FUNDS = -1;
public final static int ACCOUNT_SEIZED     = -2;
```

Then use these in **withdraw** and in **Bank**:

```java
int returnValue = account.withdraw( amount );
switch (returnValue) {
    case BankAccount.INSUFFICIENT_FUNDS:
        System.err.println("insufficient funds");
        break;
```

```
    case BankAccount.ACCOUNT_SEIZED:
        System.err.println("account has been seized");
        break;
    default:
        // do whatever you would do with a normal return
}
```

An even more flexible solution would be to declare a new class specifically designed so that its instances can hold the information the client (or perhaps the client's client) needs in order to deal with an error.

True Disaster

Sometimes there is no way to recover from an error, so there is no point in informing a method's client of a disaster. Java provides a way to shut down a program in an emergency:

```
public Whatever withdraw( int amount )
{
    if ( theBankIsBeingRobbed ) {
        System.err.println("call the cops!");
        System.exit(911);
    }
    // normal processing...
    return somethingAppropriate;
}
```

The **static exit** method in the **System** class shuts down the JVM, so program execution stops immediately. **System.exit** accepts an integer argument – in this case **911**. In some systems, the JVM provides this integer to its caller by setting a global variable in the environment – yet another technique for returning error information.

The Java Way: Throwing and Catching Exceptions

Using a method's return value is often a clumsy way to signal the client that something has gone wrong. Java provides a cleaner alternative. To guard against overdrafts, we can write this client code:

```
try {
    account.withdraw( amount ));
}
catch ( InsufficientFundsException exceptionInstance ) {
    // look at exceptionInstance and take appropriate action
}
// whatever happens next
```

This is easy to read. We **try** to withdraw the money. If there's no problem with the withdrawal, then the JVM skips the code in the **catch** block, and execution resumes after that block. The Java keywords **try** and **catch** work smoothly together. The logic resembles **if** and **else** but without the need for an explicit test here. Instead, the **withdraw** method must arrange to have the code in the **catch** block execute when something goes wrong. It does that by creating the object **exceptionInstance** of type **InsufficientFundsException** that's the argument in the **catch** block:

```
public int withdraw( int amount )
           throws InsufficientFunds Exception
{
    if ( amount > balance ) {
        throw new InsufficientFundsException();
    }
    incrementBalance( -amount );
    return amount;
}
```

There is nothing new about the **new**. It tells us that an instance of class **InsufficientFundsException** is being created. But **throws** and **throw** are two more Java keywords. **throw** is the one we are interested in now. It's what method **withdraw** does with the **InsufficientFundsException** object it has just created. Think of throwing the exception up into the air, where it hovers waiting for someone to catch it. In this case that someone is the client code we have just read.

Class **InsufficientFundsException**, like any other class, must be declared before it can be used. Here is one possible declaration:

```
public class InsufficientFundsException extends Exception
{
}
```

This **InsufficientFundsException** class does nothing more than its parent **Exception**, the class in the Java API we extend when we want to use Java's exception-handling mechanism to deal with a potential problem in our program. The most important feature of an **Exception** object is that it can be thrown and caught.

Because an **Exception** is an object, it can have fields and getters and setters that allow it to carry information from where it is thrown to where it is caught. In particular, the **Exception** class has a constructor that accepts a single **String** argument. It then saves that information in one of its fields. That means we can use our **InsufficientFundsException** to "return" a **String** by declaring an

InsufficientFundsException constructor this way:

```
public InsufficientFundsException( String message )
{
    super⁴( message );
}
```

We invoke that constructor when we create and throw the exception:

```
public int withdraw( int amount )
{
    if ( amount > balance ) {
        throw new InsufficientFundsException(
         "insufficient funds: amount exceeds balance by " +
         (amount - balance));
    }
    if ( irsHasSeizedThisAccount ) {
        throw new InsufficientFundsException(
         "account has been seized");
    }
    incrementBalance( - amount );
    return amount;
}
```

and the **Exception** class **getMessage** method when we catch it:

```
try {
    account.withdraw( amount );
}
catch ( InsufficientFundsException e ) {
    atm.println( e.getMessage() );
}
// whatever happens next
```

Exception Classes in the Java API

In our discussion of **Exception** objects so far, we have concentrated on the ones like **InsufficientFundsException** we create by subclassing **Exception** ourselves. There are some subclasses of **Exception** that come with the Java API. You may have stumbled on several in your work so far: perhaps **NullPointerException**, **ArrayIndexOutOfBoundsException**, **NoSuchElementException**, or

---

⁴ Remember: The **super** keyword here invokes the superclass constructor with this signature.

ClassCastException. These are thrown by the JVM itself when it detects the appropriate error conditions, even though you have not put an explicit **throw** in your code. But you can **catch** them just as if you had decided to **throw** them yourself. Here is a fragment of code from method **processTransactionsForAccount** in release 7 of the **Bank** class (Listing 7-1) that does just that:

```
175     else if ( transaction.startsWith( "c" ) ) {
176         int amount = readPosAmt( " amount of check: " );
177         try { // to cast acct to CheckingAccount ...
178             atm.println("  cashed check for " +
179             ((CheckingAccount) acct).honorCheck (amount));
180         }
181         catch (ClassCastException e) {
182             // if not a checking account, report error
183             atm.errPrintln(
184                 "   Sorry, not a checking account." );
185         }
186     }
```

At runtime the JVM tries to cast the abstract **BankAccount acct** to a **CheckingAccount** on line 179. If that account isn't one, the JVM throws a **ClassCastException**. The **honorCheck** message on line 179 is never sent to the **BankAccount**, nor is the **println** message on 178 sent to the **Terminal**. Control passes immediately to the **catch** on line 181. There we print a suitable message, to the **Terminal** object's error output stream.

If we had wanted to, we could have declared a **WrongKindOfAccountException** class, thrown an instance of that class, and relied on our client to catch it:

```
catch (ClassCastException e) {
    // throw a more meaningful exception
    throw new WrongKindOfAccountException("checking");
}
```

This sort of *re-throwing* is common when we catch a Java system exception but we're not yet ready to deal with the error. We replace the system exception with one that makes sense in our application.

Exception Syntax and Semantics: The Throw

A throw takes the form

```
throw exception;
```

where *exception* is an instance of **Throwable** or any of its subclasses. You commonly find a **throw** inside an **if** statement that detects an error of some kind. Usually the **Exception** is created and thrown right away:

```
throw new SomeKindOfException();
```

Exception Syntax and Semantics: The Catch

We *catch an exception* at a (safe) place where execution can resume after the error has been detected and the exception thrown. The body of the **catch** block takes action to deal with the problem. It might do some or all of the following:

- print a message
- deal with the error condition
- rethrow the same or a different **Exception**
- shut down the application
- do nothing:

```
catch (Exception e) {
}
```

The Call Stack

In the examples we have seen so far, we caught each **Exception** soon after it was thrown – either right away, as with the **ClassCastException**, or in the code that invoked the method in which the **throw** occurred, as with the **InsufficientFundsException**. The first kind of example is like a simple **if ... else**. The second is like an early return from a method. But the **throw/catch** mechanism is much more powerful and flexible than these examples suggest. Imagine a long sequence of invocations in which **method0** invokes **method1** invokes **method2** invokes **method3**, and an error is detected in **method3** that should be handled by **method0**:

```
public void method0()
{
    int answer = someObject.method1();
}

public int method1()
{
    return someObject.method2();
}
```

```
public int method2()
{
    return someObject.method3();
}

public int method3()
{
    int answer;
    // code here to compute the answer,
    // some error might occur
    return answer;
}
```

These objects and methods might be in the same class, or different classes. With Java's exception-handling API, you can cleanly manage the jump from the body of **method3** all the way back to **method0**[5]:

```
public void method0()
{
    int answer;
    try {
        answer = someObject.method1();
    }
    catch ( MyException e ) {
        // deal with exception e
    }
}

public int method1()
{
    return someObject.method2();
}

public int method2()
{
    return someObject.method3();
}
```

---

[5] If you already know about Java's exception-handling mechanism, you will know that this code won't quite compile as written. We take that matter up in a very short while.

```
public int method3()
{
    boolean disaster = false;
    int answer;
    // code here to compute the answer
    if (disaster) {
        throw new MyException();
    }
    return answer;
}
```

In this example, when **disaster** happens, control passes from the **throw** in **method3** all the way back to the **catch** in **method0**, bypassing any processing in the intermediate methods. The sequence of method invocations in this example:

1. **method0**
2. **method1**
3. **method2**
4. **method3**

is known as the *call stack*.[6] At any moment a running Java program has a call stack that starts with **main** and ends with whatever method is executing at that moment. The call stack is dynamic: It changes its shape as the program runs. Each time a method is invoked, it is added to the stack. When that method returns, it is removed from the stack.

One of the beauties of throwing exceptions is that they provide a way to transfer control to any point higher on the call stack than the point at which they are thrown.

Exception Syntax and Semantics: the throws Clause

The example above won't quite work as written. The Java compiler insists that each method on the call stack that *might* throw an uncaught exception, or be the recipient of an exception thrown by something below it, must either **catch** that exception or explicitly disclaim responsibility, automatically throwing it on up the stack. So to satisfy the compiler we must recode **method1**, **method2**, and **method3** in the example:

```
public int method1() throws MyException
{
    return someObject.method2();
}
```

---

[6] Strictly speaking, we should call this the *method invocation stack*, because in object-oriented programs we invoke methods by sending messages; we don't call them. "Call" is a phrase left over from procedural languages like C. But "call stack" is so much easier to say, and so common, that we will use it.

```
public int method2() throws MyException
{
    return someObject.method3();
}

public int method3() throws MyException
{
    boolean disaster = false;
    int answer;
    // code here to compute the answer
    if (disaster) {
        throw new MyException();
    }
    return answer;
}
```

Think of **throws** in the declaration as meaning, "might throw" while **throw** in the body means "does throw." You will sometimes be annoyed (or puzzled) by the error message from the compiler when you forget the **throws** clause when it's required. But that annoyance is worth dealing with. The compiler forces the programmer to declare that she knows what's going on: that an **Exception** might be thrown some day somewhere below this method on the call stack of a running program. The **throws** clause in the declaration says, "I know that, and have chosen not to catch that exception here."

This requirement guarantees that all thrown user-declared exceptions will be caught eventually. Some exceptions thrown by the JVM (subclasses of **RuntimeException** like the **ClassCastException** discussed above) needn't be declared in a **throws** clause, and they needn't be caught. Any **Exception** that makes it all the way up the call stack to **main** without being caught causes the program to crash.

The Bank Application, Once Again

We have rewritten the banking application, this time testing for all the errors we could think of. It's the most complicated version yet. It uses ten classes:

- The **Bank** class (Listing 7-1), modeling a single bank. When visiting the bank, a user (a banker) may open a new account (regular, checking, fee, or savings), serve an existing customer, set a new interest rate or check fee, advance time to the next month (causing interest to be credited to savings accounts and fees to be assessed where appropriate), generate a report, seek help, or leave. When serving a customer, the bank allows only those transactions permitted by the customer's account.

- The abstract class **BankAccount** (Listing 7-2) and its concrete subclasses **CheckingAccount** (Listing 7-3), **SavingsAccount** (Listing 7-4), **FeeAccount** (Listing 7-5), and **RegularAccount** (Listing 7-6) whose instances model the various kinds of accounts.

- The **Month** class (Listing 7-7) for keeping track of the current month and year.
- The remaining three classes are all subclasses of **Exception**. We create objects of type **InsufficientFundsException** (Listing 7-8) or **NegativeAmountException** (Listing 7-9) when an error occurs.

We will study how the bank application uses these exceptions.

Exception Handling in the Bank Application

Our first example is method **incrementBalance** in class **BankAccount**. That's where we detect overdrafts.

```
139    public final void incrementBalance( int amount )
140        throws InsufficientFundsException
141    {
142        int newBalance = balance + amount;
143        if (newBalance < 0) {
144            throw new InsufficientFundsException(
145                        "for this transaction" );
146        }
147        balance = newBalance;
148        getIssuingBank().incrementBalance( amount );
149    }
```

We compute the new balance on line 142. If the result is negative, we throw an **InsufficientFundsException** on lines 144–5, and execution resumes wherever this exception is caught. If all has gone well, we update our balance and the balance in our **Bank** and return normally. The **final** in the method header says that the **incrementBalance** method may not be overridden in any subclass of **BankAccount**. It casts the method in stone so we can know that those methods that depend on it always get the functionality they expect – in particular the check for insufficient funds.

Although this is the only place an **InsufficientFundsException** is thrown, we catch that exception at three different places in **Bank** and in two places in **CheckingAccount**, which correspond at runtime to different call stacks. One **catch** is in **openNewAccount** in class **Bank**:

```
112  private void openNewAccount()
113  {
114      String accountName = atm.readWord("Account name: ");
115      char accountType =
116          atm.readChar( "Type of account (r/c/f/s): " );
```

```
117      try {
118          int startup = readPosAmt( "Initial deposit: " );
119          BankAccount newAccount;
120          switch( accountType ) {

124          case 'f':
125              newAccount = new FeeAccount(startup, this);
126              break;

140      } // end of try block
141      catch (NegativeAmountException e) {
142          atm.errPrintln(
143          "can't start with a negative balance");
144      }
145      catch (InsufficientFundsException e) {
146          atm.errPrintln("Initial deposit less than fee");
147      }
148  }
```

We need the **try**/**catch** for insufficient funds because it's possible that the initial deposit for a new **FeeAccount** will be too small to cover the transaction fee the **Bank** charges for opening the account.[7] Should that happen, as a result of code executing from line 125,[8] control jumps immediately to the catch on line 145. Because we know why the **InsufficientFundsException** was thrown, we print a useful error message instead of using the generic one "for this transaction" that comes with the exception.

Here is the call stack at the moment this exception was thrown:

method	*in class*
main	**Bank**
visit	**Bank**
openNewAccount	**Bank**
constructor	**FeeAccount**
constructor (super)	**BankAccount**
deposit	**BankAccount**
incrementBalance	**BankAccount**

The exception travels up through four method invocations on the call stack until it's caught in **openNewAccount**.

---

[7] Charging a fee to open an account is not a good way to invite new business. We address this question in the exercises.
[8] We don't show the other cases in the **switch** here.

The **newMonth** method in class **Bank** can catch an
InsufficientFundsException too:

```
233     private void newMonth()
234     {
235         month.next();
236         Iterator i = accountList.keySet().iterator();
237         while ( i.hasNext() ) {
238             String name = (String) i.next();
239             BankAccount acct =
                    (BankAccount)accountList.get(name);
240             try {
241                 acct.newMonth();
242             }
243             catch (InsufficientFundsException exception) {
244                 atm.errPrintln(
245                     "Insufficient funds in account \"" +
246                     name + "\" for monthly fee" );
247             }
248         }
249     }
250
```

Again the error message offers the only interpretation possible: If informing any bank account of the passing of another month causes an **InsufficientFundsException** to be thrown, then it must be the result of an overdraft when the **Bank** tries to deduct the monthly account fee.

The overdraft discussed at the beginning of this chapter is dealt with when the **processTransactionsForAccount** method catches an **InsufficientFundsException**:

```
204     catch (InsufficientFundsException e) {
205         atm.errPrintln( "    Insufficient funds " +
206                         e.getMessage() );
207     }
```

Any one of the transactions requiring that a message be sent to a **BankAccount** can cause method **incrementBalance** to throw an **InsufficientFundsException** for some reason – because a withdrawal was too large or some fee could not be covered. So the generic error message relies on the message contained in the exception caught to provide more information.

Catching Several Exceptions in the Same Place

Method **openNewAccount** in class **Bank** illustrates another common idiom in exception handling. Two catch clauses occur in succession:

```
141    catch (NegativeAmountException e) {
142        atm.errPrintln(
143        "can't start with a negative balance");
144    }
145    catch (InsufficientFundsException e) {
146        atm.errPrintln("Initial deposit less than fee");
147    }
```

When a thrown **Exception** reaches this code, the JVM tries to match the type of the **Exception** to the types specified in the **catch** clauses in the order in which they appear. In this example it would first see if the exception were a **NegativeAmountException** and if so **catch** it; otherwise, it would see if it were an **InsufficientFundsException** and if so **catch** it. If it were neither of those, then the JVM would look further up the call stack for a **catch** block that did match the type of the exception.

The order in which we check is particularly important when the exceptions we expect come from an inheritance hierarchy. For example, if we declare:

```
class ExceptionA extends Exception {...}
class ExceptionB extends ExceptionA {...}
```

Then, in the **try/catch** statements

```
try {
    something;
}
catch (ExceptionB e) {...}
catch (ExceptionA e) {...}
catch (Exception e) {/* unanticipated error */}
```

the two specific classes of exceptions (**ExceptionA** and **ExceptionB**) are caught and dealt with first. The last **catch** clause catches any other **Exception** that might be thrown. Without that catch, an **Exception** thrown by the JVM caused by an error that the programmer failed to anticipate would crash the program. This **catch** prevents that. But it would be a mistake to reorder the **catch** clauses this way:

```
catch (ExceptionA e) {...}
catch (ExceptionB e) {...}
catch (Exception e) {/* unanticipated error */}
```

because each instance of **ExceptionB** is also an instance of **ExceptionA** and would be caught by the first catch. In fact, the compiler will not allow us to be foolish in this particular way. When one type of exception extends another, always catch the subclass first.

Re-throwing Exceptions

We also **catch** an **InsufficientFundsException** in the **honorCheck** method in class **CheckingAccount**:

```
54  try {
55      incrementBalance( - getIssuingBank().getCheck Fee() );
56  }
57  catch (InsufficientFundsException e) {
58      throw new InsufficientFundsException(
59                  "to cover check fee" );
60  }
61  try {
62      withdraw( amount );
63  }
64  catch (InsufficientFundsException e) {
65      incrementBalance( getIssuingBank().getCheck Fee() );
66      throw new InsufficientFundsException(
67                  "to cover check + check fee" );
68  }
```

We first look for an **InsufficientFundsException** when we try to subtract the check fee, and then, if we are successful, when we try to subtract the amount the check is written for. Each time we catch the exception, we throw *another* **InsufficientFundsException** with a more specific message indicating just why the transaction failed. Catching one exception in order to re-throw another that is more informative is a common exception-handling idiom.

There's one piece of subtle error recovery worth looking at in more detail. If we succeed in subtracting the check fee but then cannot honor the check, it's only fair to add back the check fee. So the code for adding back the check fee goes into the **catch** block for the second **try**, before we re-throw a new **InsufficientFundsException**.

NegativeAmountExceptions

When the bank application prompts the user for a dollar amount, it expects a non-negative response. To enforce this, **Bank** invokes its **readPosAmt** method, which wraps the **Terminal readInt** method with a check on the return value. It throws a **NegativeAmountException** if that value is negative:

```
294     private int readPosAmt( String prompt )
295         throws NegativeAmountException
```

```
296     {
297         int amount = atm.readInt( prompt );
298         if (amount < 0) {
299             throw new NegativeAmountException();
300         }
301         return amount;
302     }
```

The error message printed when a **NegativeAmountException** is caught depends on the context.

Error Handling in Juno

We have deliberately avoided handling Juno errors – until now. There are many to be dealt with. A user might attempt to **type** a **JFile** that is a **Directory**, **cd** to a **JFile** that is a **TextFile**, or refer to a **JFile** that doesn't even exist. Any of these actions will cause Juno to crash. Listings 7-10 to 7-29 define version 7 of Juno, which makes a start at catching some of these errors. You will finish the job in the exercises.

Juno 7 design calls for several kinds of Exceptions:

- We declare class **JunoException** extending **Exception** for Juno error handling. We provide information about each particular error using either a subclass of **JunoException** or the message API inherited from class **Exception**.

- We use a **BadShellCommandException** extending **JunoException** to tell the user that the arguments to a shell command have been entered incorrectly. The **BadShellCommandException** constructor accepts the misused **ShellCommand** as an argument, so the **catch** has access to the help string for that **ShellCommand**.

- We throw an **ExitShellException** extending **JunoException** in **doIt** in class **LogoutCommand** in order to tell the shell's interpreter that the user is done. In this case we are throwing an exception just to transfer control from the **doIt** back to the method above it on the call stack – in this case, **interpret** in class **Shell**. Logging out of Juno is not an error.[9]

To see how these exceptions are caught, look at the **try/catch** logic in the **Shell**'s **interpret** method (Listing 7-12):

```
73      try {
74          commandObject.doIt( st, this );
75      }
```

---

[9] Pedantic programmers sometimes assert that exceptions ought to be used only for dealing with errors (that is, exceptional behavior). We say pooh. Exceptions were designed for error handling but can be used (with care) for other purposes.

```
76      catch (ExitShellException e) {
77          return false;
78      }
79      catch (BadShellCommandException e) {
80          console.errPrintln( "Usage: " + commandName + " " +
81                              e.getCommand().getArgString() );
82      }
83      catch (JunoException e) {
84          console.errPrintln( e.getMessage() );
85      }
86      catch (Exception e) {
87          console.errPrintln( "you should never get here" );
88          console.errPrintln( e.toString() );
89      }
```

Line 74 invokes the **doIt** method of the **ShellCommand** object corresponding to the command name the user typed. That **doIt** will throw an **ExitShellException** if the command was **logout**, a **BadShellCommandException** if the arguments were entered incorrectly, or some other **JunoException** if something else went wrong.

The catches on lines 76, 79, 83, and 86 are arranged in increasing order of generality.

- When we Catch an **ExitShellException**, we return **false** from **interpret**, signaling the command-line interpreter that this **Shell** session is over.

- When we catch a **BadShellCommandException**, we construct an error message from the command name and the sample argument string for the command, in order to tell the user how to enter the command arguments correctly.

- When we catch a generic **JunoException**, we print the error message contained in the exception, relying on the thrower to provide useful information.

- After catching all the exceptions we expect to see, we catch any other **Exception** on line 86. That **catch** will execute only if some error occurred that the Juno programmer failed to imagine and deal with by throwing a **JunoException**. It's a signal that the program needs work. Catching those unanticipated exceptions here keeps Juno from crashing even though the programmer wasn't careful enough.

To see where some of these exceptions might be thrown, we will look at **doIt** in class **TypeCommand** (Listing 7-16):

```
35  public void doIt( StringTokenizer args, Shell sh )
36          throws JunoException
37  {
38      String filename;
39      try {
40          filename = args.nextToken();
41      }
```

```
42          catch (NoSuchElementException e) {
43              throw new BadShellCommandException( this );
44          }
45          try {
46              sh.getConsole().println(
47                  ( (TextFile) sh.getDot().
48                      retrieveJFile( filename) ).getContents() );
49          }
50          catch (NullPointerException e) {
51              throw new JunoException("JFile does not exist:" +
52                                      filename);
53          }
54          catch (ClassCastException e) {
55              throw new JunoException("JFile not a text file:" +
56                                      filename);
57          }
58  }
```

The declaration header on lines 35–6 includes the required **throws** clause, because this method might throw a **JunoException**. And often it does.

If the user forgets to type a file name after **type** on the Juno command line, the **nextToken** method in class **StringTokenizer** will throw a **NoSuchElementException** at line 40 because the **StringTokenizer** has no more tokens. That exception won't tell the user much, so we catch it on line 42 and throw a new **BadShellCommandException** instead, telling it that **this ShellCommand**, which happens to be a **TypeCommand** instance, is the problem command.

Once the filename argument *is* found, we send the current **Directory** (**sh.getDot()**) a **retrieveJFile** message to get the **JFile** with that name, cast that **JFile** to be (what we expect to be) a **TextFile**, and then print out the file's contents. If **retrieveJFile** returns **null** (because no file by that name exists), then sending it a message causes the JVM to throw a **NullPointerException**. We **catch** that and rethrow a **JunoException** with an appropriate message. If **retrieveJFile** finds a **Directory** instead of a **TextFile**, the cast will fail and the JVM will throw a **ClassCastException**. We catch that and re-throw a **JunoException** with an appropriate message. Note how both **catch**es illustrate how we tell our client what went wrong by catching an exception from the Java library and providing application-specific information (that is, Juno information) by throwing a new exception of our own.

This analysis of **interpret** and of **doIt** in class **TypeCommand** only begins to deal with the many ways in which Juno might break. The exercises ask you to find them all.

finally

A **finally** clause can be used to guarantee that certain *cleanup* code is executed after a **try**. The sequence

```
try {
    something
}
catch ( SomeException e ) {
    ...
}
finally {
    cleanup
}
```

ensures that the cleanup code in the **finally** clause is executed, no matter what, once the **try** commences.

Such code is most useful when system resources are allocated (for example, new disk files are opened) in the **try** block and we want to be sure they are eventually de-allocated (that is, the files are closed) no matter what happens. In Chapter 9 we will use a **finally** clause for just that purpose. We don't need **finally** clauses here in Juno, but we mention them to complete our discussion of exception handling.

Summary

In this chapter we studied design strategies that help programmers write robust programs. In particular, Java's exception-handling API provides a powerful control mechanism for dealing with exceptional events like user errors. We installed complete error handling in the bank application[10] and sketched how Juno might be made more robust. To see exception-handling syntax and semantics in a small standalone program, study **RumpelstiltskinDemo.java**[11] (Example 7-1).

Error handling is difficult even with good tools. Clean code can become clumsy. When we design programs, we try to keep related functionality in a single place – but error handling is necessarily distributed because the place where an error is found is not usually the place where it is dealt with. In commercial software, error handling can account for between a quarter and a third of all the code. In the exercises we ask you to measure the fraction of Juno code that serves that purpose.

Juno has many small classes, each with just a few methods. In the next chapter, we change pace and study the single large **String** class, which has many methods. We'll use what we learn to improve Juno.

Exercises

7-1   Create a text file for your journal for this chapter. Use your journal for questions that call for written answers and to record any observations about your work.

---

[10] If you find an error we missed, please let us know!

[11] Rumpelstiltskin is one of Jacob and Wilhelm Grimm's fairy tales. You can find a translation at http://www.fln.vcu.edu//grimm/rumpeleng.html and an interesting contemporary update at http://www.ucl.ac.uk/~zcapl61/rumple.html.

7-2   Run release 7 of the banking application. Enter erroneous input and discuss (in your journal) the results you get. Read the source code. Identify all of the **throws**, the kind of exception thrown, and the error condition that causes the **throw**. For each exception thrown, identify the places in the program that exception might be caught.

7-3   Comment out the **try/catch** for the **ClassCastException** when cashing a check in the transaction loop in **processTransactionsForAccount** and see what happens when you try to cash a check on a savings account.

7-4   Rewrite **whichAccount** so that it throws a **NoSuchAccountException** instead of returning **null** when a nonexistent account is requested. Pass that exception's constructor the name of the nonexistent account and build an appropriate error message to send along to the superclass constructor. Then rewrite the code that invokes **whichAccount** and tests for a **null** return so that it catches a **NoSuchAccountException** instead.

Alternatively, just let **whichAccount** return **null** when there is no such account. Then the client code can try to go ahead with its business. When it sends a message to that **null BankAccount**, the JVM will throw a **NullPointerException**. Catch that exception and issue the proper error message.

Decide which of these two strategies you prefer, and explain why.

7-5   Give the **InsufficientFundsException** an additional constructor that accepts two integer arguments: the current balance in the account, and the amount that some method is attempting to withdraw. Write private fields and getters for those attributes, set the fields in the constructor, and use the getters to build an appropriate error message when the exception is caught.

7-6   In several places in **BankAccount.java** you will find the two statements

```
incrementBalance( - amount - getTransactionFee() );
countTransaction()
```

That suggests that you could improve program reliability and save typing by moving the charge for the transaction fee into method **countTransaction**.

a. Make that change.
b. Test your code for a **FeeAccount** with a very small balance – sufficient to cover the transaction but not the fee.
c. Discuss what you would have to do to fix the error. (Hint: Look at how a **CheckingAccount** deals with a similar situation.)
d. Discuss whether it's better to make that change or to keep the original design, in which **countTransaction** does not handle the transaction fee.

7-7   Write class **HackerAccount** extending **BankAccount** and try to override the **incrementBalance** method in order to disable the test for an overdraft. Explain what happens.

7-8   The **Bank** has decided not to charge a transaction fee for opening a new **FeeAccount**. You are a software engineer; your manager has asked you what this change entails. Write her a memo discussing how you might modify the application code to implement the new functionality. Find at least two solutions and compare them in order to decide which would be better. Defend your decision. Your argument should take into account the complexity of the code changes required and the time it would take you to make them. (Note that this exercise does not call for any code – just a memo to your manager in response to her design question.)

7-9   Where is the **throw** for the **InsufficientFundsException** caught in the **newMonth** method in class **Bank**? What is the call stack when that **throw** takes place?

7-10   Find all the **Bank** customer inputs that might cause an **InsufficientFundsException** to be thrown and caught in **processTransactionsForAccount** and show the call stack at the moment of the **throw**.

The following exercises ask you to complete the error handling in Juno version 7. Part of what you will learn in these exercises is how difficult it is to pay attention to all the bad things that might happen in an application. At each place where you add or modify code for error detection and recovery, provide a comment flagged with the string **EEE** like this:

```
// EEE describe your change
```

so that it's easy to find your work. You will discover that we have already done this where we've begun to add error checking (for example, in **TypeCommand.java**). Use the exceptions already defined or new ones we may ask you to write.

7-11   Run Juno version 7 and experiment systematically, trying to break the program. Each time you succeed, write a short input script (complete with Juno comments) that demonstrates the error. Save all these scripts, so that you can use them for testing as you fix Juno so that it handles each error you know about. (Some of the exercises that follow discuss these errors, so don't read ahead until you have looked for them yourself.)

7-12   (*) When a user (other than root) who has not registered tries to log in, Juno crashes. If you have not already constructed an input script demonstrating this error, do so now. Then correct this behavior.

7-13   (*) The current version of **doIt** in class **TypeCommand** detects and deals with a nonexistent **JFile** by catching a **NullPointerException**. Redesign this part of the code by declaring class **JFileNotFoundException** (extending **JunoException**) whose constructor takes the filename as a parameter and constructs a suitable message. Throw an instance of this class from **retrieveJFile** in class **Directory** when appropriate. The **interpret** method in **Shell** will catch it (as a **JunoException**), so you need not catch it or a **NullPointerException** in **TypeCommand** – or in **ListCommand** or in any other place that hopes to find a **JFile**. The error message should resemble as closely as possible the one issued by the system on which you are developing Juno.

7-14   Juno allows **newfile** and **mkdir** to overwrite an existing **JFile**. Make Juno more user friendly by having the **JFile** constructor throw a **JFileFoundException** when the **JFile** being constructed already exists. That will force a Juno user to use **remove** or **rmdir** if necessary before using **newfile** or **mkdir**.

7-15   Observe that the system crashes if you try to **list** something that is not a **Directory**. Correct this behavior by declaring, throwing, and catching a suitable **JunoException**. (Hint: Look at how we solved a similar problem in **TypeCommand**.)

7-16   Carefully go through each **ShellCommand** to add error handling. (Some of this work is spelled out in previous exercises.)

7-17   Replace the test for a **null commandObject** in the **Shell interpret** method with a **throw** and **catch** of a suitable **JunoException**, which you may have to invent. Which design is better, the old one with the **if** test or the new one with an exception?

7-18   (*) Add Juno password selection to **register** in class **LoginInterpreter** and password query when a user logs in to Juno. The user should not type her password on either the registration or the login line. The **register** method should prompt for the user's password and then ask to have it typed a second time for confirmation. Ordinary login should prompt for the password. Reporting a failed login is tricky. System security requires that the error message provide no information. Each of these errors should generate the single message "sorry":

- trying to log in as a nonexistent user, with any password (Juno should prompt for a password even if it knows the user does not exist.)
- trying to log in with a correct login name but the wrong password

On most systems, a password will not appear on the screen when you type it. Unfortunately, there is no easy way to make Juno behave that way in command-line mode.

Your implementation should add a password field to **User** instances and throw a suitable **JunoException** if someone tries to log in with an incorrect password. Class **RumpelstiltskinDemo** (Example 7-1) suggests a design for this functionality that avoids the need for a public **getPassword** method in the **User** class.

Remember that **User** root needs a password too. Where will you set it?

7-19   Write the Juno command **chown newowner filename** that changes the owner of a **JFile**. Only the owner of a file should be able to change its ownership, essentially giving the file to another **User**.

7-20   Arrange for Juno's files to have access permissions, so that it is possible to mark a file as readable or unreadable, writable or unwritable. You will have to decide exactly what these terms mean and provide Juno commands to change a file from unreadable (or unwritable) to readable (or writable) and back. You may add several fields to **JFile** objects, or one new field holding an instance of the **Permissions** class (which you have designed).

7-21   How much of Juno code is for error handling? Answering this question is a lot easier if you've followed our earlier suggestion and flagged all lines that do error checking with comments of the form **// EEE**. Then you can automatically count these with commands that find and count lines in files. In Unix those commands are **grep** and **wc**. For example,

```
% grep "EEE" Shell.java | wc
```

will give a count of all lines containing the pattern "EEE" in the file **Shell.java**. We can do this for all Java source files in our directory with

```
% grep "EEE" *.java | wc
```

In the next chapter you will learn enough to write **wc** and **grep** both as standalone applications and in Juno. Then you will have those tools to use on any system.

EStore exercises

7-22   Add error handling where appropriate in the **EStore** application.

7-23   Arrange for **EStore** customers to have passwords. Follow the design sketched in Exercise 7-18.

Chapter 8

Strings

We've dealt with strings regularly since Chapter 1 without thinking too hard about what they are, learning pieces of the API from time to time, content just to use them correctly in our programs. But in order to do more sophisticated things with strings, and in order to become more expert programmers, we need to learn more about them. Now is the time. In this chapter we will:

- Study the **String** API and its implementation
- Learn about characters and internationalization
- Learn to use the **StringBuffer** class when we must process strings efficiently
- Learn about parsing strings using static methods in class **String** and the wrapper classes for primitive numerical types

Our conceptual model for a string is a finite sequence of characters. In everyday written English, we specify a string by surrounding its characters with quotation marks:

```
"spot"    // a string of four characters
"post"    // a different string with the same characters
"Dewey, Cheatham and Howe" // punctuation marks and blanks count
""        // a string of zero characters (the empty string)
```

That convention lets us distinguish between the characters that make up the string and the *meaning* of the words those characters represent; strings have no meaning.

In Java, a string is an object: an instance of class **String**. We declare variables of type **String** just as we declare variables of any other reference type:

```
String bankName;
```

If **bankName** is an instance variable, its value is **null** (**null** is not the same as the empty string!).

String.java

Our usual practice when learning a new programming concept has been to see it in an example, study the API, and then learn the implementation. We've used strings in all our examples. For variety, we'll study the API and the implementation together.

One problem with that strategy is the fact that Java is a living application.[1] So the version of **String.java** in the library as we write this may not be the one that you are working with. We shall study version 1.150 (December 3, 2001), which was distributed with J2SE version 1.4. We encourage you to find the source code for **String.java** in the Java distribution that you are using and compare it with this one.

Of the 2351 lines in this version of **String.java**, 1487 are comments and 108 are blank. Thus only 2351-1487-108=756 lines contain "real Java". Those proportions may surprise you. Beginning programmers (and many advanced ones) do not comment their code as much as they should. The first six lines contain version information and a copyright notice[2]:

```
/*
 * @(#)String.java          1.150 01/12/03
 *
 * Copyright 2002 Sun Microsystems, Inc. All rights reserved.
 * SUN PROPRIETARY/CONFIDENTIAL. Use is subject to license
 * terms.
 */
```

The javadoc comments preceding the class declaration and the similar comments preceding each public method generate the Web pages your browser interprets when you visit the online documentation. For the **String** class, that's

```
/**
 * The <code>String</code> class represents character strings. All
 * string literals in Java programs, such as <code>"abc"</code>, are
 * implemented as instances of this class.
 * <p>
 * Strings are constant; their values cannot be changed after they
 * are created. String buffers support mutable strings.
 * Because String objects are immutable they can be shared. For example:
 * <p><blockquote><pre>
 *     String str = "abc";
 * </pre></blockquote><p>
 * is equivalent to:
 * <p><blockquote><pre>
 *     char data[] = {'a', 'b', 'c'};
 *     String str = new String(data);
```

---

[1] According to John Zukowski, the number of classes and interfaces in the standard edition of the Java platform grew from 212 in version 1.0 to 504, 1781, 2130, and to 2738 in version 1.4.
[2] The license allows us to reprint portions of this file here so long as we keep the copyright notice.

```
*  </pre></blockquote><p>
*  Here are some more examples of how strings can be used:
*  <p><blockquote><pre>
*      System.out.println("abc");
*      String cde = "cde";
*      System.out.println("abc" + cde);
*      String c = "abc".substring(2,3);
*      String d = cde.substring(1, 2);
*  </pre></blockquote>
*  <p>
*  The class <code>String</code> includes methods for examining
*  individual characters of the sequence, for comparing strings, for
*  searching strings, for extracting substrings, and for creating a
*  copy of a string with all characters translated to uppercase or to
*  lowercase. Case mapping relies heavily on the information provided
*  by the Unicode Consortium's Unicode 3.0 specification. The
*  specification's UnicodeData.txt and SpecialCasing.txt files are
*  used extensively to provide case mapping.
*  <p>
*  The Java language provides special support for the string
*  concatentation³ operator ( + ), and for conversion of
*  other objects to strings. String concatenation is implemented
*  through the <code>StringBuffer</code> class and its
*  <code>append</code> method.
*  String conversions are implemented through the method
*  <code>toString</code>, defined  by <code>Object</code> and
*  inherited by all classes in Java. For additional information on
*  string concatenation and conversion, see Gosling, Joy, and Steele,
*  <i>The Java Language Specification</i>.
*
*  @author Lee Boynton
*  @author Arthur van Hoff
*  @version 1.150, 01/12/03
...
*/
```

The embedded HTML formatting commands make these comments hard to read in the source code. Figure 8-1 shows what they look like when displayed in a browser.

---

[3] The misspelling is in the source file. We reported the bug to Sun, where it has been entered into their internal bug-tracking system with the assigned Bug Id: 4635092. The state of the bug can be monitored via the The Java Developer Connection Bug Parade at `http://developer.java.sun.com/developer/bugParade/index.jshtml`. Is it still there in the version of Java on your computer?

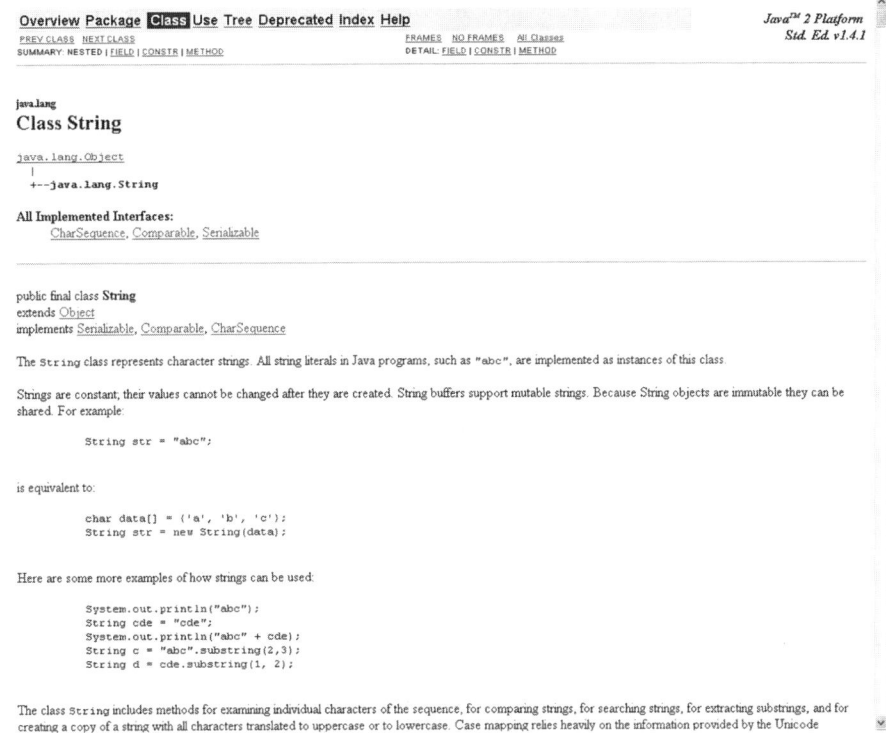

Figure 8-1: A javadoc fragment for String

The class declaration itself begins with the header

```
public final class String
     implements java.io.Serializable, Comparable, CharSequence
{
```

The Java keyword **final** means that this class may not be subclassed.[4] We will see what **implements java.io.Serializable** means in the next chapter. Declaring that **String** implements the **Comparable** interface means that you will find a **compareTo** method for comparing this **String** to other objects. Likewise, declaring that **String** implements the **CharSequence** interface means that we will find **charAt**, **length**, **subsequence**, and **toString** methods. We will study interfaces later too, in Chapter 10.

---

[4] The keyword **final** has other uses too. A **final** method may not be overridden in a subclass. The value of a **final** field may not be changed.

Each **String** object has three instance variables in which we are interested[5]:

- **private char[] value** – Java represents the actual contents of a **String** internally as an array of characters. That's no surprise. It's the natural way to think of a **String**.
- **private int count** – the number of characters in the array.
- **private int offset** – the first index (in **value**) used for a character in this **String**. As you read through the parts of **String.java** we will cover here, just assume **offset** is always 0. Pretend it's not there. Then you can also pretend that **count** is just **value.length**.

This code honors the convention that private fields hold the data that capture the object's state. Public methods access that data. For example, the **length**[6] method simply returns the value stored in the **count** variable[7]:

```
public int length()  {
    return count;
}
```

String Constructors

Java allows us to invoke a constructor for a **String** without explicitly using the keyword **new** by quoting the characters we want in the string[8]:

bankName = "Dewey, Cheatham and Howe";

That convenience sometimes confuses beginning programmers, because it suggests that strings are like **int**s: primitive types rather than objects. But they are not. A **String** is a full-fledged object in Java: We work with **String**s by sending them messages.

The **String** class has several explicit constructors as well. For example, we can construct a new **String** by making a copy of another:

String alias = new String(bankName);

---

[5] There are others, used mainly for making the **String** operations run faster, but we can safely ignore them here.

[6] If we were designing **String.java**, we might choose to call this method **getLength**.

[7] If we actually use every location in value to store a **char**, then **count** is just **value.length** and so is redundant. But the **offset** variable that we are ignoring in our discussion tells us that the implementor may want to use some part of the value array for other purposes.

[8] The literal truth is complicated and confusing at this stage of your programming career. You will not go wrong if you think of this code as saying something like

```
bankName = new String( with characters "Dewey, Cheatham and Howe" );
```

We can also construct a **String** by passing a constructor an explicit character array:

```
char[] carray = {'y', 'e', 's', '!'};
String certainly = new String(carray);
```

Here is the code for that constructor:

```
public String(char[] value)
{
    this.count = value.length;
    this.value = new char[count];
    System.arraycopy(value, 0, this.value, 0, count);
}
```

Note that the code *copies* the contents of the argument array to the **value** field after creating a new array of the necessary size. Replacing the last two lines by **this.value = value** would be a serious error, for then the **value** field would no longer be effectively private. The program that invoked this constructor would have direct access to it. Second, the copying is done with the static **arraycopy** method from the **System** class. The loop

```
for (int i = 0; i < count; i++ ) {
    this.value[i] = value[i];
}
```

would do exactly the same job, but less efficiently.

Getting at the Characters in a String

Because the **value** field inside the **bankName String** instance is private, clients cannot see the characters in it by asking about **bankName.value[i]**. But the **String** API does allow you to see those characters by sending **charAt** messages. For example, when **bankName** has value "Dewey, Cheatham and Howe"

- **bankName.charAt(0)** returns the character **'D'**,
- **bankName.charAt(5)** returns the character **','**.
- **bankName.charAt(100)** throws a **StringIndexOutOfBoundsException**

The implementation of **charAt** is just what you would expect:

```
public char charAt(int index)
{
    if ((index < 0) || (index >= count)) {
        throw new StringIndexOutOfBoundsException(index);
    }
    return value[index + offset]; // think "offset = 0"
}
```

Note that the constructor for the **StringIndexOutOfBoundsException** thrown when the request is unreasonable accepts the value of the faulty index as an argument so that when this exception is caught, that value is available for error reporting.[9]

The **String** API also allows a client to search for a character in a **String**.

- **bankName.indexOf('e')** returns 1   // since indexing is 0 based
- **bankName.indexOf('e', 6)** returns 9 // this search starts at index 6
- **bankName.indexOf('x')** returns -1   // signals failure.

What Are Characters?

Strings are composed of characters, and we have been using characters and character constants throughout the book, but we have been a little vague about what a character is. To begin with, think of a character as a letter of the alphabet, or, more generally, what we can enter at the keyboard of a computer, so that digits and punctuation marks are characters too. We know characters can be stored in Java variables of the primitive type **char**, and that we write a character literal in a Java program using single quotes: **'e'** or **' '**.

Some characters are hard to represent literally. The Enter or Return key on our keyboard represents a character. Because there is no letter of the alphabet for that key, the designers of Java have borrowed a construction from the C programming language, using the backslash (\) as an *escape character*. Thus **'\n'** represents the newline character,[10] so the **String "Hello,\nworld"** would be printed this way:

```
Hello,
world
```

The length of **"Hello,\nworld"** is 12, not 13.

There are several other uses for the escape character. The characters **'\b'** and **'\t'** represent a backspace and a tab, respectively. And you can use the escape character when you need a quotation mark in a **String** literal. For example:

```
System.out.println("She said, \"Good morning!\"");
```

would print

```
She said, "Good morning!"
```

---

[9] The method header for **charAt** does not need a **throws StringIndexOutOfBoundsException** clause. That is one of the exceptions the JVM may throw whenever necessary – even when a caller may not know that might happen. Those exceptions are in fact the ones that extend **RuntimeException**.

[10] This statement is not strictly true. The character (or characters) used to represent the creation of a new line of text may depend on the system on which Java is running. But '\n' works on Windows and on Unix.

If you want to use the escape character itself in a **String** literal, you must escape it.

```
System.out.println("The escape character in Java is '\\'.");
```

would print

The escape character in Java is '\'.

Characters are represented internally in Java as integers. Java respects the convention that integers between 0 and 255 represent the ASCII[11] characters. They include the ordinary letters 'A'–'Z' with values 65–90, 'a'–'z' with values 97–122, the digits '0'–'9' with values 48–57, and the various punctuation marks. There are also unprintable characters. For example, the character with ASCII value 7 is the bell.

```
System.out.println('\007');
```

will ring the bell on your terminal.[12] This syntax suggests that you can use the escape character to specify a character by its numerical value. That is true – just remember to use base 8 rather than base 10. In base 8, ASCII 'a' is 101, ASCII 'A' is 141, and you can convert lower- to uppercase letters by adding 40 (base 8) to their ASCII values. These details used to take up lots of time in introductory programming courses. They have become less central since modern languages like Java have made it possible to write most programs without knowing them.

Class **EscapeDemo** (Example 8-1) illustrates the use of the escape character.

In fact, the Java character set goes beyond ASCII; 256 characters are not enough when you want to make computer programs truly international. There must be a way to represent the characters used to write Chinese and Japanese, Arabic and Hebrew. Java supports the *Unicode* character set, in which characters are specified by integers in the range 0–$(2^{16} - 1)$. For example, the character **'\u0500'** is the Hebrew aleph (א). The numbers used to specify Unicode characters are usually written in *hexadecimal* (base 16) notation.

Class **Character** provides many static methods for manipulating **char**s. Among them you will find

```
public static int getNumericValue(char ch)
public static boolean isLetterOrDigit(char ch)
public static char toUpperCase(char ch)
```

Their names tell you what they do. You can find the rest by consulting the API.

Testing Strings for equality

In Chapter 5 we observed that the **String** class overrides the **equals** method in class **Object** in order to implement the idea that two **String** objects are equal if

---

[11] American Society for Computer Information Interchange.
[12] Nowadays the bell is more like a faint beep.

they contain the same characters in the same order, whether or not they are the same object.

Here is the code from **String.java** that implements the **equals** method:

```
public boolean equals(Object anObject) {
    if (this == anObject) {
        return true;
    }
    if (anObject instanceof String) {
        String anotherString = (String)anObject;
        int n = count;
        if (n == anotherString.count) {
            char v1[] = value;
            char v2[] = anotherString.value;
            int i = offset;
            int j = anotherString.offset;
            while (n-- != 0) {
                if (v1[i++] != v2[j++])
                    return false;
            }
            return true;
        }
    }
    return false;
}
```

The first **if** statement says that when we ask a **String** whether or not it's **equal** to itself, the answer is obviously "yes."

The signature in the method header shows that we can ask a **String** if it is equal to another **Object** that may or may not be a **String**. Of course the answer will be **false** if it's not. The code in the second **if** statement covers that case, using the Java keyword **instanceof**. When the test on that line fails, control passes to the **return false** statement at the end of the method.[13] In general

```
anObject instanceof AClass
```

---

[13] In this code it is hard to find the place where the **if(...)** **{...}** block ends, because that block is so long. The Java source would have been easier to read if the test had been reversed:

```
if ( !(anObject instanceof String) )
    return false;
// continue with existing code currently in the if block.
```

evaluates to **true** when **anObject** is an instance of any subclass of **AClass**, and to **false** otherwise.[14] In this case (**anObject instanceof String**) will be true only when **anObject** is actually a **String**, because the **String** class is final and so can have no subclasses. The body of that second **if** statement does the actual character-by-character comparison of the character arrays in the two strings, provided they have the same length. Note that the private fields of **anotherString** are available here even though this **String** is a different **String**. Other than that, none of this code is at all object oriented. It would look exactly the same in C. Carefully crafting loops like this used to be an important part of introductory programming courses. Now it is often postponed until later in the curriculum, so that there is room to introduce more conceptual material earlier.

Comparing Strings

When you want to alphabetize a list of **String** objects, you must do more than test them for equality. You must compare them to see which comes first. You could do this yourself, a character at a time, using the fact that the integer values of the ASCII characters increase as you move through the alphabet.[15] But the operation is so common that the **String** API has a method that does just that job for you. **string0.compareTo(string1)** returns a negative integer if **string0** precedes **string1** in alphabetical order, 0 if they are **equal**, and a positive integer otherwise. For example,

"cake".compareTo("care") returns -7

because the strings differ first at index 2, and there 'r' is 7 letters further along in the alphabet than 'k'.

Here is the code for **compareTo**. You can see how much it resembles that for **equals**. The statement **return c1 - c2** is interesting: There you see character values subtracted just as if they were integers. And note how the last line handles the case in which one **String** is a prefix of the other. If all the characters match as far as the end of the shorter of the two, then they are the same only when they have the same length.

```
public int compareTo(String anotherString)
{
    int len1 = count;
    int len2 = anotherString.count;
    int n = Math.min(len1, len2);
    char v1[] = value;
    char v2[] = anotherString.value;
```

---

[14] We could have used an **instanceof** test instead of catching a **ClassCastException** in order to prevent an attempt to cash a check on an account that's not a **CheckingAccount** in our banking simulation.
[15] Alphabetizing strings of Unicode characters is trickier. Java helps with its support for internationalization. We will not address those issues in this book.

```
      int i = offset;
      int j = anotherString.offset;

      while (n-- != 0)  {
          char c1 = v1[i++];
          char c2 = v2[j++];
          if (c1 != c2)  {
              return c1 - c2;
          }
      }
      return len1 - len2;
}
```

Substrings

A *substring* is a piece of a string. The message expression

bankName.substring(<begin index>, <end index>)

returns the substring of **bankName** that starts at **<begin index>** and ends at **<end index>** - **1**. So the length of the substring is **<end index>** - **<begin index>**. For example,

bankName.substring(7, 12)

returns the **String "Cheat"**.

There are several **substring** methods, each with a different signature. A single argument in the **substring** message denotes the starting index; the substring returned extends from that index in the target string to the end of the target string.

bankName.substring(7)

returns the **String "Cheatham, and Howe"**.

There are also **indexOf** methods that allow you discover whether a **String** contains a particular substring, a **startsWith** method that tells you about the prefixes of a **String**, and a companion **endsWith** method to look for suffixes.

Methods that seem to change the contents of a String

Here are several examples of messages sent to a **String** that suggest that they change its contents:

- **bankName.toUpperCase()**[16] returns "DEWEY, CHEATHAM AND HOWE"
- **bankName.replace('e', 'x')** returns "Dxwxy, Chxatham and Howx"
- **bankName.concat("!")** returns "Dewey, Cheatham and Howe!"

---

[16] **toUpperCase** illustrates some of the difficulties you encounter with internationalization. If you check the source code you will find that half of it is a special case to handle Turkish!

In fact, **bankName** itself is unchanged after each of these messages because each of the corresponding methods creates a brand new **String** and returns it.

   Another useful method that returns a new **String** is the one that trims leading and trailing white space:

" x y z \t\b".trim() returns "x y z"

Here is the code for **trim**:

```
public String trim()
{
    int len = count;
    int st = 0;
    int off = offset;   /* avoid getfield opcode */
    char[] val = value; /* avoid getfield opcode */

    while ((st < len) && (val[off + st] <= ' '))  {
        st++;
    }
    while ((st < len) && (val[off + len - 1] <= ' '))  {
        len--;
    }
    return ((st > 0)||(len < count))?substring(st, len) : this;
}
```

The integer variable **st** increases from 0 to skip over white space at the start of this **String**, where *white space* is any **char** whose integer value is less than that of the blank. That code relies on the fact that the ASCII ordering of characters puts tabs and newlines and backspaces before the blank. Other characters like the bell (**'\007'**) will count as white space too. The variable **len** decreases to skip over white space at the end of the **String**. The last line of code says

```
if there really is white space to trim
    return the appropriate substring of this
else
    return this
```

but it does so using the conditional expression we saw in Chapter 5.

   Here is the code for **substring**, to which **trim** has delegated its last task. If the client has requested a genuine substring (not the whole thing), then a **String** constructor is invoked and a new **String** is returned. This **String** does not change at all.

```
public String substring(int beginIndex, int endIndex)
{
    if (beginIndex < 0)  {
        throw new StringIndexOutOfBoundsException(
            beginIndex);
    }
    if (endIndex > count)  {
        throw new StringIndexOutOfBoundsException(
            endIndex);
    }
    if (beginIndex > endIndex)  {
        throw new StringIndexOutOfBoundsException(
            endIndex - beginIndex);
    }
    return ((beginIndex == 0) && (endIndex == count)) ?
            this :
            new String(offset + beginIndex,
                    endIndex - beginIndex, value);
}
```

More Methods

String has dozens of useful methods. Take some time now to browse the **String** API in your Java environment to learn about what kinds of things you can ask a **String** to do for you, so that you will know what to look for when you write programs that use strings.

StringBuffer

A **String** is constant. The methods we have studied that seem to change the contents of a **String** don't: They create and return new **String** objects with the changed contents. Because strings are *immutable*, building them up character by character can be very time consuming. For example, to read 2000 characters (about a page of typewritten text) from the standard input stream one character at a time, we might write

```
String result = "";

for( int i = 0; i < 2000; i++ ) {
    char ch = (char) System.in.read();
    result = result + ch; // result += ch
}
```

The bold concatenation in the last line of the loop body constructs a new value for **String result** *2000 times*. That's inefficient. Each time a new **String** is constructed, all the characters accumulated so far need to be copied into it. A **StringBuffer** will help us improve the performance of our program.

The StringBuffer API

A **StringBuffer** is a *mutable* sequence of characters. Both its contents and its length can change: It's like an **ArrayList** designed to handle characters. Because it can grow, we can append characters to it at will. And when we're done, we can (inexpensively) convert it to a **String**. The code fragment above will run faster if we rewrite it this way:

```
StringBuffer strbuffer = new StringBuffer(2000);
for( int i = 0; i < 2000; i++ ) {
    char ch = (char) System.in.read();
    strbuffer.append(ch);
}
String result = strbuffer.toString();
```

The integer argument passed to the constructor is optional. We provide it here because we know in advance how many characters we will be adding. When we don't, we can just use the no-argument constructor. The message **append** simply appends its argument to the contents of the **StringBuffer** it is sent to. When we finally want a **String**, we send the **StringBuffer** a **toString** message, creating an immutable **String** just once.

Method **toString** in class **StringBuffer** delegates its task to the **String** constructor that accepts a **StringBuffer** argument:

```
public String toString()
{
    return new String(this);
}
```

StringBuffer Internals

We encourage you to read the implementation of **StringBuffer**, in the file **StringBuffer.java**, supplied with Sun's J2SE. We look at only fragments of it here. A **StringBuffer** maintains two instance variables (that we are interested in). They are analogous to the ones for **String**:

*   **char[] value**: we represent a string buffer as a character array; **value** contains the buffer's characters. That both strings and string buffers use the same representation means they can share their character sequences.
*   **int count**: the number of characters in the buffer.

As with strings, the *length* of a string buffer is simply the number of characters stored in it:

```
public synchronized¹⁷ int length()
{
    return count;
}
```

The **value** array in a **String** is just long enough to hold the characters that make up the **String**. But the **value** field in a **StringBuffer** may be longer. Its length is the buffer's *capacity* – the total number of character that could be stored:

```
public synchronized int capacity()
{
    return value.length;
}
```

It's important to keep capacity ahead of length. Private method **expandCapacity** is invoked when needed to make sure there is enough capacity to store characters; if there isn't, then it allocates a new larger array and copies the characters from the old one into the new one. Notice that **expandCapacity** adds more than it has to, to minimize repeated reallocations.

```
private void expandCapacity(int minimumCapacity)
{
    int newCapacity = (value.length + 1) * 2;
    if (newCapacity < 0) {
        newCapacity = Integer.MAX_VALUE;
    } else if (minimumCapacity > newCapacity) {
        newCapacity = minimumCapacity;
    }

    char newValue[] = new char[newCapacity];
    System.arraycopy(value, 0, newValue, 0, count);
    value = newValue;
    shared = false;
}
```

The **ArrayList** objects that we first encountered in Chapter 4 use a similar mechanism in order to grow when they need to.

Now we can see how the **StringBuffer append** method works. To put a new character into the buffer, first check to see if there's room. If there's not, expand the buffer. Then insert the new character:

---

¹⁷ Ignore the keyword **synchronized** until you study parallel programming, which is beyond the scope of this book in Java.

```
public synchronized StringBuffer append(String str)
{
    if (str == null) {
        str = String.valueOf(str);
    }

    int len = str.length();
    int newcount = count + len;
    if (newcount > value.length)
        expandCapacity(newcount);
    str.getChars(0, len, value, count);
    count = newcount;
    return this;
}
```

Soon we will see an application of **StringBuffer** technology in the Java library.

Semantics

Strings have no meaning. They are just sequences of characters. But we often want to express meaning with a **String**. We suspect that someone who writes "1001" wants to say something about the number 1001, not the sequence of characters 1, 0, 0, 1. Conversely, we often have a number in mind and want to write it down. We learned how to do that in elementary school. Often we learned so well that we find it hard to distinguish between a number and the characters we use to represent it. But in programming the distinction is important. The Java API provides tools for converting primitive types and objects to printable strings, and vice versa. We will look at some of them now.

Creating String Representations

To discover the **String** representation of an object, we send it a **toString** message. We saw in Chapter 5 that if the object's class has overridden the default **toString** in class **Object**, we may find the result useful. Now we can see how the **ArrayList** class and other collection classes implement **toString**. Here is the code from class **AbstractCollection** (a superclass of class **ArrayList**) that makes that happen. It uses a **StringBuffer** to collect the strings it is concatenating and turns that **StringBuffer** into a **String** when it's done.

```
public String toString()
{
    StringBuffer buf = new StringBuffer();
    Iterator e = iterator();
    buf.append("[");
```

```
        int maxIndex = size() - 1;
        for (int i = 0; i <= maxIndex; i++) {
            buf.append(String.valueOf(e.next()));
            if (i < maxIndex)
                buf.append(", ");
        }
        buf.append("]");
        return buf.toString();
    }
```

When you want the **String** representation of an **int**, you cannot send it a message, because it is not an object. Instead, use the **static valueOf** method in the **String** class:

```
String.valueOf(1001)
```

returns the **String "1001"**.

There are many **valueOf** methods, that different signatures, that you can use when you want the **String** representations for the primitive types **long**, **double**, ... and for **Object** itself. The last of these just delegates to **toString**:

```
public static String valueOf(Object obj)
{
    return (obj == null) ? "null" : obj.toString();
}
```

In fact, **String.valueOf(int)** delegates to **toString** too – in the **Integer** wrapper class for ints:

```
public static String valueOf(int i)
{
    return Integer.toString(i, 10);
}
```

This code correctly suggests that Java provides tools to find the **String** representations of integers in bases other than 10. You will find these **static** methods in the **Integer** class:

```
String toBinaryString(int)
String toHexString(int)
String toString(int, int)
        (toString(int, 2) is toBinaryString(int))
```

Making Meaning from Strings

There are also times when you need to reverse this transformation: You have the string "1001" and need to find its numerical value. The static `parseInt` method in the `Integer` class does that job:

```
int magicNumber = Integer.parseInt("1001");
```

If you try to parse a `String` that may not represent an integer, you should prepare to catch the appropriate exception:

```
try {
    int magicNumber = Integer.parseInt("trouble");
}
catch (NumberFormatException e) {
    // take corrective action
}
```

The `readInt` method in our `Terminal` class (Listing 8-1) does just that, sending itself a `readNonNullLine` message to collect the next line from the user, trimming leading and trailing blanks and then trying to convert that text into an integer:

```
public int readInt( String prompt )
{
    while( true ) {
        try {
            return Integer.
                parseInt(readNonNullLine( prompt ).trim());
        }
        catch (NumberFormatException e) {
            println( "Not an integer. Please try again." );
        }
    }
}
```

The Java API has more static methods for converting strings to numbers: integers in bases other than the default 10, and doubles. You can find them in classes `String`, `Integer`, and `Double` when you need them.

   If you are curious about the algorithms that convert strings to numbers and vice versa, you can read them in the Java API source. You will find that the central idea in the implementation of the `static` method `String.toString(int i, int radix)` is the one we used in Chapter 2 in our change-making program. Getting the surrounding details right is tricky.

Wrapper Classes

The class **Integer** is more than a repository for static methods dealing with the primitive type **int**. It has a constructor too, that creates an **Integer** object from its **int** argument. The public getter for that argument is the **valueOf** method. You need an **Integer** (rather than an **int**) when you want to store an integer in a **TreeMap** or an **ArrayList**, because those collections deal only with objects, not with primitive types.

Java comes with wrapper classes for all seven primitive types: **Integer** for **int**, **Double** for **double**, **Boolean** for **boolean**, **Short** for **short**, **Long** for **long**, **Byte** for **byte**, **Float** for **float**, and **Character** for **char**.

Summary

In this chapter we learned (at long last) how Java handles strings by reading some of the source code for the **String** class. Class **StringDemo** (Example 8.2) exercises the API. In the next chapter we take up another strategy for representing objects outside our programs: files.

Exercises

8-1   Create a text file for your journal for this chapter. Use your journal for questions that call for written answers and to record any observations about your work.

8-2   Find out where **String.java** lives in your environment, or find the latest version at Sun. Do you have the same version we discuss in this text? If not, see if you can discover any differences in the methods we discussed in this chapter.

8-3   Why can't method **indexOf(char)** in class **String** return 0 when the character is not present in the **String**? That would seem more natural than the −1 that the API specifies.

8-4   Find the code for method **toString** in class **String** and explain it.

8-5   In Exercise 7-18 we provided password protection in Juno by implementing a private **String** field in the **User** class, to hold a user's password. We'll make passwords more secure now, in several ways[18]:

• Passwords will have a minimum length

• Passwords must use a mix of alphabetic and non-alphabetic characters and must be of mixed case

---

[18] Many systems incorporate restrictions like these for passwords. If you have access to a Unix system, check the man page for the **passwd** command to see if any apply there.

- A user's password may not have a substring that's her login name or be a substring of her real name
- Passwords must be stored in encrypted form

That is much too much specialized functionality to put into class **User**. So we will declare class **Password** to encapsulate it and then replace the **String** password field in class **User** with a field of type **Password**. Listing 8-2 provides javadoc comments and stubs for the **Password** API. Complete it, including the unit test. Then install it in Juno.

To encrypt passwords, write method

```
private final String encrypt( String s )
```

and have the **Password** constructor save the encrypted password instead of the real password. Then the public **match** method tests **encrypt(guess)** against the stored value.

Your encryption algorithm can be as simple or as complicated as you like. You might just replace **'a'** with **'b'**, **'b'** with **'c'**, and so on.

Add the command **dc** to Juno 7. "dc" stands for "desk calculator".[19] Here is a sample **dc** session:

```
mars> dc
dc> 3 + 4
7.0
dc> 0.7 * 130.0
91.0
dc> 2   8
256.0
dc> x
... informative error message ...
dc> 4 x
... informative error message ...
dc> 4 +
... informative error message ...
dc> 4 + z
... informative error message ...
dc> 4 x
```

---

[19] The Unix operating system has a desk calculator. It uses reverse Polish rather than algebraic notation. What you are used to writing as "3+5" it wants with the syntax "3 5+". If you have access to a Unix system, play with **dc**.

```
... informative error message ...
dc> q
mars>
```

That is, **dc** loops forever, prompting for input. When it sees an arithmetic expression, it evaluates it and prints the result. Legal arithmetic expressions are expressions of the form

number operator number

where **number** is a floating point number and **operator** is one of **+ * - / ^**. The operator ^ stands for exponentiation. You may assume that the numbers and the operators are separated by blanks, so the pseudocode is easy:

```
loop forever
    prompt for and read a line from the Shell's console
    make a StringTokenizer for the line
    if the line is blank, continue
    if the first token starts with q, break
    try
        convert first and third tokens into doubles,
        find the operator in the second token
        switch on the operator to do the arithmetic
        print the result
    catch any errors and report them
```

Exponentiation is not an operator in Java. There's a **static** method in class **Math** that will do the job.

After you have written **DcCommand.java** but before you edit **ShellCommandTable.java** to install it in Juno, read the next exercise.

8-6   There is magic in the Juno 7 **ShellCommandTable** class that allows Juno to add new commands at run time. You no longer need to edit **fillTable**. Just make sure your **DcCommand.class** file is there when you start Juno, log in, and try the shell command **dc**. It will be there for you!

Read **ShellCommandTable.java** to figure out how the magic works – then write pseudocode for the **lookup** method. The hardest fragment to understand is probably

```
Class.forName(classname).newInstance();
```

Don't panic. Just remember that **Class** must be a class (because it begins with an uppercase letter) and look it up in the Java API. For more examples showing how a running Java program can find out about itself, see class **ReflectionDemo** (Example 8-3).

8-7   Improve **dc** so that it accepts input like "5+3", with no blanks separating the integer operands from the operator. You will have to replace the **StringTokenizer** with code that finds the operator in the input line and extracts the numbers that surround it. Remember to handle errors.

8-8   Write class **Palindrome**, whose **main** method tells the user whether the first command-line argument is the same when looked at backward. Here is sample behavior:

```
%> java Palindrome radar
yes
%> java Palindrome reader
no
```

Invent some long palindromes, or find some (the Web is a good place to look).

8-9   Improve **Palindrome** so that the test is case-insensitive and ignores punctuation, so that it correctly detects a famous palindrome :

```
%> java Palindrome "A man, a plan, a canal: panama!"
yes
```

8-10   My Aunt Tillie is odd and queer but certainly not peculiar. She likes beets but not vegetables. She likes object-oriented programming but not Java. (She does like C++). She just loves bookkeepers. Tillie's secret? She likes words with double letters. Write class **Tillie**, whose **main** method asks Tillie about the command-line arguments

```
%> java Tillie beets vegetables
beets        yes
vegetables   no
```

8-11   Improve **Tillie** so that she expresses the strength of her likes and dislikes:

```
%> java Tillie "Harry Potter" Hogwarts bookkeeper
Harry Potter   yes!!
Hogwarts       no
bookkeeper     yes!!!
```

8-12   My Uncle Abe likes words that contain two consecutive letters of the alphabet (as in his name). He's definitely fond of "definitely". Write versions of program **Abe** corresponding to the versions of **Tillie** in the two previous exercises, the first saying just "yes" or "no", the second expressing degrees of pleasure. You'd better make **Abe** case-insensitive from the start, else he won't like himself.

8-13   Write program **Convert** that accepts two integer command-line arguments **n** and **r** and prints the **String** representation of **n** three times: in base 2 (binary), base 16 (hexadecimal), and base **r**.

8-14   Modify the Juno **Shell** so that input lines can contain the escape character '\', with its usual Java meaning. Then you will be able to create multiline text files.

8-15   Rewrite **toString** in class **Dictionary** (Listing 4-8) so that it uses a **StringBuffer**.

Chapter 9

Files, Streams, and Persistence

In the applications we have worked with so far, any changes we made to data lived only for the life of a session. Each time we opened the bank with the command

```
%> java Bank
```

we started from scratch. There was no permanent record of the accounts we created and their balances. But who would put money in a bank that started fresh each morning? To be useful, programs must be able to store information in some relatively permanent form, so that it can be retrieved later.

You know about permanent storage from your work as a programmer. Your computer keeps the Java source code you write in files. You open a file in an editor, make some changes, and then save the file. If your system is properly maintained and backed up (you should do that for yourself if your system administrator doesn't), the new version of the file is available to you the next time you want to work on your program. The class files created by the Java compiler wait in your computer, ready to be interpreted by the JVM when you run your program. The HTML pages created by javadoc wait in your computer, ready to be interpreted by your browser when you want to study your documentation.

In this chapter we will study some of the classes in the Java API that you use when your Java program reads or writes information that's stored permanently somewhere.

Working with Files

We start with the file system. On Unix and in Windows systems (and in Juno), files are organized in a hierarchy. Before we can even consider the contents of a file, we need to be able to locate it in the file system. The Java class **File** helps with that task. An instance of the **File** class models the external properties of a file: its name, a path to it, its permissions.

One of the **File** constructors accepts the name of a file as its argument. For example, the statement

```
File myFile = new File( "myfile.txt" );
```

creates a **File** object in our Java program, representing a file named "myfile.txt" in the current working directory.[1] Our program is free to create such a **File** object whether

---

[1] That's the current working directory of the real system running Java. You're not in Juno now!

or not there is a real file with that name. Once we have that object, we can send it a message to find out whether there is such a file. The expression

myFile.exists()

returns **true** if the file exists and **false** otherwise – the **exists** method in class **File** gets that information from the operating system. If no such file exists, we can ask that an empty one be created (in the current working directory) by sending the message

myFile.createNewFile();

There are dozens of methods in the **File** API for asking about

- whether the file is readable or writable
- whether it is a directory
- when it was last modified
- who is its parent in the file hierarchy
- ... and other useful information[2]

But the **File** API has no methods that deal with the *contents* of files. For that, we need another abstraction.

Working with Text Files

Programs usually read files starting at the beginning and working through to the end. That's how the **javac** compiler treats your Java source code. It's how the bank application deals with the input script **bank.in** when it's invoked with I/O redirection this way:

%> java Bank < bank.in

And in most cases, a program that writes a file does so by appending things to what is there, until the writing is done. The "read from start to finish, write new data at the end" model is called *sequential access*.[3]

To read a file sequentially, you create a **FileReader** object, starting either with a **File** object:

FileReader inStream = new FileReader(myFile);

---

[2] You can recognize here methods analogous to some we built into the **JFile** class in Juno.
[3] Your word processor does not use sequential access. It looks at the whole file all at once, allowing you to move around in it at will to make changes wherever you please.

or directly from the name of the file:

```
FileReader inStream = new FileReader( "myfile.txt" );
```

In either case, if no such file exists, then the constructor throws a
FileNotFoundException. We will see later in this chapter why we choose to call
the **FileReader** variable **inStream**.

A **FileReader** is like an **Iterator** for the contents of the file: You send it **read**
messages repeatedly; each such message returns the next character from the file.

To write to a file, you need a **FileWriter** object, which is similarly constructed.

Program **Copy1** (Listing 9-1) uses a **FileReader** and a **FileWriter** to copy the
contents of one text file to another[4]:

```
%> java Copy1 myfile.txt yourfile.txt
```

If **yourfile.txt** doesn't exist, the program will create it. If it does exist, the old
contents will be lost. Pseudocode for the **main** method in **Copy1** is straightforward:

```
create FileReader inStream for the input file
create FileWriter outStream for the output file
while there are unread characters in the input file
    read a character from inStream
    write the character to outStream
close both streams once the job is done
```

The core of the program is the **while** loop:

```
16    private static final int EOF = -1;

28    int ch;

36    while ((ch = inStream.read()) != EOF) {
37        outStream.write( ch );
38    }
```

The **read** method in class **FileReader** returns the integer value of the next character
in the file. The code on line 36 assigns that value to the integer variable **ch** and checks
to see whether that value is −1, which is the integer returned by **read** when it has
reached the end of the file and there is nothing to read. We store the magic number −1
in the **final static** variable **EOF** (a common abbreviation for "end of file") and then
use that variable rather than the number itself in the **while** loop test. That makes the
program easier to understand. The body of the loop simply asks the **FileWriter** to
write the character we have just read.

---

[4] That's the job of the **cp** command in Unix, the **copy** command in DOS, and drag-and-drop with your mouse
in Windows.

Because we use a **FileReader** and a **FileWriter** to get and put characters, our program works whatever the implementation details of the underlying file system. We don't know and don't care whether it thinks characters are old 8-bit ASCII or new 16-bit Unicode. **read** always returns an integer representing a Unicode character, and **write** always takes such an integer as its argument.

Although the three-line **while** loop does all the work, the program is 64 lines long. That's because input/output programming is error prone. Because the program interacts with the operating system outside the Java environment, many things can go wrong. A good program must guard against them. So we nest the simple **while** loop inside a **try** block followed by three **catch**es:

```
30      try {
31          // open the files
32          inStream  = new FileReader( args[0] );
33          outStream = new FileWriter( args[1] );
34
35          // copy
36          while ((ch = inStream.read()) != EOF) {
37              outStream.write( ch );
38          }
39      }
40      catch (IndexOutOfBoundsException e) {
41          System.err.println(
42              "usage: java Copy1 sourcefile targetfile" );
43      }
44      catch (FileNotFoundException e) {
45          System.err.println( e ); // rely on e's toString()
46      }
47      catch (IOException e) {
48          System.err.println( e );
49      }
```

An **IndexOutOfBoundsException** will be thrown on line 32 or 33 and caught on line 40 if the user fails to supply the name of the input and output files.

A **FileNotFoundException** will be thrown from those same lines and caught on line 44 if one of the streams can't be created, because the input file doesn't exist or can't be read or the output file can't be written. Line 45 in the **catch** block relies on the **toString** method in the **FileNotFoundException** class to provide a useful error message.

If anything else unexpected goes wrong during the reading and the writing, an **IOException** will be thrown, to be caught on line 47. The **catch** block again relies on **toString**.

We're not done yet. When you *open* a file (by creating a **FileReader** or a **FileWriter**), you ask the operating system to give your program access to that file. Then it's your responsibility to tell the operating system when you are done. You do that by *closing* the file. If you don't, it may think you still want the file even after your program is over. In that case, it might not let anyone else look at it. Some operating systems limit the number of files you may have open at any one time. So it's important to close files when you are done with them. Moreover, you want to be sure to close the files whether or not an error occurred during the copy. We use a **finally** following the **try**/**catch** to make sure this happens.[5] Recall that if in your code you

```
try {
        // something
}
catch ( SomeException e ) {
        // deal with the error condition
}
finally {
        // clean up in either case
}
```

then code in the **finally** block will execute *whether or not an exception has been thrown or caught.* Here is the rest of main:

```
50    finally { // close the files
51        try {
52            if (inStream != null) {
53                inStream.close();
54            }
55        }
56        catch (Exception e) {
57            System.err.println(
                    "Unable to close input stream.");
58        }
59        try {
60            if (outStream != null) {
61                outStream.close();
62            }
63        }
64        catch (Exception e) {
65            System.err.println(
                    "Unable to close output stream.");
66        }
67    }
```

---

[5] We discussed **finally** in Chapter 7 when we studied exception handling, but this is the first time we have needed it.

Lines 53 and 61 close the input and output streams. Those lines must themselves be protected by **try**/**catch** because the attempt to close a file may itself throw an **Exception**. The **if** test in each case prevents a **NullPointerException** should either stream not be open.

What lessons can we learn from this example?

- In theory, file I/O is simple: Open a reader or a writer and send it a **read** or a **write** message.
- In practice,[6] file I/O is messy and requires lots of error handling.
- Borrow code from a working I/O program when your program must read from or write to a file. Someone else (perhaps you yourself once upon a time) will have gotten the details right.

Buffering Character Streams

The simple read-a-character, write-a-character loop

```
36    while ((ch = inStream.read()) != EOF) {
37        outStream.write( ch );
38    }
```

may not be the most efficient way to copy text from one file to another. Each **read** message sent to the **FileReader inStream** may cause the JVM to ask the underlying operating system for the next character. Calls from the JVM to the operating system are often time consuming, so it is wise to get more than one character from each such call. A **BufferedReader** can do that, asking the system for a chunk of text that it then stores in its own buffer. Its **read** method takes its characters from this buffer. When the buffer is depleted, the **BufferedReader** quietly fills it with another chunk of text from the underlying file. Further efficiency and cleaner programs follow from the use of the **BufferedReader readLine** method, which returns a whole line of text. Java also provides a **BufferedWriter**, which buffers output and writes it out in chunks to the underlying file system.

Program **Copy2** (Listing 9-2) uses both a **BufferedReader** and a **BufferedWriter** to do the same job as **Copy1**. Here are the places where it differs from **Copy1**:

```
24    BufferedReader inStream  = null;
25    BufferedWriter outStream = null;
26    String line;
```

---

[6] Here are two amusing observations, with the best references we have been able to find for them:

"Furthermore, the gap between theory and practice in practice is much larger than the gap between theory and practice in theory." – Dr. Jeff Case

"In theory, there is no difference between theory and practice. In practice, there is no relationship between theory and practice." – Grant Gainey

```
27
28     try {
29         // open the files
30         inStream =
               new BufferedReader(new FileReader(args[0]));
31         outStream =
               new BufferedWriter(new FileWriter(args[1]));
32
33         // copy
34         while ((line = inStream.readLine()) != null) {
35             outStream.write( line );
36             outStream.newLine();
37         }
38     }
```

Lines 30 and 31 wrap the **FileReader** and **FileWriter** we used in **Copy1** with a **BufferedReader** and **BufferedWriter**, respectively. On line 34 the **BufferedReader readLine** method returns the next line in the file, as a **String**, signaling the end of the file by returning the **null String**.[7] Line 35 writes this **String** to the output file. Because the **String** returned by **readLine** does not include the newline at the end of the line, we insert the (system-dependent) line separator ourselves by sending a **newLine** message.

The error handling in **Copy2** is essentially the same as in **Copy1**.

Class Terminal

We know enough now to look at more of the code (introduced in Chapter 8 as Listing 8-1 for the **Terminal** objects we have been using all along.

Output is easy. A **Terminal** delegates that work to **System.out** or to **System.err**:

```
public void println( String str )
{
    System.out.println( str );
}


public void errPrint( String str )
{
    System.err.print( str );
}
```

---

[7] Remember that the **null String** is not the same as the empty **String** "".

A **Terminal** can print primitive types too, and arbitrary objects, by providing **println** methods with different signatures. Those methods also delegate to **System.out** and **System.err**.

If we used a **Terminal** only for output to the screen, it would hardly be worth the trouble of creating one just for this simple delegation. We would use **System.out** and **System.err** in our programs instead. The primary function of a **Terminal** is to make input easy. In general, input is harder than output. When your program needs to write, you are in control: You know what you want to say. When your program needs to read, you are at the mercy of your user and must work much harder to understand what he or she says. The **Terminal** class provides many **read*** methods that wrap **System.in** in order to collect input from the user and parse it before returning it. All of those methods parse a line that has been read from standard input.

```java
private BufferedReader in =
    new BufferedReader(new FileReader(FileDescriptor.in));
```

Terminal uses a **BufferedReader** constructed from **System.in** (hidden behind **FileDescriptor.in**) to get a whole line of text from the user at the keyboard when the **readLine** method asks for it.

```java
public String readLine( String prompt )
{
    printPrompt(prompt);
    try {
        String line = in.readLine();
        if (echo) {
            println(line);
        }
        return line;
    }
    catch (IOException e) {
        return null;
    }
}
```

The **println(line)** echoes that input to the output stream if the **Terminal** has been configured to do so.

Before reading the input, the **Terminal** prints the prompt passed to **readLine** by sending itself the **printPrompt** message. That invokes the code

```java
private void printPrompt( String prompt )
{
    print( prompt );
    System.out.flush();
}
```

which sends the prompt to **System.out** with a **print** message. There's no carriage return, so that the cursor waits on the current line after the prompt.

Because most output streams are buffered, you must *flush* them when you want to be sure the characters currently in the buffer are sent to their final destination immediately. **System.out.flush()** does that for the prompt, which would be useless if we let the JVM wait for input or more output before printing it.

Filters

When we look at the pattern of program **Copy2**, we can see how that pattern helps us build many useful file-manipulation tools. It is easy to add one line to the loop

```
while there is more text
    read aLine
    write aLine
```

to produce a more general *filter*:

```
while there is more text
    read aLine
    modify aLine
    write aLine
```

For example, if you want to convert all the characters in a file to uppercase, you could use the **Copy2** program, replacing the line

```
outStream.write( line );
```

with

```
line = line.toUpperCase();
outStream.write( line );
```

or simply with

```
outStream.write( line.toUpperCase() );
```

If you want to add line numbers to a file, you could replace that line with

```
outStream.write( ++lineNumber + " " + line );
```

where **lineNumber** is an integer variable initialized to 0.

In the exercises, we will ask you to write some other useful filters.

Reading Characters from a File into a String

If you want to read the characters from a file and put them into a **String**, rather than write them to another file, you can use the **StringBuffer** class we studied in Chapter 8. The code would look something like this[8]:

```
BufferedReader inStream =
    new BufferedReader( new FileReader( "myfile.txt" ) );
StringBuffer stringbuff = new StringBuffer();
String line;

while ((line = inStream.readLine()) != null) {
    stringbuff.append( line ).append( "\n" );
}
inStream.close();
String result = stringbuff.toString();
```

Another way that makes the code look even more like that for **copy** is to use a **StringWriter** to write to a **String** instead of the **BufferedWriter** that writes to a file.

```
BufferedReader inStream =
    new BufferedReader( new FileReader( "myfile.txt" ) );
Writer outStream = new StringWriter();
String line;

while ((line = inStream.readLine()) != null) {
    outStream.write( line );
    outStream.write( "\n" );
}
inStream.close();
outStream.close();
String result = outStream.toString();
```

The Stream Abstraction

The second example above is our introduction to the stream abstraction. A *stream* models data that occur in a sequence that can be read or written only in proper order. An input stream captures the notion of a stream from which we can read things. An output stream captures the notion of a stream to which we can write things. There are

---

[8] Of course, real code to do this job would require exception handling.

many different kinds of streams, which are characterized in several dimensions. The first distinction we have already seen:

- streams for input (read from these)
- streams for output (write to these)

A second distinction is the external data source (source or sink) the stream is connected to:

- **FileReader** and **FileWriter** read from and write to files (of course).
- **BufferedReader** and **BufferedWriter** can be used in conjunction with file readers to read from and write to files with buffered input and output.
- **StringReader** and **StringWriter** read from and write to **Strings** (of course).

Streams may even be connected to URLs, for reading and writing data across the Internet.

Finally, different kinds of streams handle different kinds of data. There are streams (or methods) for

- characters
- lines
- zipped (compressed) files
- objects
- bytes

Streams show polymorphism at work. Because input (output) streams are all subclasses of the abstract class **Reader** (**Writer**), we can often write programs that read from and write to streams without having to know what kinds of objects are being read or written, or where those objects are coming from or going to. We simply send a **read** message to read from a **Reader** and a **write** message to write to a **Writer**. It is up to the concrete subclasses to implement **read** and **write** appropriately.

Persistent Objects: Serializing the Bank

Although we have concentrated so far on files of text suitable for human eyes, we know there are other kinds.[9] In fact, Java provides tools that allow a program to read and write files containing objects. We can use those tools to save the state of a **Bank** when we shut it down, and restore the state the next time we start it up. That makes the **Bank** *persistent*. Here is pseudocode for **main** in version 9 of

---

[9] Look at a **class** file in your editor for evidence of this fact.

Bank.java (Listing 9-3):

```
Suppose the state of the Bank is to be saved in a file named
"persistent.bank"

if the file exists
    open it
    read the Bank object it contains
    close the file
else create a new bank

visit the Bank, as usual

// banker has entered "exit" to finish visit
open the file
write the state of the Bank to that file
close the file
```

An object can be persistent only if its fields (including those that refer to other objects) can be represented by characters that can be saved in a file.[10] Such objects are said to be *serializable*. So we must arrange to serialize the classes in our application. The excellent news is that Java will do the actual work for us provided we **import Serializable** and add the two magic words **implements Serializable** to the class declarations:

```
public class Bank
    implements Serializable
{
    ...
}

public abstract class BankAccount
    implements Serializable
{
    ...
}

public class Month
    implements Serializable
{
    ...
}
```

---

[10] The box-and-arrow pictures we draw showing objects with fields having arrows pointing to other objects don't provide a representation that one can save in a file.

These are the only changes to the bank application source code we last saw in Chapter 7, so only these three classes have new Listings (9-3, 9-4, and 9.5)

We will discuss the meaning of "implements" in the next chapter. For now, just use it as we have above. Most Java library classes, like **String**, **ArrayList**, and **TreeMap**, are declared to be serializable. Some are not, for good reason. For example, **FileStream** is *not* serializable because a **FileStream** object maintains internal state dependent on transient properties of the underlying operating system. (Such as its current position in a sequential file.)

Once a class has been declared serializable, we may use methods **writeObject** in class **ObjectOutputStream** and **readObject** in **ObjectInputStream** to write and read instances of that class. Here is the code called from **main** in **Bank.java** to read a **Bank** object from a file:

```
496   private static Bank readBank(String bankName,
                                   String bankFileName)
497   {
498       File file = new File( bankFileName );
499       if (!file.exists()) {
500           return new Bank( bankName );
501       }
502       ObjectInputStream inStream = null;
503       try {
504           inStream = new ObjectInputStream(
505                       new FileInputStream( file ) );
506           Bank bank = (Bank)inStream.readObject();
507           System.out.println(
508             "Bank state read from file" + bankFileName);
509           return bank;
510       }
511       catch (Exception e ) {
512           System.err.println(
513               "Problem reading " + bankFileName );
514           System.err.println(e);
515           System.exit(1);
516       }
517       finally {
518           try {
519               inStream.close();
520           }
521           catch (Exception e) {
522           }
523       }
524       return null; // you can never get here
525   }
```

Method **readBank** first creates a **File** for the given filename, on line 498. If no file with that name exists, we create and return a new **Bank** object on line 500; otherwise, we open an **ObjectInputStream** from a **FileStream** from the **File**. Line 506 then reads a single **Object** from the stream and casts that **Object** to type **Bank**. The rest of the method is the expected error handling.

One further point is worth mentioning: When we save the state of a bank, we do not want to save its **atm**, because we may want to use a different one the next time we visit. We tell Java not to save the **atm** by declaring that field **transient** (a new Java keyword):

```
31 private transient Terminal atm;
```

Lines 472–7 in main create the **Bank** or read it from a file. Then the **setAtm** message on line 480 tells it what **Terminal** to use:

```
471    // create a new Bank or read one from a file
472    if (bankFileName == null) {
473        theBank = new Bank( bankName );
474    }
475    else {
476        theBank = readBank( bankName, bankFileName );
477    }
478
479    // give the Bank a Terminal, then visit
480    theBank.setAtm(new Terminal(echo));
481    theBank.visit();
```

When the user has finished visiting the bank, **main** calls method **writeBank** to save the current state of the bank in the same file from which it read the state at the start of the program. The code parallels that in **readBank**, substituting output for input throughout.

```
483    // write theBank's state to a file if required
484    if (bankFileName != null) {
485        writeBank(theBank, bankFileName);
486    }
```

You can see all the serialization code in one small standalone example in class **SerializationDemo** (Example 9-1).

Summary

In this chapter we studied persistence: files, filters, streams, and object serialization. We've seen how to read characters from and write them to a character stream, both one character at a time and one line at a time, and how to use streams to write characters to a **String**. And we've seen how we can serialize and write objects to a file in such a way that they can be read back and deserialized.

As elegant as the stream abstraction is, the details for the concrete streams are often messy: Input and output are hard even when they are properly designed. We have learned just enough to get started. If you look at package **java.io** in the Java API, you will find many classes implementing streams. It's best to put off learning how to use them until you actually need them.

In the next chapter we will close our tour of Java from the outside in by starting the study of graphical user interface programming.

Exercises

9-1   Create a text file for your journal for this chapter. Use your journal for questions that call for written answers and to record any observations about your work.

9-2   Test **Copy1**. What happens when the file to be read doesn't exist or isn't readable? What happens when the file to be written does exist but can't be written to? What if the input or the output files happen to be directories (Unix) or folders (Windows)?

9-3   Arrange to have **main** in **Copy1** return 0 to the operating system if all goes well and 1, 2, 3, or 4 if the first, second, third, or fourth **catch** block executes. Warning: If you just put **System.exit(2)** in the second **catch** block, the **finally** block will not execute. That might leave an open input file.

9-4   Use **Copy1** and **Copy2** to copy a really big file. Is **Copy2** any faster on your system?

9-5   Write program **Type** to display the contents of a text file at your terminal. That is,

```
%> java Type myfile.txt
```

should write the contents of **myfile.txt** to the screen. Use the messages in the various Java exceptions to report possible errors to the user.

9-6   Modify the **Type** program so that it can accept an optional **-n** argument on the command line. If the **-n** argument is present, each line should be preceded by its line number.[11]

---
[11] In Unix the type command is called "cat". We prepared the programs with numbered lines for this text using the Unix **cat   -n** command.

9-7   Implement the **Fgrep** filter. The command

```
%> java Fgrep string filename
```

prints out all the lines of the named file containing the string.
For example,

```
%> java Fgrep hello myfile
```

should print out all the lines in **myfile** that contain the string "hello". (Hint: Use the **String** method **indexOf**.)

9-8   Improve **Fgrep** so that it accepts the optional command line arguments **-v**, **-i**, and **-n**, in any combination.

- The **-v** flag reverses the search, printing out the lines that do *not* contain the specified string.
- The **-n** flag prints the line number (in the original file) along with each matched line
- The **-i** flag does case-insensitive matching, so that "foo" matches "Foo".

Make sure that the options all work together. All of the following commands (and others like them) are acceptable:

```
%> java Fgrep -i -n hello myfile
%> java Fgrep -n -i hello myfile
%> java Fgrep -n -v -i hello myfile
```

9-9   Implement the **Wc** filter to count words in a file. The command

```
%> java Wc filename
```

should print three numbers

```
l w c
```

where **l** is the number of lines, **w** is the number of words, and **c** is the number of characters in the named file. (If you fuss about the definition of a word, this is an impossible problem. Just take words to be what the **StringTokenizer** says are tokens and use the **StringTokenizer** method **countTokens** to find out how many there are on each line.)

9-10   (*) Connect Juno **TextFile** objects to real files on your computer by writing shell commands **putfile** and **getfile** with Juno syntax:

```
mars> putfile junofile realfile
mars> getfile realfile junofile
```

The **putfile** command opens the named **realfile** and writes the contents of the Juno **TextFile junofile** to it. The **getfile** command opens the named **realfile** and copies its contents into (as the contents of) the Juno **TextFile junofile**. Commands **putfile** and **getfile** should complain if the target file exists or the source file does not.

Clearly **getfile** and **putfile** test each other. And together they allow you to copy files in the underlying operating system.

Of course, code for **putfile** and **getfile** belongs in the files **PutfileCommand.java** and **GetfileCommand.java** respectively.

9-11   Test persistence in the new banking system. The command

```
%> java Bank -f persistent.bank
```

will try to read from the file named "persistent.bank". No such file exists, so it will create a new **Bank** to work with. Open some accounts. Then exit. The program should save the **Bank** in the file. If you execute the same command again and ask for a report, you should see the accounts you created the first time.

Test the error handling for persistence. What happens if the specified file is read or write only? What if it does not contain a **Bank** object?

Look at file **persistent.bank** in your word processor. What strings can you pick out?

9-12   What happens if you read in a saved bank with the wrong bank name? What should happen?

9-13   Have the **Bank** program enforce the **.bank** extension for files containing **Bank** objects. That is, arrange the code so that the command

```
%> java Bank -f persistent
```

tries to work with a file named "persistent.bank".

9-14   What happens in **Bank.java** if you replace line

```
535        ObjectOutputStream outStream = null;
```

with

```
       ObjectOutputStream outStream;
```

What if you replace

```
535   ObjectOutputStream outStream = null;
536   try {
537        outStream = new ObjectOutputStream(
538                    new FileOutputStream( fileName ) );
```

with

```
    try {
        ObjectOutputStream outStream =
           new ObjectOutputStream(
              new FileOutputStream( fileName ) );
```

9-15   Explain why you can never reach line 524 in **Bank.java**:

```
524        return null; // you can never get here
```

What happens if you omit that line from the program?

9-16   Improve class **Password**.

- Make passwords persistent. Declare class **Password** (Exercise 8-5) so that it implements the **Serializable** interface. Then have the unit test save a **Password** object to a file and read it back in again. After you have done this, look at the saved file with your text editor to see if you can find the encrypted password it contains. If you looked at enough of these files, could you guess the encryption algorithm?

- Arrange to reject passwords that contain as a substring any of the words in a file. Do that by writing a **Password** constructor with signature

  public Password(String password, String filename)

  The constructor should open the named file, read the words in it (white-space-separated tokens), and reject the password when necessary.

- Design a way to provide Juno with a file of words that may not be substrings of any **User Password**. How will Juno know the name of that file? How will it arrange to pass that name to the **Password** constructor? Will you still want to exclude the **User** login name and real name as well? If so, how will you arrange for both kinds of exclusions?

  Note that this part of the exercise calls for design only, not for implementation!

9-17   Design an error-message catalog for Juno. Instead of hard coding strings like **"JFile not found"**, put those strings in a file. Have Juno read that file a line at a time into an **ArrayList** or a **TreeMap**. Then when a message must be printed, it can be retrieved and sent to the **Terminal**. When you have a message catalog, you can translate the messages into French and ship a French version of Juno without having to edit the code.

What changes and additions will you need to implement your design?

9-18   (*) Explain what must be done to make Juno persistent. Implement persistence for Juno, beginning with the most recent version of Juno you have worked on.

9-19   Explain what must be done to make the **EStore** persistent. Implement persistence for the **EStore**, beginning with the most recent version you have worked on.

Chapter 10

Graphical User Interfaces

Juno and our banking system simulation prompt the user for input, read what she types at the keyboard, and act accordingly, often prompting for additional input. The user interface is a text-based command line. These days, that's rather old fashioned. Contemporary programs have graphical user interfaces (GUIs): The user communicates with the program both with the keyboard and with the mouse (or with a touch screen or a joystick). The program responds graphically, displaying text and images on the screen.

In this chapter we explore the design and Java implementation of graphical user interfaces. Following our usual pattern, we'll work with examples. Ultimately we will provide Juno with a graphical user interface. But we begin with two simpler programs: a very small application we use to understand GUI principles and then an analysis of the traffic light system from Chapter 1.

We can't possibly cover all you need to know to become a GUI programmer. But we can touch on some of the basic principles – enough so that you can learn more for yourself when you need to.

Java Outside In/Inside Out

Figure 10-1 shows a window with one button and one message. If you follow the instructions on the button and click there with your mouse, the display changes to that shown in Figure 10-2. If you click again, you see Figure 10-1.

If your computer has a window system you can run this program. First compile the Java source code for the classes **JOIPanel** and **JOIButtonListener** (Listings 10-1 and 10-2). Then either

- issue the command

  %> `java JOIPanel`

  at the command prompt in the directory or folder containing the class files, or
- open the file **joi.html** (Listing 10-3) in your Web browser

Warning: If you run the JOI application from the command line, the normal actions you take to close windows won't work. To shut the program down, you must follow the instructions where you issued the command: Type **return** to end program execution.[1]

---

[1] Later in the chapter we will see a better way to close this window.

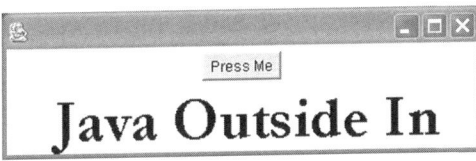

Figure 10-1: A simple GUI example (before pressing the button)

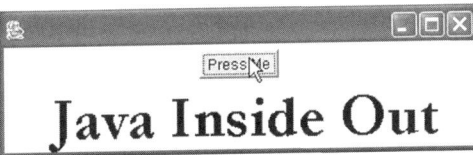

Figure 10-2: A simple GUI example (after pressing the button)

To build a graphical user interface like this one, you must address three issues:

- What will the window look like? How do you make the button and the message appear?
- How will the window behave? How do you tell the program what to do when the button is pressed?
- Who is in control?

We will examine each of these questions by studying the Java implementation of the JOI/JIO application. We look at the last one first.

Who Is in Control?

When an application has a command-line interface, the programmer is in control of what happens next: The program prints a prompt and then waits for input. The user has no choice but to provide specific information just when the program asks for it. The operating system has a simple job: Display text on the screen when the program asks the JVM to send a string to **System.out**, and read what the user types when the program asks the JVM to read from **System.in**. Graphical user interfaces are quite different. Your experience with an Internet browser shows you why. The browser program cannot know what part of the window you will choose to look at, nor where you will type or click next. It must be ready to respond to input from anyplace on the window at any time. The underlying operating system must do more than manage simple character i/o: It must be able to detect user action anywhere in the window and tell the program what has happened and where. And it must do that even when the user moves the window around on the screen or resizes it. Programs like browsers are called *event driven*. Event-driven programs are harder to write than straightforward ones that simply wait for the next string typed.

These observations show that applications with graphical user interfaces rely much more on help from other programs (the operating system and its window manager, perhaps a Web browser, libraries in Java itself) than do those with command-line interfaces.

To write a GUI, you must learn to think in an event-driven way and trust other software more than may make you comfortable. The rewards are great: snazzy, modern programs.

What Windows Look Like

The visible parts of a window, like buttons and menus and images, are *components*. To build a window you create components, and then put them in a *container*. We will illustrate this idea by studying class **JOIPanel**, which implements the window displayed in Figure 10-1.

Class **JOIPanel** extends class **java.awt.Applet**, which in turn inherits from class **java.awt.Panel**. The import statements

```
6    import java.applet.*;
7    import java.awt.*;
8    import java.awt.event.*;
```

tell the compiler where to find these classes. "awt" stands for "abstract window toolkit" – **java.awt** is the package in which you find the components and containers you need to build windows. **Panel** is one of those containers – in fact, it actually extends the Java class **Container**. We usually start constructing a GUI by extending class **Panel** (or one of its subclasses, like **Applet**) to describe the particular panel for our application. The **JOIPanel** fields and its **init** method provide an introduction to the **Container** and **Component** classes:

```
26      private Font font;        // for printing the message
27      private Button button;    // for changing messages
35      public void init()
36      {
37          // what this Panel looks like
38          button = new Button( "Press Me" );
39          this.add( button );
40          font = new Font("Garamond", Font.BOLD, 48);
41
42          // how this Panel behaves
43          button.addActionListener(
                    new JOIButtonListener( this ) );
44      }
```

Line 38 creates a new **Button** labeled "Press Me" and stores it in the **button** field declared on line 27. Class **Button** is another of the useful classes in the **awt** package in the Java API. When we use it, we rely on someone else's code to handle what buttons look like. That's a big saving of our programming time.

Next we tell this **Panel** that it contains the **Button** we have just created. We do that by sending an **add** message on line 39. Because there is no **add** method in class **JOIPanel**, we count on inheriting something from class **Panel** (or one of its superclasses) to handle the job.

Line 40 sets the **font** field declared on line 26. The value of that field determines what the message will look like when it's painted on this **JOIPanel**. We chose type style **Garamond**, bold face, size 48.

The text ("Java Outside In" or "Java Inside Out") that you see when you run the application is not a component. It's painted directly on the **Panel** – we will see how later.

How Windows Behave

Describing what the window looks like we think of as *GUI syntax*. Now we must see how the application responds to user input. That is, we must specify the *GUI semantics*.[2] We want to arrange matters so that when the user clicks on the "Press Me" button, method **changeMessage** in class **JOIPanel** executes:

```
22   private static final String MESSAGE1  = "Java Outside In";
23   private static final String MESSAGE2  = "Java Inside Out";
24   private String currentMessage = MESSAGE1;

51   public void changeMessage()
52   {
53       currentMessage =
54           currentMessage.equals(MESSAGE1) ?
                    MESSAGE2 : MESSAGE1;
55       this.repaint();
56   }
```

That method toggles the value of the **currentMessage String** and then asks the **Panel** to repaint itself. Method **repaint** is inherited from one of the **JOIPanel** superclasses. We invoke it explicitly here, but it runs at other times too. The operating system calls it whenever the user resizes the window or restores it

---

[2] These are not standard usage for "syntax" and "semantics", but we think they convey the distinction we want to make between appearance and action.

from a minimized state. Whenever it's called, it calls the **paint** method we write ourselves:

```
67    public void paint(Graphics g)
68    {
69        g.setColor(Color.black);
70        g.setFont(font);
71        g.drawString(currentMessage, 40, 75);
72    }
```

The **Graphics** object **g** passed to **paint** knows how to draw things in the current environment. You can think of it as a programmable pen. Line 69 sets the color of the ink. Line 70 sets the font. Line 71 asks **g** to draw our message[3] at location (40,75) in the **Panel**, using a coordinate system like the one we developed for our shapes package in Chapter 3.

Events

The last piece of the puzzle is understanding how the JVM knows when to send this **Panel** a **changeMessage** message. User input to a GUI usually takes the form of mouse clicks on some component like a button or a checkbox or a list entry, or keystrokes in a part of a window designed to accept them.

Whenever a user does something with the mouse or presses a key, the operating system recognizes that an *event* has occurred. It then checks the position of the cursor on the screen and notifies the component pointed to by the cursor about that event. User actions (moving the mouse, clicking or double clicking, pressing a key) are modeled by instances of classes defined in the **java.awt.event** package, which our **JOIPanel** imports.

In this program there's only one thing the user can do: press the "Press Me" button. When that happens, the operating system creates a new **ActionEvent** object. Then it looks at the **Button** where the event took place to see if anything there is waiting to be told about it. In our program, there is. Line 43

```
43    button.addActionListener( new JOIButtonListener( this ));
```

---

[3] Because we have been thinking about objects and messages throughout the text, we might expect to see **currentMessage.draw(g)** here, asking the message to draw itself using the **Graphics** object **g**. Instead we send the **Graphics** object a message telling it what to draw. This is more like what happens when we send a message to **System.out** asking it to print a **String**. In both cases the object model is not quite right when dealing with output.

creates a new object of type **JOIButtonListener** and sends the button a message telling it that the **JOIButtonListener** will know what to do when the button is pressed. The Java API provides method **addActionListener** in class **Button**.

Event Listeners

Let's look at class **JOIButtonListener** to see what it does:

```
17   public class JOIButtonListener implements ActionListener
18   {
19     private JOIPanel panel;//the Panel containing the Button

27     public JOIButtonListener( JOIPanel panel )
28     {
29         this.panel = panel;
30     }

41     public void actionPerformed( ActionEvent e )
42     {
43         panel.changeMessage();
44     }
45   }
```

Line 29 in the constructor remembers the **JOIPanel** that created this **JOIButtonListener** by storing a reference to it in the **panel** field. The only other method in this class is **actionPerformed**. That's the method called by the operating system when something happens to a **Button** this **JOIButtonListener** is listening to. The **ActionEvent** parameter tells what happened – a click or a double click. Whatever it was, this **Button** does the same thing: It sends a **changeMessage** message to the **JOIPanel** it's on.

The Event Model – Control Flow

Let's summarize what we've learned about how GUI programs can respond to user input.

The programmer

- creates a **Listener** class for each event the program must react to, containing code that specifies what should be done when that event occurs. (Our **JOIButtonListener** sends the **JOIPanel** a **changeMessage** message.)
- registers an instance of that **Listener** class with each of the components that should respond to the event. (We added the **JOIButtonListener** to the "Press Me" button.)

When the application is running

- the user types a key or does something with the mouse. (He presses the "Press Me" button.)
- the operating system detects that event and looks at the **Button** object to see if it has any registered **Listener** objects. (It finds the **JOIButtonListener**.)
- each **Listener** is sent a message asking it to do its thing. (The **JOIButtonListener** is sent an **actionPerformed** message.)
- the **Listener** does its thing. (The **JOIButtonListener** sends the **JOIPanel** the message that makes it change its message.)

Displaying Windows

The event model described above requires lots of work from the operating system on behalf of the Java program. Typically that support can be provided in the two ways we have seen to run the JOI application: from the command line or from a browser.

Java GUIs from the Command Line

The command

```
%> java JOIPanel
```

asks the JVM to begin execution in the **main** method in class **JOIPanel**:

```
78    public static void main( String[] args )
79    {
80        Terminal t      = new Terminal();
81        Frame frame     = new Frame();
82        JOIPanel panel = new JOIPanel();
83        panel.init();
84        frame.add(panel);
85        frame.setSize(400,120);
86        frame.show();
87        t.readLine("Type return to close the window ... ");
88        System.exit(0);
89    }
```

The JVM can display a **Panel** only if it's on a **Frame** – another container class in the Java library. Line 81 creates the necessary **Frame**. Line 82 creates the **JOIPanel**. Because that class has no constructor, the default no-argument constructor from class **Applet** is inherited. Then we send the **JOIPanel** an **init** message on line 83. The code there is what you would normally expect to find in a constructor – we will see soon why we put it here instead. Line 84 asks the **Frame** to **add** the **JOIPanel** to itself; line 85 tells it how big we want it to be. Now we're ready to display the **Frame** by asking it to **show** itself.

Once line 86 executes, the window system takes control of the **Frame**. The clicks and key presses on the **Panel** it contains determine what happens next.

You will have noticed that the usual ways you close a window with the mouse don't work on the **JOIPanel**. You can move the window, resize it, minimize it, and restore it, but you can't close it. That's because window closing is the responsibility of the program, not the operating system, and we have not provided listeners for the various events that you expect will close a window. We'll learn how to do that later. For now, lines 87 and 88 offer a graceful way to shut down the window by typing at the command line where you launched the application.

Java GUIs in Applets

One of the reasons Java became quickly popular when it was introduced in 1996 was the fact that Java programs could be embedded in Web pages as *applets*: tiny applications whose class files live on a Web server to be downloaded by a browser with a built-in JVM and executed there. Java applets displayed by browsers have even less use for standard flow control than do applications with GUIs. They don't have **main** methods, or constructors. When you display the **JOIPanel** as an applet, the browser executes the **init** method and then waits for user input as before. We put all the usual constructor kinds of things into **init** so that we could display our **JOIPanel** either as an application by running **main**, or with a browser as an applet.

A browser knows there is an applet on a Web page when it sees the **<applet>** html tag. The relevant lines in **joi.html** (Listing 10-3) are

```
<applet
code="JOIPanel.class" height=100 width=400>
</applet>
```

The **code** parameter names the class file in which execution starts. The **height** and **width** parameters tell the browser how big the applet wants to be. It will stay that size however the user resizes the browser window.

Interfaces

This section is a digression from the primary purpose of the chapter, which is to introduce GUI programming. It provides insight into *interfaces*: a useful software construction principle provided by Java. These interfaces are not "command line" or "graphical." They refer to another concept entirely. We hope that's not too confusing.

When we introduced the **JOIButtonListener** class, we deliberately ignored the unfamiliar keyword **implements** in the declaration header

```
17   public class JOIButtonListener implements ActionListener
```

In order to understand it now, we look at **ActionListener** in the Java API. Because its name begins with an uppercase letter, we expect it to be a class, but it's not. The javadoc in Figure 10-3 shows that it is an interface with just one method, **actionPerformed**, and nothing else.

A class like **JOIButtonListener** that declares that it **implements Action-Listener** will not compile unless it contains an implementation of the **action-Performed** method declared in that interface. Our **JOIButtonListener** does that. Because it does, when the user presses our button the JVM can safely send our listener an **actionPerformed** message.

You should think of an interface as like a very abstract class: one with only abstract methods (no instance fields, and no implementations of anything). A class that implements an interface promises to provide implementation for all the interface's methods.

We can use our new knowledge of Java to put the **JOIButtonListener** functionality into **JOIPanel** itself, so that we no longer need a second class. We call the revised version **JOIApplet** (Listing 10-4). The declaration header now reads:

```
24   public class JOIApplet extends Applet
            implements ActionListener
```

In the body of the class we replace the **changeMessage** method that used to be invoked from the **JOIButtonListener** with an **actionPerformed** method that

---

public interface **ActionListener**
extends EventListener

The listener interface for receiving action events. The class that is interested in processing an action event implements this interface, and the object created with that class is registered with a component, using the component's addActionListener method. When the action event occurs, that object's actionPerformed method is invoked.

Since:
   1.1
See Also:
   ActionEvent, Tutorial: Java 1.1 Event Model, Reference: The Java Class Libraries (update file)

Method Summary

void	actionPerformed(ActionEvent e)
	Invoked when an action occurs.

Figure 10-3: The javadoc for interface ActionListener

does the same job:

```
60   public void actionPerformed( ActionEvent e )
61   {
62       currentMessage =
63           currentMessage.equals(MESSAGE1 ) ?
                    MESSAGE2 : MESSAGE1;
64       this.repaint();
65   }
```

and we register *this* object as an **ActionListener** for the **Button**:

```
47           button.addActionListener( this );
```

The interface concept is more flexible than inheritance. A class can extend just one parent class but can implement as many interfaces as needed. Our **JOIApplet** extends class **Applet**, so that it has access to all the tools a real **Applet** needs. It implements **ActionListener** so that the runtime system knows it will find an **actionPerformed** method here when the button is pressed.

Interfaces We Have Seen Before – Comparable

When we studied class **String** in Chapter 8, we ignored the part of the declaration that asserts that the **String** class implements the **Comparable** interface. But we did look at the method

```
public int compareTo(Object o)
```

that returns a positive **int** when **o** is a **String** that precedes this **String** alphabetically, a negative **int** if it follows it, and 0 if the two strings are **equal**. That is in fact the only method in the interface, so it is all we need to provide in **String** to fulfill the promise in the declaration header.

The wrapper class **Integer** for the primitive type **int** also implements the **Comparable** interface. Its **compareTo** method makes the obvious comparison between integers: It subtracts one from the other.

In general, we want a class to implement the **Comparable** interface whenever we hope to be able to put instances of that class in some kind of sorted order. The keys in a **TreeMap** must be objects from a class that implements this interface.

Interfaces We Have Seen Before – Serializable

In Chapter 9 we observed that Java could serialize only those objects whose classes implement the **Serializable** interface. If you look at that interface in the API, you will see that it has no methods. So all you need do to implement it is to say you have done so!

In general, we want a class to implement the **Serializable** interface whenever we intend to ask Java to save its instances to a file. We don't have to tell it how to save them, just that we want them saved.

Collections, Again

We learned about collections in Chapter 4 and have used them regularly since then. We will look now at the Java collections *framework*, a unified architecture of interfaces and abstract and concrete classes that allow us to represent and manipulate collections. It consists of the two hierarchies illustrated in Figure 10-4.

The italicized names are the names of interfaces, and the boldfaced names are the names of classes. The solid arrow from one interface to another indicates that the originating interface **extends** the other. A dashed arrow from a class to an interface indicates that the class **implements** the interface. Thus, for example, the interface *List* **extends** the interface *Collection*, and the class **ArrayList implements** the interface *List*.

Recall that a Juno **Directory** (Listing 10-20) has a private **TreeMap** field that maintains the list of **Jfile**s in the **Directory**, keyed by their names:

private TreeMap jfiles; // table for JFiles in this Directory

Once we know about interfaces, we see that we could rewrite that declaration as

private Map jfiles; // table for JFiles in this Directory

Then when it is time to initialize the **Map**, we can choose between a **TreeMap** and a **HashMap** – that is

jfiles = new TreeMap();

or

jfiles = new HashMap();

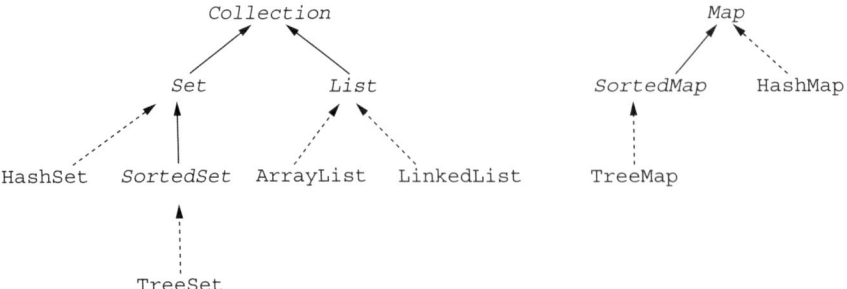

Figure 10-4: A Simplified Collections Framework

Because the interface methods **put** and **get** are declared in the common **Map** interface, either kind of **Map** will work, even though **TreeMap** and **HashMap** implement **put** and **get** quite differently. We chose to use a **TreeMap** because it gives us the keys (the **JFile** names) in alphabetical order when we ask it for an **Iterator**. There are other places and times when a **HashMap** would be a better choice. The point is that we can view either as a **Map** and write the same application program no matter which implementation we choose to use.

There are many algorithms (represented as static methods in class **Collections**) for sorting, searching, and finding the maximum and minimum elements in various collections. The design using interfaces means these algorithms may be written and used without knowing how any particular class implements an interface.

In general, it's a good idea to declare a variable as generally as possible – for example, **List** as opposed to **ArrayList** or **Map** as opposed to **TreeMap**, so long as the more general interface supports all of the necessary methods.

Why Interfaces?

We use interfaces because

- they allow us to capture similar behavior among classes without complicating the class hierarchy. **String** and **Integer** both implement **Comparable** but have no common ancestor (superclass) other than **Object**.
- they serve as a tool for data abstraction as they further separate the specification of behavior from its implementation. One may use an interface as a type in a variable declaration and (later) assign to the variable any object implementing the interface, thus allowing "plug-in" implementations.
- they promote re-usability. Different classes implementing a common interface may share many algorithms (procedures) whose implementations depend only on the common interface. The **Collections** hierarchy provides an example.

When we study Juno release 10 later in this chapter, we will declare our own interfaces, designed so that both the command-line and graphical user interfaces can talk to the various command interpreters using the same language.

The Traffic Light Simulation

In Chapter 1 we introduced a traffic light simulation as an example of a Java application with a graphical user interface. We looked at the program architecture and discussed what classes we had to write in order to model the traffic light. But we did not study the implementations of those classes. Now we are ready to do that.

Layouts

Class **TrafficLight** (Listing 1-3) resembles the **JOIPanel** class we have just studied. It too extends **Panel**. A **TrafficLight** has private fields for its three lenses and its **Button**. The constructor adds those objects to the **TrafficLight** and adds a listener to the **Button** to respond when the **Button** is pressed.

```
20    private Lens red          = new Lens( Color.red );
21    private Lens yellow       = new Lens( Color.yellow );
22    private Lens green        = new Lens( Color.green );
23    private Button nextButton = new Button("Next");

30    public TrafficLight()
31    {
32        this.setLayout(new BorderLayout());
33
34        // create a Panel for the Lenses
35        Panel lensPanel = new Panel();
36        lensPanel.setLayout( new GridLayout( 3, 1 ) );
37        lensPanel.add( red );
38        lensPanel.add( yellow );
39        lensPanel.add( green );
40        this.add( lensPanel, BorderLayout.NORTH );
41
42        // configure the "Next" button
43        Sequencer sequencer = new Sequencer( this );
44        NextButtonListener payAttention =
45        new NextButtonListener( sequencer );
46        nextButton.addActionListener( payAttention );
47        this.add( nextButton, BorderLayout.CENTER );
48    }
```

The **Panel** syntax is a little more complicated than in the JOI/JIO application. On line 35 we create a new **Panel** object and tell it (on line 36) that we plan to put three components on it that we want stacked one above the other. That's what a **GridLayout** object does – class **GridLayout** is in the **awt**. Then we add the lenses to the **lensPanel** (lines 37, 38, and 39) and add the **lensPanel** to this **Panel** in the **NORTH** position, at the top (line 40). That makes sense because on line 32 we set the layout of this **Panel** to be a **BorderLayout**. That's a layout with five places at which you may add components: **NORTH**, **SOUTH**, **EAST**, **WEST**, and **CENTER**. On line 47 we add the **Button** at the **CENTER** position. We leave the other three positions empty. When we display the **Frame** later, they will not use up any space on the screen.

Lines 43–6 create a **Sequencer** for the **TrafficLight** and an **ActionListener** for the **Button** that knows about the **Sequencer**, so that **Listener** can send the **Sequencer** a message when the **Button** is pressed.

Closing a Window

You will recall that the mouse clicks on the **JOIPanel** window, which should have closed the window, did nothing. In the **TrafficLight** window, they work. Reading the **main** method shows us why.

```
104    public static void main( String[] args )
105    {
106        JFrame frame       = new JFrame();
107        TrafficLight light = new TrafficLight();
108        frame.getContentPane().add(
                        BorderLayout.CENTER, light );
109        frame.setDefaultCloseOperation
                        (JFrame.EXIT_ON_CLOSE);
110        frame.pack();
111        frame.show();
112    }
113 }
```

This code resembles main in class **JOIPanel** but uses a **JFrame** instead of a **Frame**. Class **JFrame** is part of the Swing package we will discuss below. A **JFrame** is easier to close than a **Frame**: Line 109 sets its default closing operation.

Canvas

So far, we've learned how to put buttons and text on our windows. Neither of those gives much opportunity for artistic creativity. The **Lens** objects on our **TrafficLight** are different. Let's see how they are drawn.

```
15  public class Lens extends Canvas
16  {
17      private Color onColor;
18      private Color offColor = Color.black;
19      private Color currentColor;
20
21      private final static int SIZE = 100;
22      private final static int OFFSET = 20;

32      public Lens( Color color )
33      {
34          this.setBackground( Color.black );
```

```
35              this.onColor = color;
36              this.setSize( SIZE , SIZE );
37              this.turnOff();
38          }

46          public void paint( Graphics g )
47          {
48              g.setColor( this.currentColor );
49              g.fillOval( OFFSET, OFFSET,
50                          SIZE - OFFSET*2, SIZE  - OFFSET*2 );
51          }

57          public void turnOn()
58          {
59              currentColor = onColor;
60              this.repaint();
61          }

67          public void turnOff()
68          {
69              currentColor = offColor;
70              this.repaint();
71          }
72      }
```

The declaration header tells us that class **Lens** extends **Canvas**, an **awt** class whose instances are objects that can be painted on. Line 34 sets the background of this **Lens** to black using the **setBackground** method inherited from class **Canvas**. Line 35 remembers in field **onColor** the **color** argument passed to the constructor. Line 36 determines the size of this **Canvas**: It's a square with side 100.[4] The next line sends this **Lens** a message to turn itself off. The **turnOff** method on line 67 does the job, setting the **currentColor** to the **offColor** (which is the same as the black background), and then asks the **Canvas** to **repaint** itself. Recall from our study of the JOI application that **repaint** in the superclass calls **paint**, which is here on line 46. The **paint** method uses the **Graphics** object **g** it's passed as a kind of paintbrush, whose color is set to the **currentColor** (black or red/yellow/green, depending on the **Lens**). Then the paintbrush is told to paint an oval. An oval is an egg-shaped figure in an imaginary box. The javadoc for **fillOval** (Figure 10-5) in class **Graphics** explains the meanings of its four parameters.

---

[4] The units are pixels. A pixel is the smallest dot making up an image on a screen; its size depends on the screen's resolution.

fillOval

```
public abstract void fillOval(int x,
                              int y,
                              int width,
                              int height)
```

Fills an oval bounded by the specified rectangle with the current color.

Parameters:
   x - the x coordinate of the upper left corner of the oval to be filled.
   y - the y coordinate of the upper left corner of the oval to be filled.
   width - the width of the oval to be filled.
   height - the height of the oval to be filled.
See Also:
   drawOval(int, int, int, int)

Figure 10-5: Javadoc for fillOval

In this case, the oval is a circle centered in the square **Canvas**.

Designing a GUI for Juno

We will end this chapter – and our study of Java from the outside in – by studying a graphical user interface for Juno. We begin with the design and then briefly discuss some interesting features of the implementation.

The Juno command-line interface is a login loop with a nested shell command loop. Each will require a GUI that provides a way to get all the information it needs when it needs it while leaving the user in control of the process.

The login: Console

Recall that Juno's login loop allows for four responses:

- **help** – where the user asks for what responses are available to him
- **exit** – to shut down Juno
- **register** – to register a new Juno user
- login-name – supplied by a registered user to log in and create a shell to listen for shell commands

In our GUI, the user should choose an action by clicking or typing in a window. With so few responses allowed, help should not be necessary. The design of the window should provide all the clues the user needs to select correct actions.

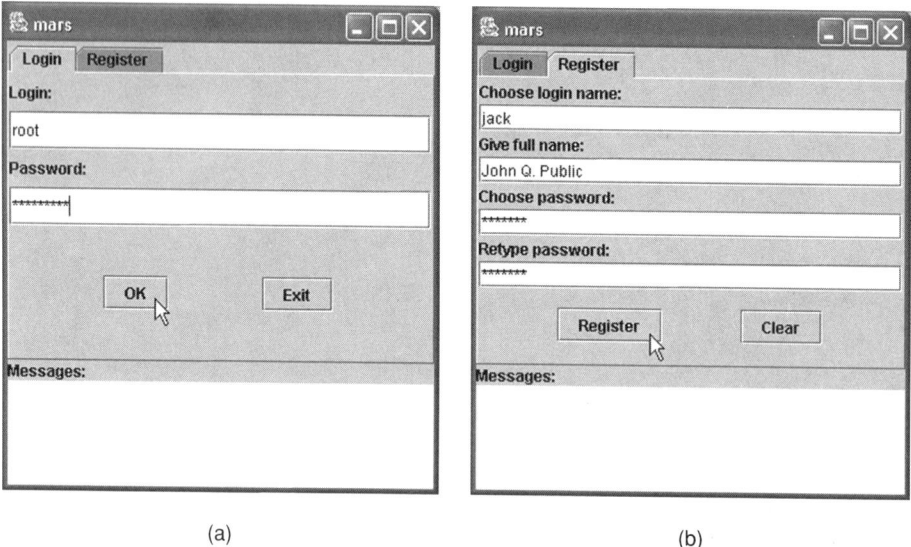

(a)   (b)

Figure 10-6: The login console GUI: (a) the login pane is selected (b) the registration pane is selected

For **exit**, we will offer a simple button with that label. We will also arrange for the normal window-closing actions to shut down Juno too.

That leaves registration and logging on to the system. These are completely separate functions, each requiring its own interface. There must also be some way for Juno to inform the user of progress and errors. Figure 10-6 illustrates the design we have chosen. The window displays a *tabbed pane* with two tabs, one for Login and one for Register. The user selects a pane by clicking on the corresponding tab. Because the login activity is performed more often than the registration activity, its pane (Figure 10-6a) is the default. Underneath the tabbed pane is a *text area*, labeled **Messages**, for displaying both progress and error messages.

The Login Pane

The login pane has two labeled *text fields*, one for the login name and one for the password. The password field is configured so that it echoes just a * for each character typed, to hide the password from someone looking over the user's shoulder. There's an **OK** button to send the login name and password to Juno, and an **Exit** button to exit from Juno altogether. Pressing **Exit** causes the window to disappear and the program to stop. In the illustration, the user has typed in "root" for a login name and "swordfish" for a password and is about to push the **OK** button to log on.

The Registration Pane

The registration pane (Figure 10-6b) has four text fields and two push buttons. The first two text fields take a login name and a full name. The other two are password fields: Asking a user to type a brand-new password twice is a common convention that confirms the fact that the user can remember his or her password for at least a few seconds and can type it correctly even when it contains a mix of upper- and lowercase and non-alphanumeric characters (as it should). Pushing the Register button sends the information in the text fields to Juno. Pushing the Clear button simply clears these fields so that a user can start from scratch. In the illustration, the user has entered the information required to register a new user with login name `jack`, full name `John Q. Public`, and a password (twice); he's about to click on the Register button.

The Shell Console

When a user has logged in, he should see an entirely different interface that allows him to enter shell commands. Juno provides that interface in a new window. Figure 10-7 shows user jack's shell – he registered, successfully logged in, and has begun work.

The title bar of the window says, "Juno shell for jack", identifying the user associated with the shell. The window itself starts with two menus labeled `Command` and `Help`.

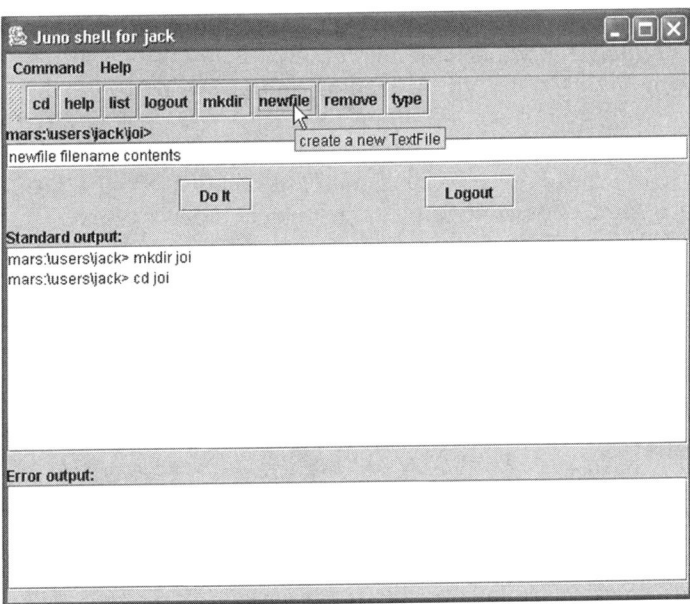

Figure 10-7: The shell console GUI

Below the menus is a toolbar with a button for each shell command. Below that is a text field, whose label shows the current computer ("mars") and the current directory, where jack can type his Juno shell command. Then there are two buttons: clicking on **Do It** submits the command line in the text field to Juno for interpretation; clicking on **Logout** logs the user out of the shell (causing this shell window to disappear). Finally, there are two output text areas: one for displaying shell-command output and one for Juno error messages.

The output textfield shows that jack created a directory called "joi" and changed to it. He just clicked on the **newfile** toolbar button (because he left the cursor there, the button's tool tip shows). His click caused the command template **newfile filename contents** for shell command **newfile** to appear in the command text field – now he is ready to edit that command, replacing **filename** with the name of the file he wants to create and replacing `contents` with its text before clicking on **Do It**. (Selecting the **newfile** menu item in the command menu has the same effect.)

Design Critique

The shell window goes only part way toward a true graphical user interface. It still shows its command-line roots. Jack should really have to type only the filename and the contents when he wants to create a new file. The fact that the underlying command is called "newfile" should never appear: **newfile** should be just an informative label on a button or a menu item. Clicking that button or selecting that item from the command menu should bring up another window with two text fields, one for the filename and one for the contents. That window should have its own OK button to create the file and close the window, a Cancel button to abort, and a Clear button so that the user can start again.

Moreover, the label "Do It" for the button that submits the command typed in the shell window's text field exposes even more of Juno's internals. We know that's the name of the method each **ShellCommand** implements to accomplish its task. But "Submit" or "OK" might be a better label for someone who does not know Juno internals.

User interface design is a serious subject in its own right, best left to professionals. Programmers usually don't do it well. Our Juno GUI suffices to teach the essentials of GUI programming but falls far short of what would be required for good GUI design.

Multiple Shells

In command-line mode, Juno is a single-user system. One user must log out before another can register or log in. In GUI mode, Juno supports simultaneous logins. Figure 10-8 shows three windows: the original login console, the shell window for jack, and a third window displaying a shell for user jill.

The record in jill's output window shows she has moved to jack's directory and can see the **joi** subdirectory he created.

Figure 10-8: Multiple user shells

Implementing the Juno GUI

Using Java Interfaces to Preserve Modularity

When we equip Juno with a second user interface, it's important to keep the **LoginInterpreter** and the **Shell** and its commands ignorant of which interface is currently in use. We would not want to have to edit code throughout Juno to add structure like this:

```
if the interface is command line
    do something
else // it must be graphical
    do something else
```

In fact, this version of Juno has a third interface that can talk over the Internet to a remote user. So the pseudocode for what we don't want to write would be even more complicated:

```
if the interface is command line
    do something
else if the interface is graphical
    do something else
else if the interface is to the Internet
    do yet another thing
else // perhaps there will be a fourth interface some day
```

In particular, when a **Shell** sends its console a **println** message, it should not have to know whether the **String** it is printing is going to an ordinary **Terminal** (which sends it to **System.out**) or to a **TextField** in a window. In our previous versions of Juno, the **Shell** had a console of type **Terminal**:

```
private Terminal console; // The console for this shell
```

In this version, that won't do. Fortunately, interfaces come to the rescue. In **Shell** (Listing 10-7) we replace the **Terminal console** with a field declared as an object of type **OutputInterface**:

```
25    private OutputInterface console;
```

after having declared **println** in **OutputInterface** (Listing 10-32) this way:

```
11  public interface OutputInterface

20      public void println(String str );
```

Then we implement that method (and others from the interface) in our **GUILoginConsole** (Listing 10-28):

```
15  public class GUILoginConsole extends JFrame
16      implements OutputInterface

31      private JTextArea messages;

97      public void println(String str )
98      {
99          messages.append( str + "\n" );
100     }
```

To preserve the correct behavior for the command-line interface, we declare class **JunoTerminal** implementing the **OutputInterface**. A **JunoTerminal**

(Listing 10-33) has a **Terminal** field to which it delegates **println** requests:

```
12   public class JunoTerminal
13       implements InputInterface, OutputInterface
14   {
15       private Terminal terminal; // the delegate terminal

56       public void println(String str )
57       {
58           terminal.println( str );
59       }
```

When **Juno** (Listing 10-5) instantiates a login console (and later a **Shell**), we tell it what kind of console we have:

```
82   if (isGUI) {
83       console = new GUILoginConsole( hostName,
84                   this, interpreter, echoInput);
85   }
86   else if (isRemote) {
87       console = new RemoteConsole(this, echoInput, junoPort);
88   }
89   else {
90       console = new JunoTerminal( echoInput );
91   }
```

There's also an **InputInterface**, whose use and structure you can discover for yourself by reading the code (Listing 10-31).

Finally, we use the **InterpreterInterface** (Listing 10-30):

```
16   public interface InterpreterInterface
17   {
25       public boolean interpret( String str );
```

so that all three user interfaces (and any others we might choose to design some day, like an applet interface to a remote Juno system) can send strings either to a **LoginInterpreter** or to a **Shell** command interpreter.

Remote Juno

To run Juno as a server prepared to listen for requests over the network, start it with the **-remote** flag:

```
%> java Juno -remote
```

Then you can connect to Juno from a remote location on the Internet with the command

```
%> telnet your.computers.internet.address 2001
```

You should not try this unless you know what you are doing – on a shared system, the administrator may not allow a user's programs to accept connections from the outside world this way.

Swing

The AWT with its panels and buttons and frames dates back to Java's beginnings. When programmers started using it, they discovered that it was too rudimentary to do lots of the GUI things they wanted to do. So the designers of Java created a richer set of graphics primitives that they called the "swing set." Swing classes now come with Java, in package **javax.swing**. When a Swing component corresponds to an old AWT component, its name begins with "J". So Swing GUI programmers create **JPanel** and **JFrame** and **JButton** objects instead of **Panel** and **Frame** and **Button** objects. Each of these Swing classes enhances the functionality of its AWT counterpart. Our Juno GUI uses the extra power of Swing.

Programming WindowClosing Actions

In our traffic light simulation, closing the single window closed down the application, so we simply set the default **JPanel** closing action to do just that. In Juno, window closing is more subtle. Closing a **Shell** window kills that **Shell** but does not shut down Juno, while closing the Login/Register window stops all running shells, saves the Juno state if necessary, and exits from Juno. So the window-closing code must be different in those different cases. Here is the inner class[5] that does the job for the Login/Register window managed by class **GUILoginConsole** (Listing 10-28):

```
346    private static class WindowCloser extends   WindowAdapter
347         implements ActionListener
348    {
349         Juno system;
350
351         public WindowCloser( Juno system )
352         {
353             this.system = system;
354         }
355
356         public void windowClosing (WindowEvent e)
```

---

[5] The scope of this *inner class* is just the **GUILoginConsole** class. It's wise to make this an inner class, because only the **GUILoginConsole** uses it.

```
357        {
358            this.actionPerformed( null );
359        }
360
361        public void actionPerformed(ActionEvent e)
362        {
363            if (system != null) {
364                system.shutDown();
365            }
366            System.exit(0);
367        }
368    }
```

Lines 363–6 do the real work: sending the system a **shutDown** message and ending the application.

This class implements the **ActionListener** interface, so it can legally be added as a listener for the exit button in the Login pane:

```
159    private WindowCloser closeMe
```

```
210            exit.addActionListener( closeMe );
```

Because we want the same behavior when the user closes the window with the standard system tools, we add this object as a listener for the whole window:

```
80            this.addWindowListener( closeMe );
```

Then on line 358 we have the **windowClosing** method delegate to the **actionPerformed** method.

A **WindowListener** for a window is like an **ActionListener** for a **Button**. Whenever the user does something, like click on the close button or minimize a window, the operating system creates a **WindowEvent** for the action and tells all the listeners for the window about that **WindowEvent**. Then the listeners can do whatever they are supposed to do.

You might expect this class to implement the **WindowListener** interface. In fact, we could have written

```
346    private static class WindowCloser implements
            WindowListener
```

But we chose to extend class **WindowAdapter** instead. That's because there are six abstract methods in the **WindowListener** interface and we wanted to code only one, the **windowClosing** method. But to implement the interface we'd have had to write them all, even though the other five would do nothing. The **WindowAdapter** class saves us the trouble: It implements the **WindowListener** interface by providing six methods that do nothing. We extended that class and overrode the one we needed.

The corresponding window closer in the **GUIShellConsole** (Listing 10-29) class is

```
255     private static class WindowCloser extends WindowAdapter
256         implements ActionListener
257     {
258         Frame myFrame;
259
260         public WindowCloser( Frame frame ) {
261             myFrame = frame;
262         }
263
264         public void windowClosing( WindowEvent e )
265         {
266             this.actionPerformed( null );
267         }
268
269         public void actionPerformed( ActionEvent e )
270         {
271             myFrame.dispose();
272         }
273     }
```

That **WindowCloser** is told the current **Frame** when it is constructed, and it disposes of that **Frame** when asked.

Summary

In this chapter we briefly explored some of the issues in building graphical user interfaces. In particular, we

- Saw a simple example (JOI/JIO) of a graphical user interface (GUI) built using the AWT framework and learned how event-driven programs turn program control flow over to the user.
- Introduced interfaces. An interface describes behavior but provides no implementation of that behavior. A class that implements an interface promises to implement all of its behavior.
- Revisited the traffic light application from Chapter 1, reading the code in greater detail.
- Studied the design of Juno's GUI and the interfaces that make Juno code modular.

If you want to learn Java GUI programming in earnest, you might start with the trail on constructing GUIs in Sun's online tutorial for Java, which can be found at http://java.sun.com/tutorial/.

Exercises

10-1   Create a text file for your journal for this chapter. Use your journal for questions that call for written answers and to record any observations about your work.

10-2   Look at some windows for applications running on your computer and list the things you see that you think might be components. Then look at the Java API and see if you can find classes that are good candidates to model the components you've identified. You might want to change what you first named a component so that your name matches the one in the Java API.

10-3   Experiment with different fonts and type sizes in the JOI application. For some you may want to adjust the size of the **Frame**. Can you figure out a way to compute the right frame size from the type size? An approximation will do.

10-4   Arrange to have the strings "Java", "Outside" and "Out", "Inside" and "In" display themselves in different colors – perhaps black for "Java", red for "Outside" and "Out", and green for "Inside" and "In".

10-5   Comment out the line in the **JOIPanel** constructor that adds the **ActionListener** to the **Button**. Compile and run the code and describe what does and doesn't happen.

10-6   The single button on the **JOIPanel** toggles the message that appears. Add a second button whose action is to leave the message the same but toggle the color of the message – perhaps from red to green and back. (Don't try to do both this exercise and the one that varies the colors of the words in the message.)

10-7   Arrange matters so that single and double clicks on the "Press Me" button behave differently. Perhaps one can toggle the message and the other can write the message backward.

10-8   Change the declaration of the Juno **Directory** list of **JFile**s to **Map** from **TreeMap** and change the implementation from **TreeMap** to **HashMap**. Run Juno and write about any differences you observe in its behavior.

10-9   What does the **compareTo** method in class **String** do if you send a message to a **String** asking it to compare itself to an **Object** that is not a **String**?

10-10   Do the exercises in Chapter 1 that ask you to modify the traffic light simulation program.

10-11   Instead of setting the layout of the **TrafficLight** to a **BorderLayout** and adding the **lensPanel** and the **nextButton** at **NORTH** and **CENTER**, we could set it to a **GridLayout** with four rows and one column. Then we could add the three **Lens** objects and the **nextButton** directly to the **TrafficLight** and not need the **lensPanel**. Try that and comment on the result. Or we could still use the **lensPanel** and set the layout of the **TrafficLight** to a **GridLayout** with two rows and one column. Then we could add the **lensPanel** and the **Button** directly to the **TrafficLight** without specifying their positions. Try that and comment on the result.

10-12   Study the relationship between classes **JOIPanel** and **JOIApplet** and use what you learn to construct a **TrafficLight** that can be displayed both as an application and as an applet.

10-13   Fix **JOIApplet** so that when **main** there is invoked from the command line, the actions that should close the window do so.

10-14   When you compile the source code in file **GUILoginConsole.java**, which contains a declaration of class **GUILoginConsole**, the compiler creates the class file **GUILoginConsole.class**. What class file does the compiler create for the inner class **WindowCloser**? For the inner inner class **Registration**? (You can't figure this one out. You have to look at a directory or folder listing after you have compiled **GUILoginConsole.java** to see what's there.)

10-15   Run Juno version 10 with and without the **-g** command-line option. Describe in your journal how the system behaves in both cases. When running the graphical user interface, log in at least twice so that there are two different shell consoles for two users visible at the same time. Observe how changes made to the **JFile** system by one user can be seen by the other.

Evaluate Juno's GUI. What features do you like? What features do you dislike? What improvements would you like to see?

10-16   You will have noticed that the message area in the **GUILoginConsole** echoes everything that has been typed (including passwords!). We put that feature in for debugging. Remove it. Moreover, the message area is editable: The user can type there. Fix the code so that is impossible. You can find out how by consulting the API.

10-17   Currently, a user signals his intention to log in by pressing the OK button in the Login pane (after filling in the login name and password fields). Modify the program so that the user can signal the same intention by pressing the Enter key on his keyboard while the mouse cursor is in either **TextField**. (Hint: Pressing the Enter key while the mouse cursor is in a **TextField** causes the window system to generate an **ActionEvent** for that **TextField**. Your program can have a listener for that event.)

10-18   Add the behavior described in the previous exercise to both the Register pane and the shell console.

10-19   Add a Clear button to the Login pane.

10-20   Read the Juno code and then explain how menu items are created in the **Help** menu in the shell console. What happens (in the code) when the user chooses one of these menu items?

10-21   In doing the previous exercise, you will have noticed that the help provided says nothing about usage – that is, no prototype is provided. Change the body of the **actionPerformed** method in class **HelpMenuCommand** to correct this.

10-22 Currently, clicking on "Do It" in the shell console doesn't clear the command line from the command-line text field. It should. Change **GUIShellConsole** so it does.

10-23 Create a **TextFile** editor for Juno to use in GUI mode. The shell command **edit** (implemented in class **EditCommand**) should accept the name of a **TextFile** as an argument and open a window for editing a file with that name in the current directory. If no such file exists, it should create the window anyway so that the user can create the file. The window can be quite simple. All it needs is a **TextArea** to display the file's contents for editing, and two buttons, one to **Save** the text in the **TextArea** and one to **Quit** from the editor. A third button for Clear might be nice.

The **doIt** method should figure out whether the user is interacting with the CLI (local or remote) or with the GUI and politely refuse to edit a file in the former case. Once you have written this command, you can disable the **newfile** command in GUI mode or make it an alias for **edit** in that mode.

You can make your editor as complicated as you have time and talent for. One feature that might be nice would be a query about whether the user really wanted to quit if the contents of the file had been changed in the editor but not saved. You might learn how to use a modal window for that purpose.

What bad thing might happen if the user opened two edit windows simultaneously for the same file? Can you design a way to prevent this from happening?

10-24 There is a flaw in the implementation of the remote (Internet) interface to Juno. The only way to shut down the server is to ask the operating system to do so. That means the code that is intended to save the Juno state (in method **shutDown** in class **Juno**) does not run. To remedy this state of affairs,

- Write the Juno shell command **shutdown** (in file **ShutdownCommand.java**) to shut the whole system down, gracefully.
- Arrange matters so that only user root may issue the shutdown command from a shell.

10-25 Now that Juno is a multiuser system (in graphical or remote mode), it would be nice if it had an instant messaging service. That can be arranged.

- a. Add a field to Juno that keeps track of all the active shells. A **Set** will do the job nicely. When a user logs in, add his **Shell** to the set. When he logs out, remove it.
- b. Write the Juno shell command **talk** so that when user **bill** issues the command

  mars> talk someone hello there

  the string "message from bill: hello there" appears on the console of every active **Shell** for user **someone**.
- c. Write the Juno command **broadcast** so that when user **bill** issues the command

  mars> broadcast hello everyone

the string "broadcast from bill: hello everyone" appears on the console for every active **Shell**.

d. If you did the previous exercise on shutting down Juno, modify the shutdown command so that it broadcasts a warning that the system is shutting down, then waits a minute before actually doing so, so that logged-on users have a chance to log out.

10-26   Design a GUI for the Bank.

• Design a graphical user interface for the Bank simulation. Use pencil and paper. What will the windows look like? You can draw a sequence of pictures showing how the windows change as the user enters various kinds of information: choosing from menus, checking boxes, and typing input. Use your own experience as a user of a real ATM and of other GUIs to guide your design.

• In the previous part of the exercise, you wrote an ambitious design based on what you would like to see as a user. You probably invented something that's very hard to program. Now simplify your design a lot, decide what classes you will need for the window syntax and semantics, and implement your design. Your bank should work with either a command-line or a graphical user interface, as does the current version of Juno.

10-27   Answer the previous exercise for the **EStore** simulation.

Glossary

One of our students (Zengyuan Zou) asked, "Why is English more complicated than Java?" Any human language will be more complicated than any programming language because human languages must be flexible and extensible and capable of expressing subtle ideas and shades of meaning. Programming languages need only express precisely the particular things their designers decide are important. This glossary includes entries for the official parts of Java (those are easy to explain) and for some of the more difficult concepts we have introduced in order to be able to think clearly about programs at a level appropriate for beginning students of computer science. It's more than an index (though it does provide references to the text) and less formal than a dictionary. For the official definitions of terms with official meanings in Java, consult James Gosling, Bill Joy, Guy Steele, and Gilad Bracha, *The Java Language Specification (Second Edition)*, Addison-Wesley, 2000, also available online at `http://java.sun.com/docs/books/jls/second_edition/html/j.title.doc.html`. For more informal definitions and generally interesting information, consult one of several online dictionaries of computer science like the one at `http://foldoc.doc.ic.ac.uk/foldoc/`.

Entries in **this Font** are reserved words in Java.

abstract The Java keyword used as a modifier to declare a class or method as abstract. Any method whose implementation is left to a subclass is abstract and must be identified as such. Any class containing an abstract method is itself abstract and must be declared as such. Abstract classes can't be instantiated – only their children can.

If you forget to implement an abstract method when writing a child class, the Java compiler will tell you that the class you are writing must be declared abstract. Of course you won't do that – you'll write the method you forgot.

We discuss abstract classes and methods in Chapter 5.

abstraction (common) When you find yourself copying code from one part of a program to another with your editor, look for a common abstraction. You may be able to design a class or a method that captures the common code and use that class or method instead of the copies.

access, access modifier In Java declarations, the access modifier determines who may refer to the members (methods and fields) of a class. Java offers several possible access modifiers:

- **public** – access to a member is granted to all other classes.
- **private** – access to a member is restricted to the member's own class.

- **protected** – access to a member is granted to all subclasses of the member's class.

The precise definitions are a little more complicated. The complications are related to Java's concept of a package. Because we don't discuss packages in this book, we've left out the details.

actual argument   See *argument*.

alternate   See *conditional expression*.

application   A program written to perform a specific task or related set of tasks. An Internet browser, Juno, and a word processor are examples.

application programming interface (API)   The public methods in a collection of classes – what clients for the services provided by those classes need to know in order to use them. Sometimes the documentation for the API is also called the API. The Java API is (or describes) the public methods in the classes supplied with Java.

argument   (sometimes called *actual argument*) The value (or expression denoting a value) in a message invoking a method. That value becomes the value of the corresponding method parameter. For example, in the message expression

```
foo.setValue( "e", e )
```

the values denoted by "**e**" and **e** are the actual arguments. (We expect that the value of the variable **e** is the double **2.71828**.) The header in the declaration of the method invoked by this expression will be

```
setValue( String name, double val )
```

where **name** and **val** are the parameters. See *parameter*.

array   An object managing a collection of values of like type. Values in an array can be set or retrieved by specifying their integral position, called an index. The index of the first value is 0. Unlike other kinds of collections, the values stored in an array must all be of the same type – either one of the primitive built-in types, or a class type. Declaring arrays and accessing array locations uses special syntax involving the square braces (**[** and **]**). That sometimes makes it hard to remember that arrays are objects. Arrays are introduced in Chapter 4. See example program **ArrayDemo.java**.

ASCII   An acronym for American Society for Computer Information Interchange. The ordinary characters on a traditional (English) keyboard are represented by numbers in the range 0–127. Those numbers are the ASCII values of the characters. The numbers between 0 and 127 just fit into the lower seven bits of an 8-bit byte. ASCII values are less important to programmers than they used to be. Moreover, Java replaces ASCII character encoding with 16-bit Unicode.

assert   The Java keyword used to specify a condition that must be true at a particular place in program execution. We do not discuss **assert** in this book.

assignment statement   An expression in Java that has the side effect of assigning a value to a variable; for example in,

```
x = y + z;
```

the value denoted by the expression **y + z** is stored in (becomes the new value of) variable **x**.

The assignment expression itself has a value: the value assigned to **x**. So in the expression

```
u = (v = 6)      // or u = v = 6;
```

the value 6 is first assigned to **v** and then to **u**.

binary operator   An operator that takes two operands. For example, the operators *****, **+=** and || are binary operators. See *operator*.

bit   A single piece of information, usually thought of as 0 or 1. The term comes from *b*inary dig*it*.

block   A fragment of code delimited by braces (**{ }**).

boolean   The Java keyword used when declaring a variable or return type to be of type **boolean**. A **boolean** variable can take on one of just two values: **true** or **false**.

body   The code executed in each iteration of a **for** or a **while** loop, or the part of a class or method declaration containing the executable code. See *declaration*.

box-and-arrow picture   A visual representation of the state of objects and variables in a Java program – in this text, drawn using a particular set of conventions. Box-and-arrow pictures appear first in Chapter 1; we discuss them explicitly in Chapter 3.

break   The Java keyword used to leave (break out of) a **for** loop, a **while** loop or a **switch** statement. See *switch*, and example programs **Forever.java** and **SwitchDemo.java**.

byte, **byte**   In general, 8 bits of information: just enough to represent any one of $2^8 = 256$ values. The Java keyword used to declare a variable or return value to be of type **byte**, an integer in the range $-128\ldots127$. We have not used this data type. See *bit*.

call   When we send a message to an object to invoke a method, we sometimes say we are *calling* the method. That phrase is inherited from older programming languages that were not object oriented. It is still common because it is easier to say than "invoke".

call stack   The sequence of method invocations, giving a dynamic history of the methods invoked (messages sent) to get to a particular point in the execution of a program. When the Java Virtual Machine (JVM) runs a Java program, the call stack starts with the **main** method in some class. If the program crashes, the JVM prints the current call stack. A better name might have been *method invocation stack* or *message stack*, but *call stack* is used for historical reasons. The call stack is discussed in Chapter 7; understanding it is important when figuring out where exceptions may be caught.

case   The Java keyword used in a **switch** statement to label the start of a set of statements. See *switch*, and example program **SwitchDemo.java**.

cast   A cast tells the JVM about the type of an object when it might not be able to guess correctly. Its primary use is to identify the type of an object retrieved from a collection, as in

(String) myArrayList.get(i).

Casts can also be used for conversion – perhaps to convert a character to its (integer) internal representation – **(int) ch** – or to convert a **double** to an **int** (with possible loss of precision).

catch   The Java keyword to indicate the beginning of a **catch** clause (for catching exceptions) after a **try** statement. See *exception*.

char   The Java keyword that declares a variable or a value return from a method to be of type **char**. **char**s are really integers between 0 and $2^{16} - 1$, providing enough integers to represent characters from all the alphabets of the world. Type **char** is discussed in Chapter 8.

class   In object-oriented programming, a class can be thought of as a blueprint or template for an object. The **BankAccount** class specifies the properties of bank accounts. **class** is the Java keyword that asserts that the definition which follows describes the fields and methods of all objects of a certain kind.

class file   When the Java compiler successfully compiles the source code in file **Foo.java** in which class **Foo** has been declared, it produces the *class file* **Foo.class**. If you examine the contents of a class file in your text editor, what you see will make little sense. It's the Java Virtual Machine that reads class files when it runs a Java program.

class method   A static method – a method that responds to messages sent to the class itself, rather than to instances (objects) of the class. An example from the Java API is the method **isWhiteSpace** in class **Character**. For example,

Character.isWhitespace(ch)

returns **true** if the character **ch** is considered white space by Java and **false** otherwise. The most common example is the **main** method in any class that has one.

CLI   See *command-line interface.*

client   In object-oriented programming, the user of another object – that is, the object sending a message to another object. For example, in Chapter 1 a **Bank** is a client for the services provided by its **BankAccount** objects. In Chapter 3 the various shapes (**HLine** and **Box**) are clients for the services provided by a **Screen**. Most of the programs in this book are clients for a **Terminal**.

collection   Most serious applications must deal with collections of objects. Java provides several kinds of objects that help programmers manage collections. We introduce array, **ArrayList**, and **TreeMap** in Chapter 4. See example programs **ArrayDemo.java**, **ArrayListDemo.java**, and **TreeMapDemo.java**.

command line-interface (CLI)   A program that prompts for input and responds by displaying lines of text has a *command-line interface.* DOS and the Unix shells provide command-line interfaces, as do most of the programs in this book. See *graphical user interface.*

comment   Most programming languages provide a way for programmers to convey information about a program to human readers (as opposed to compilers or interpreters). Because people read programs, comments are important even though the compiler ignores them. Java offers several ways to write comments. See *javadoc.*

compiler   An application that translates programs written in a programming language into programs that can be executed by a general-purpose computer. The Java compiler reads Java source code and writes its output to Java *class files.*

compile-time error   A fault in a program that can be detected by the compiler. Missing semicolons and misspelled identifiers are examples of compile-time errors. See *runtime error; error of intent.*

Component   **Component** is a class in the part of the Java API that supports graphical user interfaces. Instances of class **Component** occupy space on a display. **Panel**, **Applet**, **Frame**, and **Button** are **Component**s. Components, and graphical user interfaces in general, are discussed in Chapter 10.

concrete class   A class that is not abstract. An object (class instance) is always an instance of some concrete class. See *abstract class.*

conditional expression   An expression of the form

```
<test> ? <consequent> : <alternate>
```

where `<test>` is a boolean expression and `<consequent>` and `<alternate>` are expressions having the same type. The `<test>` is evaluated. If its value is true, then the value of the conditional expression is that of the `<consequent>`; otherwise, its value is that of the `<alternate>`. For example,

```
int max = (x > y) ? x : y;
```

assigns to variable **max** the larger of the values of **x** and **y**.

consequent   *See conditional expression.*

`const`   A Java keyword that has been reserved but is not currently used in the language.

constructor   A special method used to construct instances of a class. The keyword **new** invokes a constructor. If you think of a class declaration as describing a factory that makes objects, you can think of a constructor as the code that describes what happens when the factory receives an order to manufacture an object. Constructors are first discussed in Chapter 3.

container   In the Java API that supports graphical user interfaces, a container is an object that contains **Component** objects or other containers. Class **Frame** provides an example: A **Frame** may contain components like menus, buttons, and canvases, and other containers like panels. See *component.*

`continue`   The Java keyword used to transfer control immediately to the test in a **for** loop or a **while** loop. See example program **Forever.java**.

convention   A rule for program design and implementation that codifies standards agreed to by a community of programmers even though it may not be enforced by a compiler. Good programmers honor conventions. See *prettyprinting; name.*

data abstraction   The design principle that calls for separating the user interface for a class from its implementation. The idea is to expose the interface by judicious use of **public** and to hide the implementation details. We practice data abstraction systematically with our convention of private fields accessed by public getters and setters.

declaration   The place in a Java program where the compiler is told the name and properties of an entity. Classes, methods, and variables must all be declared.

A variable declaration provides the variable's type and name and may initialize its value.

A method declaration provides a *header* specifying the access allowed, the return type, the name and the declarations of the formal parameters, and the exceptions the method may throw. If the method is not abstract, the header is followed by the body, delimited by braces (`{ }`) containing the code that tells what the method does.

A class declaration provides a header specifying the access allowed, the name, the parent class (unless that defaults to **Object**), and the interfaces the class implements. The header is followed by the body, delimited by braces (**{ }**) containing the code that describes the fields and methods of that class.

declaration body, declaration header   See *declaration*.

decrement operator   The **--** operator decreases a variable's value by one. The **--** may come before or after the variable. The expression

    --x

first decrements the value of variable **x** and then returns the result, while the expression

    x--

returns the value of **x** and then decrements the value of **x**.

default, **default**   In general, program behavior when no special action is taken – "what happens naturally." In Java, the keyword used to label the case clause in a **switch** statement that control transfers to (by default) when no other labels match the value of the **switch** expression. See example program **SwitchDemo.java**.

defensive programming   The process of writing one's programs so that they detect and act on errors before harm is done.

delegation   A term used in object-oriented programming to describe an implementation in which an object responds to a message just by sending a message (perhaps the same message, or a related one) to another object. In this way, an object might complete a task much in the way a manager does: by delegating all or some of the work to someone else. For example, a **TextFile** object delegates the computation of its length to its **String** contents.

development environment   The set of tools (e.g., editor, compiler) that one uses to write programs.

directory   A file that can contain files and other directories. In Windows systems, folders are directories. See *hierarchical file system*.

do   The Java keyword used to start a **do-while** loop of the form

```
do {
    <statements>
}
while ( <boolean expression> );
```

We have not used **do-while** loops in this book.

double   The Java keyword used to declare a variable or the return type of a method to be the primitive type **double** – that is, a double precision floating point number.

else   The Java keyword used in an **if-then-else** statement to indicate an alternate course of action when the conditional test is false. See *if*, and example program **IfDemo.java**.

error   We discuss programming errors in Chapter 7. See *compile-time error; runtime error; error of intent.*

error of intent   A program that compiles successfully and runs without crashing commits an error of intent when it does what its programmer told it to do but the programmer told it to do the wrong thing. The software that crashed the Mars probe failed because the programmer confused the metric and English systems of units – an error of intent.

escape character   In Java, the escape character is ****. In a literal **String** or character constant, the **** followed by a special character (or number) may be used to represent a character that is otherwise difficult to type. For example, in **'\n'**, the **\n** represents the single newline character. Common escape sequences include:

```
'\n' — the newline character
'\t' — the tab character
'\b' — the backspace character
```

See the example program **EscapeDemo.java**.

event   Something that happens. The Java API for graphical user interfaces uses event objects to model various actions a user takes with her mouse or keyboard. For example, the depressing (and releasing) of a button is modeled as an event; the API allows the programmer to specify listeners that respond to such events. That is, the Java mechanism for responding to user actions is *event driven*.

event driven   An event-driven program is one that responds to asynchronous events (as opposed to a regime where the program is always in control – asking for input only when it wants it). Event-driven programs give the user both the fact and the feeling of more control over program behavior.

exception   Java programs use instances of the **Exception** class in the API to handle unexpected things that may happen when a program runs. Typically a program throws an instance of a subclass of class **Exception** in a **try** block and catches it in a **catch** block somewhere on the call stack. A common idiom in input/output programming is

```
try {
    ... <read something from a file> ...
}
catch (IOException e) {
    System.err.println( "I/O error: " + e );
}
```

```
finally {
    < close the file >
}
```

Exceptions are discussed in Chapter 7.

exception handling   The design and implementation of that part of an application which deals with errors and unexpected events. A surprisingly large fraction of well-written code is devoted to exception handling. See Chapter 7.

`extends`   The Java keyword used in a class (or interface) declaration header to indicate that the class (or interface) being defined is a subclass (or subinterface) of another class (or interface). A class that does not explicitly extend another class extends `Object` by default.

extension   A class (interface) that extends another class (interface).

`false`   The Java reserved word that denotes the `boolean` literal value `false`.

field   A variable belonging to either an instance (an instance field or instance variable) or to a class (a class field or class variable). The `balance` is an instance field in a `BankAccount`. The `double PI` is a class field in class `Math`.

file   A place in your computer system where things can be saved so that they are there when you need them. Files are discussed in Chapter 9.

`final`   The Java keyword used in a declaration to indicate that something cannot be modified. The value of a `final` field cannot be changed. A `final` method cannot be overridden. A `final` class cannot be extended.

`finally`   The Java keyword used to indicate the start of a `finally` clause in a `try` statement. The statements in the `finally` clause are guaranteed to be executed, even after an exception is thrown from inside the `try` block. The `finally` clause is discussed in Chapter 9, where it's used to ensure that opened files are closed when an exception is thrown. See *exception*.

`float`   The Java keyword used to declare a variable or the return type of a method to be the primitive type `float` – that is, a single precision floating point number. Because the cost of doubles is usually only a little more than the cost of floats (in program time and space) and the accuracy is much greater, we use only `double` in this book.

flow control   The parts of a programming language that determine the order in which statements execute. In Java, statements execute in the order in which you read them in the source code except when a message is sent to an object or a looping or conditional construct changes the order.

font   The style of typeface used for displaying text.

for   The Java keyword that starts a **for** statement, as in

```
for (int i = 0; i < args.length; i++)
{
    Terminal.println( args[i] );
}
```

See the example program **ForDemo.java**.

formal parameter   See *parameter*.

framework   In object-oriented programming, a collection of associated classes, which taken together apply to some problem domain. They supply the *structure* of a solution in that domain, leaving space for the programmer to supply additional application-specific details. Examples include the AWT framework and the Swing framework, both of which help programmers construct graphical user interfaces, and the collections framework that helps programmers manage grouped data.

goto   A Java keyword, reserved for use by Java but currently with no meaning. The Java language specification says it's reserved because that may allow a Java compiler to produce better error messages when this C++ keyword incorrectly appears in programs. We prefer to think the designers of Java reserved it just to prevent a programmer from using it as an identifier.

graphical user interface (GUI)   A program that offers its user a graphical display and receives its input from actions the user takes on that display (mouse clicks, typing in forms) has a *graphical user interface*. Most PCs provide such an interface. A program with a GUI waits for user actions (modeling those actions as events) and then executes code to respond to those events. This gives the user a sense of control when interacting with the program. We discuss Java GUIs in Chapters 1 and 10. See *command-line interface*.

GUI semantics   How a GUI behaves: the actions that a program takes in response to user actions (such as clicking on a button with the mouse); such actions are usually specified by the code invoked by a **Listener** – an object whose purpose it is to respond to the event.

GUI syntax   What a GUI looks like, the code responsible for how the graphical user interface is constructed and displayed.

hardware   The physical machinery that is part of a computer system. We take hardware for granted in this text.

hierarchy   A set of objects arranged so that each is (conceptually) contained in or subordinate to another object of the set – with the exception of the first object. The parts of a book like this one are arranged in a hierarchy, with the whole book at the top containing chapters that contain sections that are divided into paragraphs. The classes in Java form an inheritance hierarchy, with class **Object** at the top level. Hierarchies are often described using metaphors from botany (a tree with a root – at the top – and branches and leaves) or from family structure (parents and children).

hierarchical file system   A file system organized into directories (folders) each of which may contain a group of directories (folders) and files. Both Unix and Windows offer hierarchical file systems. The **JFile** class and its child classes introduced in Chapter 5 and later incorporated in Juno model such a system.

identifier   A word chosen by a programmer as the name of a class, method, or variable in a Java program. Reserved words (including keywords) may not be used as identifiers. **String**, **main**, and **args** are identifiers, even though Java beginners often think they are keywords. Identifiers are discussed in Chapter 2.

if   The Java keyword used to indicate the start of an **if** statement, as in

```
if (x > y)
    max = x;
else
    max = y;
```

See the example program **IfDemo.java**.

immutable   The property of being constant or unchangeable. In Java, literals and **String** instances are immutable, so when one substitutes one substring for another in a **String**, a new **String** is created. **StringBuffer** instances are mutable. **String**s and **StringBuffer**s are discussed in Chapter 8.

implementation   A computer program that allows a real computer to run an application. On a small scale, a method implements the actions its documentation promises. On a larger scale, the **Bank** and **BankAccount** classes implement our banking system simulation. In the *software development cycle*, application design comes first, implementation second.

implements   The Java keyword used in a class definition to indicate that the class implements an interface – that is, that it provides implementations for all the methods declared in the interface. See *implementation*.

import   The Java keyword that tells the compiler where to find a class (or interface) that is defined elsewhere – either by the user or in the Java API. For example, to use an **ArrayList** we must import it, telling the compiler where it is in the Java API package hierarchy:

```
import java.util.ArrayList;
```

increment operator   The **++** operator increases a variable's value by one. The **++** may come before or after the variable. The expression

```
++x
```

first increments the value of variable **x** and then returns the result, while the expression

x++

returns the value of **x** before it was incremented.

inherit, inheritance   In object-oriented programming, inheritance is the relationship between classes that allows objects of one class (the child class) to inherit the properties (state and behavior) of another class (the parent class). Java supports inheritance. See *object-oriented programming*.

inner class   A class declared in the body of another class, providing convenient access in the inner class to the fields and methods of the containing class. We use inner classes only occasionally in this text.

input output redirection   Programs with a command line interface read from the keyboard (standard input) and usually write to the screen (standard output). Unix and Windows systems allow the user tell the program at runtime to read from a file (instead of from standard input) or write to a file (instead of to standard output). We have often taken advantage of that feature to automate tests for our programs. If we put a sequence of Juno commands in file **junotest.in** we can exercise those Juno commands and capture the output in the file **junotest.out** this way:

```
%> java Juno -e < junotest.in > junotest.out
```

Then we can read **junotest.out** to see whether the commands behaved properly, or compare **junotest.out** with a file known to contain the correct output. The **-e** flag tells Juno to echo its input to its putput so that **junotest.out** contains a complete record of the Juno session.

instance   An object. Every object is an instance of some class. "**foo** is an instance of class **Foo**" and "**foo** is an object of type **Foo**" are synonymous.

instanceof   The Java keyword used to test if an operand is an instance of some class (or interface). For example, the boolean expression

```
b instanceof BankAccount
```

evaluates to **true** if and only if **b** is an instance of class **BankAccount**; otherwise, its value is **false**.

instance method   A method belonging to an object.

instance variable   A variable (field) belonging to an object.

int   The Java keyword used to declare a variable or the return type of a method to be the primitive type **int** – that is, a 32-bit integer in the range $-2^{31} \ldots 2^{31} - 1$.

interactive   An application that requires ongoing input from a user is interactive. So our banking system is interactive, but the Java compiler is not. In general, unit tests for classes should not be interactive.

interface   In general, the way a user interacts with a program. In object-oriented programming, the set of messages that may be sent to an object (or class). See *API*.

interface   The Java keyword that indicates the start of an interface declaration. An interface is like a purely abstract class with no fields (except those that are **static** and **final**) and no method implementations. Interfaces are discussed in Chapter 10.

interpreter   A program that interprets (or executes) another program directly without first translating it to machine code. The JVM is an interpreter for Java class files. Another example of an interpreter is the Unix shell or Windows command interpreter. Juno uses several interpreters, one for login commands and one for shell commands.

invoke   A method is invoked when an object receives a message whose signature matches that of one of its methods. Then the code in the method body runs. See *call*.

iterator   An object (an instance of class **Iterator**) providing the functionality necessary for looping through (obtaining each element of in turn) a **Collection** of objects.

Java™   A justifiably popular language supporting object-oriented programming. James Gosling designed Java at Sun Microsystems.

Java Virtual Machine (JVM)   The abstract machine, implemented as a software program, that interprets the code the compiler has written to class files.

javadoc comment   A comment, beginning with **/**** and ending with ***/**, possibly extending over several lines. Java source code containing javadoc comments may be processed using the **javadoc** command tool to generate API documentation viewable in a browser. The Java compiler ignores all comments. Javadoc comments are introduced in Chapter 3.

Juno   An application written in Java that models some of the functionality provided by a multi-user operating system that manages a hierarchical file system. A central example in this text, first introduced in Chapter 6. In ancient mythology, the goddess of women and the wife of Jupiter. An acronym for *J*uno's *U*nix, *not*.

JVM   See *Java virtual machine*.

keyword   One of the tokens in Java with predefined meanings. All of Java's *reserved words* except for **true, false**, and **null**, are keywords. **true, false**, and **null** are *literals*. **String**, **main**, and **args** are just *identifiers*. See *reserved word*. Keywords are discussed in Chapter 2.

left associative   A property of operators, where the operator is applied left-to-right, that is

```
x - y + z
```

is interpreted as

```
(x - y) + z
```

See *operator*.

line comment   A comment starting with **//** and extending to the end of the current line. The Java compiler ignores all comments. Programmers study them.

literal   A token denoting a literal value in Java. Examples are the integer literal **5**, the character literal **'5'**, the **String** literal **"five"**, and the boolean literal **true**.

local variable   A variable declared in a block (enclosed in braces, **{** and **}**). That block is usually a *method body*. The *scope* of a local variable (where it is visible) is from its declaration to the end of the block – that is, to the next unmatched **}**.

long   The Java keyword used to declare a variable or the return type of a method to be the primitive type **long** – that is, a 64-bit integer in the range $-2^{63} \ldots 2^{63} - 1$.

main   The class method the JVM looks for when you start a Java program from the command line with the **javac** command.

member   A field, method, or inner class defined in a class or interface.

message passing   In object-oriented programs, work is done when one object sends a message to another. That is one of the main features that distinguish object-oriented programs from procedural programs, in which one function or procedure calls another.

message   A request sent to an object. A message may have arguments that provide information for its recipient.

method   The code that provides the instructions for responding to a message. A method consists of a method header, followed (if the method is not abstract) by a method body. Methods are first discussed in Chapter 3.

method body   The *block* of statements that defines the implementation of a method. Methods are discussed in Chapter 3. See *declaration*.

method header   The specification of a method's access permissions, return type, and signature – its name and the types of its parameters and any Exceptions it may throw.

mutable   The property of being changeable. A **StringBuffer** is mutable; a **String** is not.

name   The identifier used to identify a variable, class, interface, or method. What's in a name? Choose the names of things in your program wisely, honoring the conventions set out in Chapter 2. See *convention; identifier*.

native   The Java keyword used to qualify the declaration of a method to indicate that the method is implemented in some language other than Java (usually C or C++). We don't discuss native methods in this text.

new   The Java keyword used to construct new instances (objects) of some class. See *constructor*.

null   The Java literal for the **null** reference type. **null** is the default value of a field of reference type before it has been assigned a value. **null** is a reserved word but not a keyword.

object   A construct in a computer program that models something from the real world. An object has internal state and responds to messages sent to it by either changing its state or by returning values.

Object   The class in the Java API from which all classes (ultimately) inherit.

object-oriented programming (OOP)   A contemporary software design philosophy that views a computer application as a collection of communicating objects. The hallmarks of OOP are *message passing* and *inheritance*. Java supports OOP.

object model   The design of the classes and objects in an object-oriented program, specifying the kinds of objects that will be needed and the way in which they will communicate.

operating system   A computer program that makes the services built into hardware available to a user. Examples include the Unix operating system, Microsoft's Windows operating systems, and the operating systems on various handheld computing devices – including (in the broadest sense) things like cell phones and even smart cards.

operator, operand   An operator combines the values of one or more operands to produce a new value. The following table lists the Java operators in order of precedence. For example, multiplication is evaluated before addition – that is:

`a + b * c` is evaluated as   `a + (b * c)`

For operators of equal precedence, the order of evaluation depends on associativity. Operators that are left associative group to the left; operators that are right associative group to the right; and operators that are non-associative don't group at all. So,

`a = b += c` is evaluated as   `a = (b += c)`

and

`a - b + c` is evaluated as `(a - b) + c`

but `x -- --` is not allowed.

Precedence rules are often complicated and hard to remember. It's best not to rely on them. Use parentheses to tell the compiler just what you mean.

Precedence	Operators	Semantics	Associativity
1	*expr*++ *expr*--	post-increment, post-decrement	non-associative
1	*expr*(*params*)	message expression	left-associative
1	*expr*. *message*	message expression	left-associative
1	`var[` *expr*`]`	array indexing	left-associative
2	~ !	bitwise not, logical not	unary, right-associative
2	++*expr* --*expr* +*expr* - *expr*	pre-increment, pre-decrement, positive, negative	unary, right-associative
2	`new,` (*type*) *expr*	object creation, cast	non-associative
3	* / %	multiply, divide, modulo	left-associative
4	+ -	add, subtract	left-associative
5	<< >> >>>	arithmetic left-shift, arithmetic right-shift, unsigned right-shift.	
6	`instanceof`	relational	non-associative
6	> < >= <=	relational	left-associative
7	== !=	equal, not equal	left-associative
8	&	bitwise and	left-associative
9	^	bitwise exclusive or	left-associative
10			bitwise inclusive or	left-associative
11	&&	logical and	left-associative
12	||	logical or	left-associative
13	`test ? expr : expr`	conditional	right-associative
14	= += -= *= /= %= >>= <<= >>>= &= ^= |=	assignment	right-associative

overloading   Using the same method name in different contexts to accomplish similar goals. See *signature*. One can also say that Java overloads the **+** operator, because it can be used to add numbers and to concatenate strings.

overriding   The redefinition of an inherited member (variable or method). A field or method definition in a subclass overrides any definition inherited from a superclass. Overriding is discussed in Chapter 5.

***package*, `package`**   A collection of related classes and interfaces defining its own name space, with its own access rules. The Java keyword for specifying package access. We don't discuss packages in this text.

parameter   (Sometimes called *formal parameter*.) A variable declared in a method (or constructor) declaration header that acts as a placeholder for actual arguments (values) passed along with a message (or new-expression). A parameter acts like a local variable in the method. See *argument*.

parsing   The process of recognizing and determining the structure of a text or program. More generally, the process of breaking a string into pieces that make sense in a particular context.

pixel   The smallest rectangular spot on a display device that can be instructed to display a value. In our shapes package, the **Screen** consists of an array of character pixels. Your computer screen is an array of thousands of pixels, each of which can be independently programmed to display a particular color.

precedence rules   See *operator*.

prettyprinting   Arranging the text of a program so that it is easy to read. Prettyprinting conventions dictate the amount and placement of white space (blanks, tabs, and newlines) – in particular, the proper indentation of methods and the bodies of loops. See *convention*.

primitive type   One of the eight built-in types **int**, **long**, **short**, **byte**, **double**, **float**, **char**, **boolean**. All other types are reference types.

`private`   The Java keyword used to restrict access to a class's members to the code in the class body.

programming language   A language like Java in which one writes a computer program.

`protected`   The Java keyword used to restrict access to a class's fields and methods to the class itself and its subclasses. (Technically, to other classes in the package, too, but we do not discuss packages in this book.)

pseudocode   A language more formal than narrative in English (or your native language) but less formal than that in a computer program. We use pseudocode to sketch the outline of a program or an algorithm in a form that makes it easy to see the structure of the program we intend to write. For example, here is pseudocode from Chapter 9 describing a file filter:

```
while there is more text
    read aLine
    modify aLine
    write aLine
```

public   The Java keyword used to grant access to a class's fields and methods to code in any other class.

reference, reference type   When the type of a variable is a class (not a primitive type), the value of that variable is a reference to an object of that class, not the object itself. In the JVM, references are implemented as addresses. You can see a hint of that fact in the strings returned by the default **toString** method in class **Object**. In our box-and-arrow pictures we draw references as arrows. In some languages, references are implemented using pointers. Java has no pointers.

regression tests   A set of tests that can be easily repeated as a program is modified. Their purpose is to ensure that modifications, including fixes to other errors, do not introduce additional errors.

reserved word   A word in a programming language that is reserved for special use and so cannot be used as an identifier. The reserved words in Java are:

```
abstract    double       int         strictfp
assert      else         interface   super
boolean     extends      long        switch
break       false        native      synchronized
byte        final        new         this
case        finally      null        throw
catch       float        package     throws
char        for          private     transient
class       goto         protected   true
const       if           public      try
continue    implements   return      void
default     import       short       volatile
do          instanceof   static      while
```

Each of these is discussed in its own entry in this glossary.

return   The Java keyword used in a return statement to return control from a method back to where the message was sent from. A simple return is used for returning from void methods (where no value is to be returned). When a value is to be returned, the return statement takes the form

return *expression;*

right associative   Used to refer to operators that are evaluated from right to left. For example, the assignment operator **=** is right associative; the expression

a = b = c is evaluated as **a = (b = c)**

runtime error   A fault in a program that can be detected only when the program runs (not when it compiles). Overdrafts on a **BankAccount** and division by zero are examples of runtime errors. See *compile-time error; error of intent.*

scope   The scope of an identifier is that part of the program where the compiler recognizes the entity named by the identifier. Scope is discussed in Chapter 3.

semantics   The semantics of a piece of program is its meaning. "Semantics refers to what we wish to say, and syntax is how we have to say it." (Professor Christopher Stratchey)

sequential access   The requirement that items of interest be examined one at a time in order. Typically, files are read that way – a line or a character at a time, beginning at the beginning. Streams, discussed in Chapter 9, model sequential access.

serializable, **Serializable**   In general, data is serializable if it can be put in a form that can exist outside the program that creates it. In Java, a class implementing the **Serializable** interface announces to the world that it is willing to have its instances serialized.

shell   The program in the Unix operating system that interprets a user's commands. Juno **Shell**s, introduced in Chapter 6, simulate Unix shells.

shell command   An operating system command that is available to users. Juno **ShellCommand**s, introduced in Chapter 6, simulate Unix shell commands.

short   The Java keyword used to declare a variable or the return type of a method to be the primitive type **short** – that is, a 16-bit integer in the range $-2^{15} \ldots 2^{15} - 1$.

signature   A method's signature is defined by its method name and the number and types of its formal parameters. It's too bad the method's return type is not part of its signature. The number and types of formal parameters define a constructor's signature. Java allows (and good design takes advantage of) different methods with the same name as long as they have different signatures.

software development cycle   The process that creates applications. That process starts with conception and continues through implementation, testing, maintenance, and new conception. We discuss the software development cycle in Chapter 1 and illustrate it with the examples that grow through the text.

source code   Computer programs written by programmers and read by programmers and compilers.

source file   A file containing source code.

standard error   The output character stream (**System.err**) to which error messages should be written. Unless redirected on the command line, text written to **System.err** goes to the same terminal as does text written to **System.out**.

standard input   The input character stream (**System.in**) from which input, typed at a terminal, may be read.

standard output   The output character stream (**System.out**) to which output to be displayed on a terminal should be written.

state   The state of an object is the list of the values of all of its fields. The state of a **BankAccount** (from Chapter 3 on) is its balance and its transaction count.

static   The Java keyword used to modify a member (field or method) declaration to indicate that the member is a class member, as opposed to an instance member.

strictfp   The Java keyword used as a class modifier to indicate that all floating point arithmetic performed by the class must conform to the IEEE 754 standard for arithmetic, as opposed to the native floating point arithmetic of the underlying computer. We don't discuss **strictfp** in this text.

String   A class in the Java library whose instances model character strings. A **String** in Java is an object, not a primitive type. We use strings starting in Chapter 1 and discuss them in Chapter 8. A set of characters within double quotes represents a string: **"hi"**.

stub, stub programming   A stub is a class or method with a header and just enough body to allow it to be compiled and referred to (but to no effect) by its potential clients. For example, a stub for a method returning **void** might have an empty body, while a stub for a method returning an **int** might consist of the single statement **return 0;**. Stub programming is the practice of writing classes with method stubs and then filling in the implementations, testing as you proceed.

subclass   A relationship between classes. A class that extends another class; the class that is extended is called the superclass.

substring   A string that is a portion of another string. For example, the string "not" is a substring of "another". Substrings are discussed in Chapter 8.

super   A Java keyword having several purposes. **super** can be used as a message in a constructor to invoke the constructor of a superclass; it can be used as the target of a message in a method to invoke the superclass version of that method on the current object (**this**). The **super** keyword is discussed in Chapter 5.

superclass   A relationship between classes. A class that is extended by another class; the class extending the superclass is called a subclass.

switch   The Java keyword used to start a **switch** statement. Switch statements are discussed in Chapter 5 and illustrated in the example program **SwitchDemo.java**.

symbolic constant   A field whose value is intended to be fixed throught a program. It is wise to create a symbolic constant rather than repeatedly type the value. That makes the program easier to modify and more likely to be correct. **PI** is a symbolic constant declared this way in class **java.lang.Math**:

```
public static final double PI = 3.14159265358979323846;
```

Symbolic constants are usually declared final. By convention their names are all upper case, as in

```
public static final string NORTH = "North";
```

in class **java.awt.BorderLayout.** But that's only a convention, for we also see

```
public final static Color orange = new Color (255, 200, 0);
```

in class **java.awt.Color**.

synchronized   The Java keyword used to prescribe synchronization (of threads) on an object or method. We do not discuss threads and synchronization in this text.

syntax   The rules for how we must write things down. See *semantics*.

this   The Java keyword meaning "the object we are writing about right now". **this.someField** refers to a field of the object. **this.someMethod** sends a **someMethod** message to **this** very object. **this( )** is how the object invokes one of its own constructors. Using **this** as the value of an argument in a message allows this object to send a reference to itself to one of its clients. We first discussed **this** in Chapter 3. There are additional uses for **this**, not discussed in this text.

throw   The Java keyword that starts a **throw** statement, to be followed by the **Exception** being thrown. Exceptions are discussed in Chapter 7.

throws   The Java keyword used in a method declaration to declare that either the method explicitly throws an exception of some type or does not catch an exception that might be thrown by some method further down the call stack. Exceptions are discussed in Chapter 7.

token   A *token* is the smallest part of a program that has meaning in its own right. Examples are **5**, **myMethod**, **class**, **super**, and **"catfish"**. See Chapter 2.

traditional comment   A Java comment of the form **/* ..<any text> ... */** . This kind of comment may extend over several lines. Traditional comments exist in Java because Java borrows lots of syntax from C. We never (well, only rarely) use traditional comments. Of course, the Java compiler ignores all comments.

transient   The Java keyword used in the declaration of a field to say that field is not part of the persistent state of an object. We touch on transient fields only transiently in **SerializationDemo.java**.

TreeMap   A collection defined in the Java API for storing sorted key–value pairs. **TreeMap**s are introduced in Chapter 4.

trim   To trim a **String** is to remove all leading and trailing white space from that **String**. The **String** API provides method **trim** to do that job.

true   The Java reserved word that denotes the literal **boolean** value **true**.

try   The Java keyword that starts a **try** statement. See *exception*.

type   An attribute of variables and expressions. In general, variables are declared to be of a certain type in order to limit the kind of expressions that may be assigned to them. There are primitive types, such as **int** and **char**, and reference (class) types, such as **String** and classes defined by a user.

unary operator   An operator that takes a single operand. See *operator*.

Unicode   An agreed-upon standard for representing characters using 16 bits. Java supports the Unicode character set. Unicode extends the ASCII 7-bit character set. We discuss Unicode (briefly) in Chapter 8.

unit testing   The process of testing a single component of a system – for example, a single class in a program, as opposed to testing the system as a whole. You will often find the unit test for a class in its **main** method.

user interface   The protocol by which a user (usually a human being) interacts with an application.

value   An assigned or computed datum that can be stored in a variable. We often speak of the value stored in a variable or the value computed for an expression.

variable   A location where a value can be stored. In Java, a variable must be declared before it can be used; the compiler then knows both its name and its type. Variables may be fields in instances and classes, local in method bodies or blocks, or formal parameters for methods.

void   The Java keyword used to denote the return type of methods that return no value.

volatile   The Java keyword to indicate that a variable can be changed asynchronously (by another thread). Neither threads nor **volatile** variables are discussed in this text.

while   The Java keyword used to start a **while** statement – for example,

```
while (i<j) {
    <do something with i>;
    i++;
}
```

See the example programs **WhileDemo1.java** and **WhileDemo2.java**.

white space   The characters that separate tokens: ASCII spaces, horizontal tabs, form feed characters, and line terminators. The Java API provides the static method **Character.isWhitespace(char)**, which can be used to test any character to see if it is a white space character.

window semantics   How a window behaves in response to actions taken by the user.

window syntax   How we make components appear on a window.

Examples

The examples in this section are meant to demonstrate various features of the Java programming language but are not necessarily discussed in the text.

Example 2.1 While1Demo.java

```
1  // Example 2.1 While1Demo.java
2  //
3  //
4  // Copyright 2003 Bill Campbell and Ethan Bolker
5
6  // A class for illustrating the while-statement. A typical run:
7  //
8  // %> java While1Demo
9  // Enter integer (a negative to stop): 4
10 // 4 is non-negative.
11 // Enter integer (a negative to stop): -3
12 //
13 // Enter integer (a negative to stop): 5
14 // 5 is non-negative.
15 // Enter integer (a negative to stop): -2
16 // Finally, enter integer you want to count to: 12
17 // Count 1 to 12: 1 2 3 4 5 6 7 8 9 10 11 12
18
19 public class While1Demo
20 {
21     public static void main( String[] args )
22     {
23         Terminal terminal = new Terminal(); // for input and output
24
25         // while tests a condition
26         int n = terminal.readInt("Enter integer (a negative to stop):");
27         while ( n >= 0 ) {
28             terminal.println( n + " is non-negative." );
29             n = terminal.readInt("Enter integer (a negative to stop): ");
30         }
31         terminal.println();
32
33         // while tests a boolean variable
34         boolean more = true;
```

```
35          while ( more ) {
36              n = terminal.readInt("Enter integer (a negative to stop): ");
37              if ( n >= 0 ) {
38                  terminal.println( n + " is non-negative." );
39              }
40              else {
41                  more = false;
42              }
43          }
44
45          // while used for counting
46          n = terminal.
47              readInt("Finally, enter integer you want to count to: ");
48          int i = 1;
49          terminal.print( "Count 1 to " + n + ":" );
50          while ( i <= n ) {
51              terminal.print( " " + i );
52              i++;  //  same as i = i + 1
53          }
54          terminal.println();
55      }
56  }
```

Example 2.2 While2Demo.java

```
 1  // Example 2.2 joi/examples/While2Demo.java
 2  //
 3  //
 4  // Copyright 2003 Bill Campbell and Ethan Bolker
 5
 6  // A class for illustrating the while-statement. A typical run:
 7  //
 8  // %> java While2Demo
 9  // Enter integer: 10
10  // Fibonacci numbers <= 10: 1 1 2 3 5 8
11  // Fibonacci numbers <= 10: 1 1 2 3 5 8
12  // First 10 Fibonacci numbers: 1 1 2 3 5 8 13 21 34 55
13
14  public class While2Demo
15  {
16      public static void main( String[] args )
17      {
18          Terminal terminal = new Terminal(); // for input and output
```

```
19
20          // Prompt for and read a single integer.
21          int n = terminal.readInt( "Enter integer: " );
22
23          // while tests a condition
24          terminal.print( "Fibonacci numbers <= " + n + ":" );
25          int thisOne = 1;
26          int lastOne = 1;
27          while ( lastOne <= n ) {
28              terminal.print( " " + lastOne );
29              int nextOne = thisOne + lastOne;
30              lastOne = thisOne;
31              thisOne = nextOne;
32          }
33          terminal.println();
34
35          // while tests a boolean variable
36          terminal.print( "Fibonacci numbers <= " + n + ":" );
37          thisOne = 1;
38          lastOne = 1;
39          boolean more = true;
40          while ( more ) {
41              if ( lastOne > n ) {
42                  more = false;
43              }
44              else {
45                  terminal.print( " " + lastOne );
46                  int nextOne = thisOne + lastOne;
47                  lastOne = thisOne;
48                  thisOne = nextOne;
49              }
50          }
51          terminal.println();
52
53          // while used for counting
54          terminal.print( "First " + n + " Fibonacci  numbers:" );
55          thisOne = 1;
56          lastOne = 1;
57          int i = 1;
58          while ( i <= n ) {
59              terminal.print( " " + lastOne );
60              int nextOne = thisOne + lastOne;
61              lastOne = thisOne;
```

```
62              thisOne = nextOne;
63              i++;  // same as 'i = i + 1;'
64          }
65          terminal.println();
66      }
67 }
```

Example 2.3 IfDemo.java

```
 1  // Example 2.3 IfDemo.java
 2  //
 3  //
 4  // Copyright 2003 Bill Campbell and Ethan Bolker
 5
 6
 7  // A class illustrating the if-statement. A typical run:
 8  //
 9  // %> java IfDemo
10  // Enter an integer: 0
11  // If 0 is negative, say hello:
12  // isNegative is false
13  // The integer 0 is zero
14  // Finally: 0 is still nonnegative
15  // because it's zero
16
17  public class IfDemo
18  {
19      public static void main( String[] args )
20      {
21          Terminal terminal = new Terminal(); // for input and output
22
23          // Prompt for and read a single integer.
24          int var = terminal.readInt( "Enter an integer: " );
25
26          // simple if statement
27          terminal.println( "If " + var + " is negative, say hello:" );
28          if (var < 0) {
29              terminal.println( "hello" );
30          }
31
32          // an if-else statement testing a boolean variable
33          boolean isNegative = ( var < 0 );
34          if (isNegative) {
```

```
35                    terminal.println( "isNegative is true" );
36              }
37              else {
38                    terminal.println( "isNegative is false" );
39              }
40
41              // if-else-if statement
42              terminal.print( "The integer " + var + " is " );
43              if (var > 0) {
44                    terminal.println("positive");
45              }
46              else if (var < 0) {
47                    terminal.println( "negative" );
48              }
49              else { // just one case left!
50                    terminal.println( "zero" );
51              }
52
53              // finally, nested if-(if)-else: note the indenting
54              terminal.print( "Finally: " + var + " is still " );
55              if (var >= 0) {
56                    terminal.println("nonnegative");
57                    if (var == 0 ) {
58                          terminal.println("because it's zero ");
59                    }
60              }
61              else {
62                    terminal.println( "negative" );
63              }
64        }
65  }
```

Example 3.1 StaticDemo.java

```
1  // Example 3.1 joi/examples/StaticDemo.java
2  //
3  //
4  // Copyright 2003 Bill Campbell and Ethan Bolker
5
6  // Demonstrate the interplay between static members (fields and methods)
7  // and instance (non-static) members.
8  //
9  // %> java StaticDemo
```

```
10  // 0: counter = 1; objectField = 0
11  // StaticDemo.classMethod() = 100
12  // classMethod() = 100
13  // 1: counter = 2; objectField = 1
14  // StaticDemo.classMethod() = 101
15  // classMethod() = 101
16  // 2: counter = 3; objectField = 2
17  // StaticDemo.classMethod() = 103
18  // classMethod() = 103
19  // 3: counter = 4; objectField = 3
20  // StaticDemo.classMethod() = 106
21  // classMethod() = 106
22  // 4: counter = 5; objectField = 4
23  // StaticDemo.classMethod() = 110
24  // classMethod() = 110
25  //
26  // last classMethod() = 110
27
28  public class StaticDemo
29  {
30      // Declare three (static) class variables
31      // A class variable is associated with the (one) class.
32
33      private static int counter = 0;
34      private static int classVar = 0;
35      private static Terminal terminal = new Terminal();
36
37      int objectField = 0;      // an instance variable; one per object
38
39      // The constructor keeps track of how many StaticDemo objects
40      // have been constructed.
41
42      public StaticDemo( int objectFieldValue )
43      {
44          objectField = objectFieldValue;  // set the instance variable
45          counter++;  // increment counter (counting the StaticDemos made)
46      }
47
48      public void instanceMethod()
49      {
50          // Instance methods can refer to both instance variables
51          // and class variables.
52
```

```
53          terminal.println( "counter = " + counter +
54                              "; objectField = " + objectField );
55          classVar = classVar + objectField;
56
57      }
58
59      public static int classMethod()
60      {
61          // Class methods may refer only to class variables
62          // (and other class methods), as well as to local variables.
63
64          // What happens if we comment out the next line?
65          int counter = 100;
66
67          return counter + classVar;
68      }
69
70      public static void main ( String[] args )
71      {
72          for (int i = 0; i < 5; i++)  {
73              StaticDemo sd = new StaticDemo( i );
74              terminal.print( i + ": " );
75              sd.instanceMethod();
76
77              // classMethod()
78              //   is equivalent to
79              // StaticDemo.classMethod()
80              terminal.println( "StaticDemo.classMethod() = "
81                              + StaticDemo.classMethod() );
82              terminal.println( "classMethod() = "
83                              + classMethod() );
84          {
85          terminal.println();
86          terminal.println( "last classMethod() = " + classMethod() );
87      }
88  }
```

Example 3.2 ForDemo.java

```
1  // Example 3.2 joi/examples/ForDemo.java
2  //
3  //
4  // Copyright 2003 Bill Campbell and Ethan Bolker
```

```
5
6    // A class illustrating the For-statement. A typical run:
7    //
8    // %> java ForDemo
9    // Enter integer: 7
10   // 7 integers starting at 0: 0 1 2 3 4 5 6
11   // First 7 Fibonacci numbers (for): 1 1 2 3 5 8 13
12   // First 7 Fibonacci numbers (while): 1 1 2 3 5 8 13
13   // 49 @'s:
14   // @@@@@@@
15   // @@@@@@@
16   // @@@@@@@
17   // @@@@@@@
18   // @@@@@@@
19   // @@@@@@@
20   // @@@@@@@
21
22   public class ForDemo
23   {
24       public static void main( String[] args )
25       {
26           Terminal terminal = new Terminal(); // for input and output
27
28           // Prompt for and read a single integer.
29           int n = terminal.readInt( "Enter integer:" );
30
31           terminal.print( n + " integers starting at 0:" );
32           for ( int i = 0; i < n; i++ ) {
33               terminal.print( " " + i ); // all one one line
34           }
35           terminal.println();              // the newline
36
37           // Build Fibonacci numbers 1, 1, 2, 3, 5, 8,
38           // by adding last two together to make the next
39           // Use three int variables and a loop:
40
41           int thisOne, lastOne, nextOne;
42           terminal.println( "First " + n + " Fibonacci numbers:" );
43
44           terminal.print("(for): " );
45           thisOne = 1;
46           lastOne = 1;
47           for ( int i = 1; i <= n; i++ ) {
```

```
48              terminal.print( " " + lastOne );
49              nextOne = thisOne + lastOne;
50              lastOne = thisOne;
51              thisOne = nextOne;
52          }
53          terminal.println();
54
55          // Since i is never used in the body of the previous loop
56          // we can count down to get the same output:
57          terminal.print("(for, counting down):" );
58          thisOne = 1;
59          lastOne = 1;
60          for ( int counter = n; counter > 0; counter-- ) {
61              terminal.print( " " + lastOne );
62              nextOne = thisOne + lastOne;
63              lastOne = thisOne;
64              thisOne = nextOne;
65          }
66          terminal.println();
67
68          // Replace the for loop with a while loop
69          terminal.print("(while):               " );
70          thisOne = 1;
71          lastOne = 1;
72          int i = 1;
73          while ( i <= n ) {
74              terminal.print( " " + lastOne );
75              nextOne = thisOne + lastOne;
76              lastOne = thisOne;
77              thisOne = nextOne;
78              i++;
79          }
80          terminal.println();
81
82          terminal.println("Nested for loops: " + (n*n) + " @'s:" );
83          for ( int row = 1; row <= n ; row++ ) {
84              for ( int col = 1; col <= n; col++ ) {
85                  terminal.print( " @" );
86              }
87              terminal.println();
88          }
89      }
90  }
```

Example 3.3 BreakAndContinueDemo.java

```
 1   // Example 3.3 joi/examples/BreakAndContinueDemo.java
 2   //
 3   //
 4   // Copyright 2003 Bill Campbell and Ethan Bolker
 5
 6   public class BreakAndContinueDemo
 7   {
 8       private static Terminal t = new Terminal();
 9
10       public static void main( String[] args )
11       {
12           t.println("invoking loop");
13           BreakAndContinueDemo.loop(); // could say just loop();
14           t.println("returned from loop, leaving main");
15       }
16
17       private static void loop()
18       {
19           t.println("starting infinite loop");
20           while( true ) {
21               String command = t.readWord(
22                 "normal, break, continue, return, exit, oops ? > ");
23               if (command.startsWith("n")) {
24                   t.println("normal flow of control");
25               }
26               if (command.startsWith("b")) {
27                   t.println("break from looping");
28                   break;
29               }
30               if (command.startsWith("c")) {
31                   t.println("continue looping");
32                   continue;
33               }
34               if (command.startsWith("r")) {
35                   t.println("return prematurely from loop method");
36                   return;
37               }
38               if (command.startsWith("e")) {
39                   t.println("exit prematurely from program");
40                   System.exit(0);
41               }
```

```
42                  if (command.startsWith("o")) {
43                      t.println("program about to crash ...");
44                      Terminal foo = null;
45                      foo.println("crash the program");
46                  }
47                  t.println("last line in loop body");
48              }
49          t.println("first line after loop body");
50          t.println("returning normally from loop method");
51      }
52 }
```

Example 4.1 CommandLineArgsDemo.java

```
1  // Example 4.1 joi/examples/CommandLineArgsDemo.java
2  //
3  //
4  // Copyright 2003 Bill Campbell and Ethan Bolker
5
6  // A class illustrating the use of command line arguments.
7  //
8  // %> java CommandLineArgsDemo foo      bar "b q"
9  // Echo command line arguments,
10 // surrounded by |...|
11 // |foo|
12 // |bar|
13 // |b q|
14 //
15 // Note the use of quotes to get embedded blanks.
16
17 public class CommandLineArgsDemo
18 {
19     public static void main( String[] args )
20     {
21         System.out.println("Echo command line arguments, ");
22         System.out.println("surrounded by |...| ");
23         for (int i = 0; i < args.length; i++) {
24             System.out.println('|' + args[i] + '|');
25         }
26     }
27 }
```

Example 4.2 ArrayDemo.java

```
1  // Example 4.2 joi/examples/ArrayDemo.java
2  //
3  //
4  // Copyright 2003 Bill Campbell and Ethan Bolker
5
6  // A class illustrating arrays
7  //
8  // Build an array of Fibonacci numbers 1, 1, 2, 3, 5, 8, ...
9  // and play with it. Sample output:
10 //
11 // %> java ArrayDemo 8
12 // Sum first 8 Fibonacci numbers
13 // 1 1 2 3 5 8 13 21
14 // total: 54
15 //
16 // First 8 Fibonacci numbers (reverse order)
17 // 21 13 8 5 3 2 1 1
18 // Every other fib
19 // 1    1
20 // 3    2
21 // 5    5
22 // 7    13
23
24 public class ArrayDemo
25 {
26     public static void main( String[] args )
27     {
28         int n = 6; // default
29         if (args.length > 0) {
30             n = Integer.parseInt(args[0]);
31         }
32
33         int[] fibs = new int[n];  // declare and create array
34
35         fibs[0] = fibs[1] = 1; // fill first two positions
36         for ( int i = 2; i < n; i++ ) { // fill the rest
37             fibs[i] = fibs[i-1] + fibs[i-2];
38         }
39
40         // standard idiom for accumulating total of an array
41         int total = 0;
```

```
42              System.out.println("Sum first " + n + " Fibonacci numbers");
43              for ( int i = 0; i < n; i++ ) {
44                  System.out.print(fibs[i] + " ");
45                  total += fibs[i];
46              }
47              System.out.println("\ntotal: " + total);
48              System.out.println();
49
50              System.out.
51                  println("First " + n + " Fibonacci numbers (reverse order)");
52              for ( int i = n-1; i >= 0 ; i-- ) {
53                  System.out.print(fibs[i] + " ");
54              }
55              System.out.println();
56
57              System.out.println("Every other fib");
58              for ( int i = 0; i < n ; i += 2 ) {
59                  System.out.println((i+1) + "\t" + fibs[i]);
60              }
61              System.out.println();
62          }
63  }
```

Example 4.3 ArrayListDemo.java

```
1   // Example 4.3 ArrayListDemo.java
2   //
3   //
4   // Copyright 2003 Bill Campbell and Ethan Bolker
5
6   // Tell the java compiler that the ArrayList class is in
7   // the java.util part of the library.
8
9   import java.util.ArrayList;
10
11  // Exercise the most important parts of the ArrayList API.
12  //
13  // %> java ArrayListDemo
14  // Create a list containing three SimpleObjects.
15  // 0      zero
16  // 1      one
17  // 2      two
18  // Replace the object at position 0.
```

```
19   // Put a new object at 2 and push the rest along.
20   // Print out the list again.
21   // 0     new zero
22   // 1     one
23   // 2     one point five
24   // 3     two
25
26   public class ArrayListDemo
27   {
28      public static void main( String[] args )
29      {
30         System.out.println("Create a list containing three SimpleObjects.");
31
32         // Create a new, empty ArrayList
33         // with the ArrayList constructor.
34         ArrayList myList = new ArrayList();
35
36         // Put three things on it with the add()
37         // method - each add appends to the list.
38         myList.add(new SimpleObject("zero"));
39         myList.add(new SimpleObject("one"));
40         myList.add(new SimpleObject("two"));
41
42         // Print the list with a for loop.
43         // size() method tells how long the list is.
44         // get(int index) method retrieves value stored at position index
45         // The (SimpleObject) cast tells Java what type of thing you got
46         for (int i = 0; i < myList.size() ; i++ ) {
47            SimpleObject foo = (SimpleObject)myList.get(i);
48            System.out.println(i + "\t" + foo.name);
49         }
50
51         // set(int index) method changes value stored at position index
52         System.out.println("Replace the object at  position 0.");
53         myList.set(0, new SimpleObject("new zero"));
54
55         System.out.println("Put a new object at 2 and push the rest along
56         myList.add(2, new SimpleObject("one point five"));
57
58         System.out.println("Print out the list again.");
59         for (int i = 0; i < myList.size() ; i++ ) {
60            SimpleObject foo = (SimpleObject)myList.get(i); // note cast
61            System.out.println(i + "\t" + foo.name);
```

```
62          }
63      }
64
65     // This really simple class exists only to provide
66     // things to put in the ArrayList.
67     //
68     // It's an inner class, declared inside the ArrayListDemo
69     // class, which is its scope.
70     //
71     // Since it's visible only here, we are using a public
72     // name field rather than a private field and a public
73     // getName()
74
75     private static class SimpleObject {
76
77         public String name;
78
79         public SimpleObject( String name ) {
80             this.name = name;
81         }
82     } // end of body of inner class SimpleObject
83
84 } // end of body of ArrayList Demo
```

Example 4.4 TreeMapDemo.java

```
 1    // Example 4.4 joi/examples/TreeMapDemo.java
 2    //
 3    //
 4    // Copyright 2003 Bill Campbell and Ethan Bolker
 5
 6    import java.util.TreeMap;
 7    import java.util.Iterator;
 8    import java.util.Set;
 9    import java.util.Collection;
10    import java.util.Map;
11
12    // A class illustrating the use of TreeMap.  A typical run:
13    //
14    // %> java TreeMapDemo
15    // Store 3 wrapped ints, keys "one", "two", "three".
16    // The wrapped int stored for "two" is 2
17    //
```

```
18   // Iterate over keys, get each value.
19   // Note that key order is aphabetical:
20   // The value for key one is 1
21   // The value for key three is 3
22   // The value for key two is 2
23   //
24   // Iterate over the values:
25   // 1
26   // 3
27   // 2
28   //
29   // Iterate over the key-value pairs:
30   // The value for the entry with key one is 1
31   // The value for the entry with key three is 3
32   // The value for the entry with key two is 2
33   //
34   // How a TreeMap represents itself as a String:
35   // {one=1, three=3, two=2}
36   //
37   // Store a different value at key "two"
38   // {one=1, three=3, two=2222}
39   //
40   // Store map.get( "one" ) at key "two"
41   // {one=1, three=3, two=1}
42   //
43   // A TreeMap with Integer keys mapping to String values
44   // {1=I, 2=II, 3=III}
45   // %>
46
47   public class TreeMapDemo
48   {
49      public static void main( String[] args )
50      {
51         Terminal terminal = new Terminal(); // for input and output
52
53         TreeMap map = new TreeMap();
54
55         // Put in some ints (each wrapped up as an Integer object)
56         terminal.println(
57           "Store 3 wrapped ints, keys \"one\", \"two\", \"three\".");
58         map.put("one",   new Integer(1) );
59         map.put("two",   new Integer(2) );
60         map.put("three", new Integer(3) );
```

```
61
62              // get the value associated with a key;
63              // notice the required cast.
64              Integer wrappedInt = (Integer) map.get( "two" );
65
66              // And print the wrapped int
67              terminal.println( "The wrapped int stored for \"two\" is "
68                                  + wrappedInt);
69
70
71              // The set of keys.
72              Set keys = map.keySet();
73              // The iterator over this "set" of keys will return
74              // the keys in key-order.
75              terminal.println( "\nIterate over keys, get each value." );
76              terminal.println( "Note that key order is aphabetical:" );
77              Iterator keysIterator = keys.iterator();
78              while ( keysIterator.hasNext() ) {
79                  String key = (String) keysIterator.next();
80                  terminal.println( "The value for key " + key + " is "
81                                      + ((Integer) map.get( key)) );
82              }
83
84              // Iterate over the collection of values;
85              // notice the order is the same (ie the key-order).
86              terminal.println( "\nIterate over the values:" );
87              Iterator valuesIterator = map.values().iterator();
88              while ( valuesIterator.hasNext() ) {
89                  terminal.println( ((Integer) valuesIterator.next()));
90              }
91
92              // The set of Map.Entry objects (key-value pairs);
93              // Map.Entry is an inner class of Map.
94
95              // Iterate over the entries.
96              terminal.println( "\nIterate over the key-value pairs:" );
97              Iterator entriesIterator = map.entrySet().iterator();
98              while ( entriesIterator.hasNext() ) {
99                  Map.Entry entry = (Map.Entry) entriesIterator.next();
100                  terminal.println( "The value for the entry with key "
101                              + entry.getKey() + " is "
102                              + ((Integer) entry.getValue()));
103              }
```

```
104
105            // how a TreeMap represents itself as a String:
106            terminal.println(
107                "\nHow a TreeMap represents itself as a String:");
108            terminal.println(map.toString());
109            terminal.println();
110
111            // We can overwrite the value stored under a key
112            terminal.println(
113                "Store a different value at key \"two\"");
114            map.put("two", new Integer(2222));
115            terminal.println(map.toString());
116            terminal.println();
117
118            // We can store the same value under two keys
119            terminal.println(
120                "Store map.get( \"one\" ) at key \"two\"");
121            map.put("two", map.get( "one" ) );
122            terminal.println(map.toString());
123            terminal.println();
124
125            // And keys don't necessarily have to be Strings;
126            // Here's a TreeMap mapping Integers to strings.
127            terminal.println(
128                "A TreeMap with Integer keys mapping to String values");
129            map = new TreeMap();
130            map.put( new Integer( 1 ), "I" );
131            map.put( new Integer( 2 ), "II" );
132            map.put( new Integer( 3 ), "III" );
133            terminal.println(map.toString());
134            terminal.println();
135        }
136 }
```

Example 5.1 SwitchDemo.java

```
1  // Example 5.1 joi/examples/SwitchDemo.java
2  //
3  //
4  // Copyright 2003 Bill Campbell and Ethan Bolker
5
6  // A class illustrating the Switch statement
7
```

```
 8   // %> java SwitchDemo
 9   // Enter an integer: 2
10   // two
11   // Notice the importance of the breaks!
12   // The same statement without the breaks:
13   // two
14   // three
15   // Not one, two or three!
16   // Enter a character: y
17   // yes
18   // %>
19
20   public class SwitchDemo
21   {
22       public static void main( String[] args )
23       {
24           Terminal terminal = new Terminal();
25
26           int i = terminal.readInt( "Enter an integer: " );
27
28           switch (i) {
29           case 1:
30               terminal.println( "one" );
31               break;
32           case 2:
33               terminal.println( "two" );
34               break;
35           case 3:
36               terminal.println( "three" );
37               break;
38           default:
39               terminal.println( "Not one, two or three!" );
40           }
41
42          terminal.println( "Notice the importance of the breaks!" );
43          terminal.println( "The same statement without the breaks:" );
44
45           switch (i) {
46           case 1:
47               terminal.println( "one" );
48           case 2:
49               terminal.println( "two" );
50           case 3:
```

```
51              terminal.println( "three" );
52          default:
53              terminal.println( "Not one, two or three!" );
54          }
55
56          switch (terminal.readChar( "Enter a character: " )) {
57          case 'y':
58              terminal.println( "yes" );
59              break;
60          case 'n':
61              terminal.println( "no" );
62              break;
63          default:
64              terminal.println( "Neither yes nor no." );
65          }
66      }
67  }
```

Example 5.2 OverridingDemo.java

```
1   // Example 5.2 joi/examples/OverridingDemo.java
2   //
3   //
4   // Copyright 2002 Bill Campbell and Ethan Bolker
5
6   // Small program to illustrate overriding and toString()
7   //
8   // Here's what the output looks like:
9   //
10  // %> java OverridingDemo jessica benjamin
11  // Terminal t = new Terminal();
12  // nobj = new NamedObject( args[0] );
13  // nobj.toString():          jessica
14  // nobj:                     jessica
15  // nobj.toStringfromObject(): NamedObject@206fdf64
16  // nobj = new NamedObject( args[1] );
17  // nobj.toString():          benjamin
18  // nobj:                     benjamin
19  // nobj.toStringfromObject(): NamedObject@2103df64
20  //
21  // toString():               Terminal@201bdf64
22  // t:                        Terminal@201bdf64
23
```

```
24  public class OverridingDemo
25  {
26      public static void main( String[] args )
27      {
28          Terminal t = new Terminal();
29          NamedObject nobj;
30
31          t.println("Terminal t = new Terminal();");
32          t.println("nobj = new NamedObject( args[0] );");
33          nobj = new NamedObject( args[0] );
34          t.println( "nobj.toString():          " + nobj.toString() );
35          t.println( "nobj:                     " + nobj );
36          t.println( "nobj.toStringfromObject(): " +
37                      nobj.toStringfromObject());
38
39          t.println("nobj = new NamedObject( args[1] );");
40          nobj = new NamedObject( args[1] );
41          t.println( "nobj.toString():          " + nobj.toString() );
42          t.println( "nobj:                     " + nobj );
43          t.println( "nobj.toStringfromObject(): " +
44                      nobj.toStringfromObject());
45
46          t.println( "\ntoString():            " + t.toString() );
47          t.println( "t:                       " + t );
48      }
49  }
50
51  // A simple class whose instances have one field
52  // and several toString methods. Visible only inside
53  // the OverridingDemo class.
54
55  // you can put two classes in one file as long as only one of them
56  // is public
57
58  class NamedObject // extends Object, by default
59  {
60      private String name;
61
62      // constructor does the obvious thing
63
64      public NamedObject( String name )
65      {
66          this.name = name;
```

```
67      }
68
69      // override toString in class Object
70
71      public String toString()
72      {
73          return name;
74      }
75
76      // access to the overridden method using super
77
78      public String toStringfromObject()
79      {
80          return super.toString();
81      }
82  }
```

Example 5.3 EqualsDemo.java

```
 1  // Example 5.3 joi/examples/EqualsDemo.java
 2  //
 3  //
 4  // Copyright 2003 Bill Campbell and Ethan Bolker
 5
 6  // A class illustrating == and equals().
 7  //
 8  // %> java EqualsDemo
 9  // Different objects, same field:
10  // e1 == e1LookAlike ->        false
11  // e1.equals( e1LookAlike ) -> true
12  // Same object:
13  // e1 == e1Too ->              true
14  //
15  // Different ArrayLists with equal (but not ==) elements:
16  // alist0 == alist1 ->       false
17  // alist0.equals(alist1) -> true
18  //
19  // Different TreeMaps with equal keys
20  // mapping to equal (but !=) values:
21  // tmap0 == tmap1 ->        false
22  // tmap0.equals(tmap1) -> true
23  //
24  // tmap0.toString() -> {sillykey = EqualsDemo value 1}
```

```
25  // tmap1.toString() -> {sillykey = EqualsDemo value 1}
26  // Are these Strings == ?    false
27  // Are these Strings equal ? true
28
29  import java.util.ArrayList;
30  import java.util.TreeMap;
31
32  public class EqualsDemo
33  {
34      // Properties of an EqualsDemo object.
35      //
36      // Override equals: two of these objects are equal if
37      // their integer field has the same (i.e. ==) value.
38      //
39      // When you override equals it's customary to override
40      // toString too, so that equal objects return the equal
41      // Strings, so we do.
42
43      private int field;
44
45      public EqualsDemo( int field )
46      {
47          this.field = field;
48      }
49
50      public boolean equals( Object other )
51      {
52          return (other instanceof EqualsDemo)
53              && (this.field == ((EqualsDemo)other).field);
54      }
55
56      public String toString()
57      {
58          return " EqualsDemo value " + field;
59      }
60
61      public static void main( String[] args )
62      {
63          Terminal t = new Terminal();
64
65          // EqualsDemo object == vs equals()
66          EqualsDemo e1          = new EqualsDemo( 1 );
67          EqualsDemo e1LookAlike = new EqualsDemo( 1 ); // same field.
```

```
68              EqualsDemo e1Too        = e1;                        // same object
69
70          t.println("Different objects, same field:");
71          t.println("e1 == e1LookAlike ->          " + (e1 == e1LookAlike));
72          t.println("e1.equals( e1LookAlike ) -> " + e1.equals( e1LookAlike
73          t.println("Same object:");
74          t.println("e1 == e1Too ->              " + (e1 == e1Too));
75          t.println();
76
77          // Arrays and Maps
78          ArrayList alist0 = new ArrayList();
79          ArrayList alist1 = new ArrayList();
80
81          alist0.add( e1);
82          alist1.add( e1LookAlike );
83
84          t.println( "Different ArrayLists with equal (but not ==) elements
85          t.println( "alist0 == alist1 ->        " + (alist0 == alist1));
86          t.println( "alist0.equals(alist1) -> " + alist0.equals(alist1));
87          t.println();
88
89          TreeMap tmap0 = new TreeMap();
90          TreeMap tmap1 = new TreeMap();
91
92          tmap0.put( "sillykey ", e1 );
93          tmap1.put( "sillykey ", e1LookAlike );
94
95          t.println( "Different TreeMaps with equal keys" );
96          t.println( "mapping to equal (but !=) values:" );
97
98          t.println( "tmap0 == tmap1 ->        " + (tmap0 == tmap1));
99          t.println( "tmap0.equals(tmap1) -> " + tmap0.equals(tmap1));
100         t.println();
101
102         // Test Strings for == and equal
103         String s0 = tmap0.toString();
104         String s1 = tmap1.toString();
105         t.println( "tmap0.toString() -> " + s0);
106         t.println( "tmap1.toString() -> " + s1);
107         t.println( "Are these Strings == ?    " + (s0 == s1) );
108         t.println( "Are these Strings equal ? " + (s0.equals(s1)) );
109     }
110 }
```

Example 7.1 RumpelStiltskinDemo.java

```
1 // Example 7.1 joi/examples/RumpelStiltskinDemo.java
2 //
3 //
4 // Copyright 2003 Bill Campbell and Ethan Bolker
5
6 // Practice with simple exceptions - some from the API, one declared here.
7
8 public class RumpelStiltskinDemo
9 {
10     public static void main( String[] args )
11     {
12         Wizard rumpelstiltskin = new Wizard("RumpelStiltskin");
13         Wizard aNullWizard     = null;
14
15         // see if the first command line argument ( args[0] )
16         // is the right name
17         try {
18             System.out.println("Is your name " + args[0] +'?');
19             rumpelstiltskin.guessName(args[0]);
20             System.out.println("Yes! How did you guess?");
21             System.exit(0);
22         }
23         // come here right away if there is no args[0]
24         catch (IndexOutOfBoundsException e) {
25             System.out.println( "usage: java RumpelStiltskinDemo guess");
26             System.exit(0); // leave the program gracefully
27         }
28         // come here from guessName if exception thrown
29         catch (BadGuessException e) {
30             System.err.println("sorry - " + args[0] + " is not my name");
31         }
32
33         System.out.println(
34             "\nIntentionally generate a NullPointerException, \n" +
35             "see what the Exception's toString method returns");
36         try {
37             aNullWizard.guessName("who am I?");
38         }
39         catch (Exception e) {
40             System.out.println(e);
41         }
```

```
42
43          System.out.println(
44              "\nExperiment with the printStackTrace() method:");
45          try {
46              rumpelstiltskin.makeMischief();
47          }
48          catch (Exception e) {
49              e.printStackTrace();
50          }
51
52          // perhaps throw an uncaught IndexOutOfBoundsException
53          System.out.println(
54              "\nLook for a second command line argument,\n" +
55              "see what happens if it's not there:" );
56          System.out.println(args[1]);
57      }
58
59  // two inner classes, used only in this file
60  private static class Wizard
61  {
62      private String name;
63
64      public Wizard( String name )
65      {
66          this.name = name;
67      }
68
69      public void guessName( String name )
70          throws BadGuessException
71      {
72          if (!name.equals(this.name))
73              throw new BadGuessException( );
74      }
75
76      public void makeMischief()
77          throws BadGuessException
78      {
79          this.guessName("??");
80      }
81  }
82
```

```
83    private static class BadGuessException extends Exception
84    {
85        // empty body
86    }
87 }
```

Example 8.1 EscapeDemo.java

```
1  // Example 8.1 joi/examples/EscapeDemo.java
2  //
3  //
4  // Copyright 2003 Bill Campbell and Ethan Bolker
5
6  // A class illustrating the escape character '\' in quoted Strings
7  //
8  // %> java EscapeDemo
9  // argument to println    output
10 // "hello world"          hello world
11 // "hello\nworld"         hello
12 // world
13 // "\"hello world\""      "hello world"
14 // "hello\tworld"         hello    world
15 // "hello\bworld"         hellworld
16 //
17 // Note the use of quotes to get embedded blanks.
18
19 public class EscapeDemo
20 {
21     public static void main( String[] args )
22     {
23         System.out.println("argument to println\toutput");
24
25         System.out.print("\"hello world\"\t\t");
26         System.out.println("hello world");
27
28         System.out.print("\"hello\\nworld\"\t\t");
29         System.out.println("hello\nworld");
30
31         System.out.print("\"\\\"hello world\\\"\"\t");
32         System.out.println("\"hello world\"");
33
34         System.out.print("\"hello\\tworld\"\t\t");
35         System.out.println("hello\tworld");
```

```
36
37              System.out.print("\"hello\\bworld\"\t\t");
38              System.out.println("hello\bworld");
39      }
40  }
```

Example 8.2 StringDemo.java

```
 1  // Example 8.2 joi/examples/StringDemo.java
 2  //
 3  //
 4  // Copyright 2003 Bill Campbell and Ethan Bolker
 5
 6  // A class illustrating Strings
 7  //
 8  // %> java StringDemo
 9  // certainly = "yes!"
10  // bankName = "Dewey, Cheatham and Howe"
11  // bankName.charAt( 0 ) = D
12  // bankName.charAt( 5 ) = ,
13  // bankName.indexOf('e') = 1
14  // bankName.indexOf('e', 6) = 9
15  // bankName.indexOf('x') = -1
16  // "cake".compareTo("care") = -7
17  // bankName.substring( 7, 12 ) = Cheat
18  // bankName.substring( 7 ) = Cheatham and Howe
19  // bankName.toUpperCase() = "DEWEY, CHEATHAM AND HOWE"
20  // bankName.replace('e', 'x') = "Dxwxy, Chxatham and Howx"
21  // bankName.concat("!") = "Dewey, Cheatham and Howe!"
22  // " x y z \t\b".trim() = "x y z"
23  // %>
24
25  public class StringDemo
26  {
27      public static void main( String[] args )
28      {
29          Terminal t = new Terminal();
30
31          String bankName = "Dewey, Cheatham and Howe";
32          String alias = new String( bankName );
33          char[] carray = {'y', 'e', 's', '!'};
34          String certainly = new String(carray);
35
```

```
36              t.println( "certainly = \"" + certainly + "\"" );
37
38              t.println( "bankName = \"" + bankName + "\"" );
39              t.println( "bankName.charAt( 0 ) = " + bankName.charAt( 0 ) );
40              t.println( "bankName.charAt( 5 ) = " + bankName.charAt( 5 ) );
41
42              t.println("bankName.indexOf('e') = " + bankName.indexOf('e'));
43              t.println("bankName.indexOf('e', 6) = " +
44                      bankName.indexOf('e', 6));
45              t.println("bankName.indexOf('x') = " + bankName.indexOf('x'));
46
47              t.println( "\"cake\".compareTo(\"care\") = " +
48                      "cake".compareTo("care") );
49
50              t.println( "bankName.substring( 7, 12 ) = " +
51                      bankName.substring( 7, 12 ) );
52              t.println( "bankName.substring( 7 ) = " +
53                      bankName.substring( 7 ) );
54
55              t.println( "bankName.toUpperCase() = \"" +
56                      bankName.toUpperCase() + "\"" );
57              t.println( "bankName.replace('e', 'x') = \"" +
58                      bankName.replace('e', 'x') + "\"" );
59              t.println( "bankName.concat(\"!\") = \"" +
60                      bankName.concat("!") + "\"" );
61              t.println( "\" x y z \\t\\b\".trim() = \"" +
62                      " x y z \t\b".trim() + "\"" );
63      }
64  }
```

Example 8.3 ReflectionDemo.java

```
1  // Example 8.3 joi/examples/ReflectionDemo.java
2  //
3  //
4  // Copyright 2003 Bill Campbell and Ethan Bolker
5
6  import java.lang.reflect.*;
7
8  // A short program to illustrate how Java uses
9  // class information dynamically.
10 //
11 // This file declares class Greeting as well as class
```

```
12   // ReflectionDemo. Java requires that a public class be
13   // declared in a file that matches its name, but Greeting
14   // is not marked public.
15   //
16   // %> java ReflectionDemo
17   // Greeting@93dee9 is an instance of class Greeting
18   // classOfG.toString(): class Greeting
19   // classOfG.getName(): Greeting
20   // fields in class Greeting (not inherited):
21   // name: message, type: class java.lang.String
22   // methods in class Greeting (not inherited):
23   // invoking hello
24   // hello, world!
25   // Creating an object when you know the name of its class:
26   // g = (Greeting)Class.forName("Greeting").newInstance();
27   // g.toString(): Greeting@6f0472
28   // Try to create an instance of nonexistent class Foo:
29   // java.lang.ClassNotFoundException: Foo
30
31   public class ReflectionDemo
32   {
33       public static void main( String[] args )
34       {
35           Greeting g = new Greeting();
36           Class classOfG = g.getClass();
37           out(g.toString() + " is an instance of " +
38                           classOfG.toString());
39           out("classOfG.toString(): " + classOfG.toString());
40           out("classOfG.getName():  " + classOfG.getName());
41
42           out("fields in class Greeting (not inherited):");
43
44           Field[] greetingFields = classOfG.getFields();
45           for (int i=0; i < greetingFields.length; i++) {
46               Field f = greetingFields[i];
47               if (f.getDeclaringClass() == classOfG) {
48                   out("name: " + f.getName() + ", type: " + f.getType());
49               }
50           }
51
52           out("methods in class Greeting (not inherited):");
53
54           Method[] greetingMethods = classOfG.getMethods();
```

```
55              for (int i=0; i < greetingMethods.length; i++) {
56                  Method m = greetingMethods[i];
57                  if (m.getDeclaringClass() == classOfG) {
58                      out("invoking " + m.getName());
59                      try {
60                          m.invoke(g, null);
61                      }
62                      catch( Exception e) {
63                          out(e.toString());
64                      }
65                  }
66              }
67
68              out("Creating an object when you know the name of its class:");
69              out("g = (Greeting)Class.forName(\"Greeting\").newInstance();");
70              try {
71                  g = (Greeting)Class.forName("Greeting").newInstance();
72                  out( "g.toString(): " + g.toString());
73              }
74              catch (Exception e) { // couldn't find class
75                  out(e.toString());
76              }
77
78              out("Try to create an instance of nonexistent class Foo:");
79              Object o;
80              try {
81                  o = Class.forName("Foo").newInstance();
82              }
83              catch (Exception e) { // couldn't find class
84                  out(e.toString());
85              }
86      }
89
90      // too lazy to type "System.out.println()
91      public static void out( String s )
92      {
93          System.out.println(s);
94      }
95  }
96
97  class Greeting
98  {
99      public String message = "hello, world";
```

```
100
101      public void hello()
102      {
103           System.out.println(message + "!");
104      }
105  }
```

Example 9.1 SerializationDemo.java

```
 1   // Example 9.1 SerializationDemo.java
 2   //
 3   //
 4   // Copyright 2003 Bill Campbell and Ethan Bolker
 5
 6   import java.io.*;
 7   import java.util.*;
 8
 9   // Test of Java serialization.
10   //
11   // %> java SerializationDemo
12   // Wrote: round blue Mon Jan 06 20:14:44 EST 2003
13   // Read:  round null Mon Jan 06 20:14:44 EST 2003
14   //
15   // interesting observations:
16   //
17   // %> wc -c SerializationDemo* tmp
18   //    1207 SerializationDemo$Circle.class
19   //    1611 SerializationDemo.class
20   //    3221 SerializationDemo.java
21   //     271 tmp
22   //
23   // the "strings" command finds ascii strings in a file
24   //
25   // %> strings SerializationDemo.class | wc
26   //    45      45      813
27   //
28   // %> strings tmp
29   // SerializationDemo$Circle?
30   // attributest
31   //     Ljava/util/Map;L
32   // selft
33   //     LSerializationDemo$Circle;xpsr
34   // java.util.HashMap
```

```
35   // loadFactorI
36   // thresholdxp?@
37   // datesr
38   // java.util.Datehj
39   // thisq
40   // namet
41   // roundxq
42   //
43   // %> strings tmp | wc -c
44   // 180
45
46   public class SerializationDemo
47   {
48       public static void main (String[] args)
49       {
50           Circle circle = new Circle("round");
51           write(circle,"tmp");
52           System.out.println("Wrote: "+ circle);
53
54           Circle circleCopy = (Circle)read("tmp");
55           System.out.println("Read:   " + circleCopy);
56       }
57
58       public static void write (Object obj, String pathname)
59       {
60           try {
61               FileOutputStream f = new FileOutputStream(pathname);
62               ObjectOutput s = new ObjectOutputStream(f);
63               s.writeObject(obj);
64               s.flush();   s.close();   f.close();
65           } catch (Exception e) { e.printStackTrace(); }
66       }
67
68       public static Object read(String pathname)
69       {
70           try {
71               Object obj;
72               FileInputStream in = new FileInputStream(pathname);
73               ObjectInputStream s = new ObjectInputStream(in);
74               obj = s.readObject();
75               s.close(); in.close();
76               return(obj);
77           }
```

```
 78              catch (Exception e) {
 79                  e.printStackTrace();
 80              }
 81          return(null);
 82      }
 83
 84      // To implement the Serializable interface you just _say_ so.
 85      // You don't have to _do_ anything, although you may choose to
 86      // overwrite the writeObject() and readObject() methods.
 87
 88      private static class Circle implements Serializable
 89      {
 90          private Circle self;     // a circular reference
 91          private Map attributes; // saved with its contents
 92
 93          // Don't bother saving whatever the current color
 94          //(user settable) happens to be:
 95          transient private String color;
 96
 97          Circle(String name)
 98          {
 99              attributes = new HashMap();
100              attributes.put("this", this); // a circular reference
101              attributes.put("name", name);
102              attributes.put("date", new Date());
103              this.color = "blue";
104              self = this;
105          }
106
107          public void setColor(String color)
108          {
109              this.color = color;
110          }
111
112          // NOTE: serialization does not call toString-- it calls
113          // a smarter serialization method.
114          public String toString()
115          {
116              return( (String)attributes.get("name") + " " +
117                      color + " " + (Date)attributes.get("date") );
118          }
119      }
120  }
```

Index

Page references to definitions in the glossary are shown in **boldface**. **Bold monospaced font** is used for keywords, class names in the Java API, class names in our listings, and Java filenames.